Guide To
Working Capital
Management

The McGraw-Hill Finance Guide Series

Bowlin, Martin, and Scott   Guide to Financial Analysis
Smith   Guide to Working Capital Management
Weston and Sorge   Guide to International Finance

Guide To Working Capital Management

Keith V. Smith

Graduate School of Management
University of California
Los Angeles, California

McGraw-Hill Book Company

New York   St. Louis   San Francisco   Auckland   Bogotá
Düsseldorf   Johannesburg   London   Madrid
Mexico   Montreal   New Delhi   Panama
Paris   São Paulo   Singapore
Sydney   Tokyo   Toronto

this book is dedicated
to
Jamie Lynne Smith
and
Julie Anne Smith,
with
fond memories of our 8,000 mile
family journey during summer 1977

Library of Congress Cataloging in Publication Data

Smith, Keith V.
Guide to working capital management.

Includes bibliographical references and index.
1.   Business enterprises—Finance.   2.   Working
capital.   I.   Title.
HG4026.S6   658.1'52   78-17532
ISBN 0-07-058546-6
ISBN 0-07-058545-8 pbk.

1234567890   KPKP   7865432109

The editors for this book were Bonnie Lieberman,
W. Hodson Mogan, and Joan Zseleczky, the
designer was Elliot Epstein, and the production
supervisor was Teresa F. Leaden. It was set in Melior
by University Graphics, Inc.

Printed and bound by The Kingsport Press.

CONTENTS

Preface
vii

1
INTRODUCTION
1

Some Definitions • Some Statistics • Some Goals • Some Perspective • Problems • Suggested Readings

2
PLANNING WORKING CAPITAL
21

Rationale for Planning • Responsibility for Planning • Forecasting Procedures • Planning Financial Feasibility • Ongoing Financial Planning • Computerized Financial Planning Systems • Summary • Problems • Suggested Readings

3
MANAGING CASH
67

Rationale for Cash • Responsibility for Cash • Some Further Perspective • Collecting Cash • Lockbox Analysis • Mobilizing Cash • Disbursing Cash • Benefits Versus Costs • Establishing Cash Balances • Electronic Funds Transfer System • Summary • Problems • Suggested Readings

4
MANAGING MARKETABLE SECURITIES
93

Rationale for Marketable Securities • Responsibility for Marketable Securities • Characteristics of Marketable Securities • Characteristics of the Money Market • Cost-Balancing Models • Strategies for Managing Marketable Securities • Summary • Problems • Suggested Readings

5
MANAGING ACCOUNTS RECEIVABLE
115

Rationale for Receivables • Responsibility for Receivables • Establishing Credit Policy • Credit Terms • Credit Analysis • Credit-Scoring Systems • Monitoring Receivables • Collecting Receivables • Changing Credit Policies • Some Important Linkages • Summary • Problems • Suggested Readings

6
MANAGING INVENTORY
141

Rationale for Inventory • Responsibility for Inventory • Different Types of Inventory • Overview of an Inventory System • Inventory Costs • Cost-Balancing Approaches • Seasonal Demand • Inventory Replenishment • Purchase Discounts • Inflation Effects • Uncertainty and Shortage • Strategy Implementation • Summary • Problems • Suggested Readings

7
MANAGING PAYABLES AND ACCRUALS
173

Rationale for Payables and Accruals • Responsibility for Payables and Accruals • Purchasing on Credit • Types and Terms of Trade Credit • Cost of Open-Account Trade Credit • Cost of Trade Credit Involving Discounts • Disbursement Analysis • Supplier Relationships • Managing Other Accruals • Summary • Problems • Suggested Readings

8
MANAGING SHORT-TERM BORROWING
193

Rationale for Borrowing • Responsibility for Borrowing • Types of Borrowing • Collateral for Borrowing • Cost of Borrowing • Appraising Borrowing Potential • Lender Relationships • Summary • Problems • Suggested Readings

9
CONTROLLING WORKING CAPITAL
215

Rationale for Controlling • Responsibility for Controlling • Liquidity Ratios • Profitability Ratios • Composite Ratios • Monitoring Financial Ratios • Multiple Trade-offs • Corrective Actions • Control in Perspective • Summary • Problems • Suggested Readings

Glossary
243

Index
249

PREFACE

The field of finance has made great progress in recent years, both in the development of better decision-making tools and in their application to business problems. Much of the progress has focused on longer-range financial decisions such as capital budgeting, capital structure, leasing, bond refunding, and mergers. Many books and articles have been devoted to shorter-term financial decisions, but it would seem that progress in working capital management has not kept pace. Regardless of the extent to which that assertion is true, it is clear that many business difficulties and ultimate firm failures can be traced to the mismanagement of certain current assets and current liabilities.

It also can be asserted that the state of the art for working capital management is a dichotomy between qualitative discussion of institutional procedures and practices, and a series of analytical models that have been proposed as relevant to short-term financial decisions. The purpose of *Guide to Working Capital Management* is to provide a more comprehensive treatment of the subject that helps to reduce the dichotomy between theory and practice, and which places working capital in proper perspective within the broader scope of financial management. The *Guide* is aimed at students of management who are likely to have been well trained in the theory of finance, but whose experience and hence perspective is limited. The *Guide* is also aimed at financial and other managers who have an appreciation of the important role of working capital within the firm, but for whom mathematical notation and modeling may seem obscure if not frightening. While my aim at a dual audience may end up satisfying neither students nor managers in full, hopefully the *Guide* is constructive to both and helps to reduce the gap between theory and practice.

The format of the *Guide* is designed to make it a useful manual for both students and managers. Each important term or concept is carefully defined in the text and is also included in a glossary at the end of the book.

Numerical examples are used to illustrate the concepts presented in each chapter. A series of problems is presented at the end of each chapter. Solutions are provided for the first group of problems, while the second group is left entirely to the reader. A list of suggested supplemental readings is also included at the end of each chapter.

Many talented individuals contributed to the completion of this *Guide*. Charles D'Ambrosio, the McGraw-Hill series editor, provided initial motivation, critical review, and encouragement throughout the project. Constructive suggestions and perspective were provided by several financial managers, including Winston Bowman (Bullocks), Brian Hamill (United California Bank), Norman Metcalfe (Kaufman and Broad), and Richard Rockhold (Del Monte). Helpful reviews were also provided by Haskel Benishay, John Leahy, and Bradley Shuster. As always, M.B.A. students together with my finance colleagues at the UCLA Graduate School of Management provided intellectual stimulation and feedback. I especially acknowledge my friend and colleague David Eiteman for help in development of parts of the material in Chapters 2 and 3 of the *Guide*. Nancy Peterson helped with the numerical examples and exhibits, Patt Bennett expeditiously typed several drafts of the manuscript, and Karen Niskanen ably handled all secretarial matters concerned with the project. Finally, I am pleased to follow the customary practice of absolving all of the above individuals from any errors that remain.

KEITH V. SMITH
Los Angeles
October 1978

Guide To
Working Capital
Management

INTRODUCTION

Sufficient working capital must be provided in order to take care of the normal process of purchasing raw materials and supplies, turning out finished products, selling the products, and waiting for payments to be made. If the original estimates of working capital are insufficient, some emergency measures must be resorted to or the business will come to a dead stop.

W. H. Lough, *Business Finance* (New York: Ronald Press, 1917), p. 355.

Furthermore, I believe, owing to the confusion of terms, the expression "working capital" had better be omitted altogether.

A. S. Dewing, *The Financial Policy of Corporations,* 5th ed. (New York: Ronald Press, 1953), vol. 1, p. 689.

We begin this introductory chapter on the subject of working capital management with two quotations. The first, published six decades ago, reminds us that working capital is not a new subject. It reveals the scope of the subject in terms of the purchasing, marketing, and financing activities of the firm. It also provides a brief glimpse of the critical nature of working capital management within the firm. The second quotation alerts us to possible difficulties with the semantics of working capital management.

Today, the scope of working capital management continues to be large and the semantic difficulties persist. The subject has become more complex because of competition within our economy, because of the expansion of many firms into international markets, and because of higher interest rates in recent years. The subject has also become more complex because of improvements in techniques for managing working capital. This is a result of greater attention to working capital by management, as well as the larger capabilities for information processing within firms. In this first chapter we establish a perspective for the chapter-by-chapter coverage of working capital management that follows.

SOME DEFINITIONS

In order to avoid semantic problems ourselves, it is useful to provide definitions at the outset. Important terms are working capital, net working capital, working capital management, funds, and cash flow.* To illustrate, we use the financial statements of Crescent Corporation, a manufacturer and distributor of electrical appliances for home cleaning. Crescent products are sold both wholesale through distributors and retail through a subsidiary company, Speedy Cleaners. Although Crescent products have thus far been marketed only in the continental United States, management recently has considered the possibility of expanding to certain international markets. Exhibits 1-1 and 1-2 are the 1977 income statement and balance sheet for Crescent Corporation.

Working capital includes cash, marketable securities, accounts receivable, inventory, and other current assets of the firm. A broader view of working capital would also include current liabilities such as accounts payable, notes payable, and other accruals. More precisely, *working capital* is defined as the dollar sum of the current assets of the business. *Net working capital* is defined as current assets minus the current liabilities. In Exhibit 1-2, we see that Crescent Corporation had $1,381,018 (total current assets) in working capital at the end of 1977. Net working capital for Crescent at that time would be calculated as follows:

Total current assets	$1,381,018
− Total current liabilities	−614,400
Net working capital	$ 766,618

Generally speaking, *working capital management* involves the managing of individual current assets, the managing of individual current liabilities, and the managing of all interrelationships that link current assets with current liabilities and with other balance sheet accounts. Later in the chapter, after considering the goals of the firm, we will offer a more operational definition of working capital management.

Funds is a frequently used but otherwise rather vague term. To some managers funds means money or cash, to other managers funds is synony-

---

*Where appropriate, additional terms will be defined in successive chapters. A glossary of all definitions is included at the end of the *Guide*.

EXHIBIT 1-1

CRESCENT CORPORATION
INCOME STATEMENT FOR THE YEAR 1977

Net sales	$8,110,900
Cost of goods sold	4,216,700
Gross profit	$3,894,200
Selling expenses	2,383,000
Administrative expenses	850,300
Earnings before interest and taxes	$ 660,900*
Interest	20,500
Earnings before taxes	$ 640,400
Federal taxes payable	288,000
Earnings after taxes	$ 352,400
Common stock dividends (on 40,000 shares)	80,000
Added to retained earnings	$ 272,400

*After deducting $60,000 of depreciation included in cost of goods sold, selling expenses, and administrative expenses.

---

mous with financing, and to still others it simply means working capital. The firm's statement of changes in financial position (formerly, the "funds statement") often has two sections: in one, changes in net working capital is included as a separate item; in the other, it is further broken down into changes in each current asset and current liability. This is illustrated in Exhibit 1-3. For Crescent Corporation, the largest use of funds in 1977 was to increase net working capital by $332,400. Among the current assets, accounts receivable and inventory were increased, while cash was decreased. Notes payable also was decreased in 1977.

For the purposes of this book, we will define funds simply as value within the organization. *Funds flow* is thus the flow of value within the firm—both between the various facilities of an organization, and between its working capital and other financial accounts.

Cash flow, which is very important to working capital management, has

EXHIBIT 1-2

CRESCENT CORPORATION
BALANCE SHEET FOR YEAR-END 1977

Assets

Cash		$ 98,836
Accounts receivable		504,000
Installment notes receivable		201,600
Inventory		
Raw material		347,600
Finished goods		182,960
Prepaid expenses		46,022
Total current assets		$1,381,018
Land		$ 91,600
Buildings	$800,000	
Acc. depreciation	360,000	440,000
Machinery	$672,000	
Acc. depreciation	372,000	300,000
Net fixed assets		$ 831,600
Total Assets		$2,212,618

Liabilities and Equity

Accounts payable	$ 126,400
Notes payable	200,000
Federal taxes payable	288,000
Total current liabilities	$ 614,400
Common stock and surplus	$ 400,000
Retained earnings	1,198,218
Total equity	$1,598,218
Total liabilities and equity	$2,212,618

EXHIBIT 1-3

CRESCENT CORPORATION
STATEMENT OF CHANGES IN FINANCIAL POSITION FOR THE YEAR
1977

Sources of funds		*Uses of funds*	
Earnings	$352,400	Cash dividends	$122,500
Depreciation	60,000	Increased net working capital	332,400
Sale of used machinery	42,500	Total	$454,900
Total	$454,900		

Summary of changes in wording capital position

Decreased cash	($ 23,400)
Increased accounts receivable	152,480
Increased inventory	103,320
Decreased notes payable	100,000
Increased net working capital	$332,400

---

two definitions. The first, a precise definition, is based on the firm's income statement and states that cash flow is equal to the sum of earnings (after taxes) and depreciation. For Crescent, cash flow for 1977 would be calculated as follows:

Earnings	$352,400
+ Depreciation	+60,000
Cash flow	$412,400

The cash flow generated by a business during a year is often an important source of funds for that year. As seen in Exhibit 1-3, cash flow for Crescent Corporation was a large part of its total sources of funds in 1977.

The concept that depreciation contributes to cash flow and thus is a source of funds to the firm has baffled many students and managers. Because of the importance of the cash-flow concept, it is well to explore it in detail.

Exhibit 1-4 provides an example. There are two parts to the cash-flow concept. The first part is to demonstrate why the precise definition of cash flow does in fact hold. The first column of Exhibit 1-4 goes through the accounting procedure for a firm that depreciates its fixed assets. Depreciation of $200 is added to earnings of $180 in order to obtain cash flow of $380. The second column of Exhibit 1-4 goes through a similar procedure based only on cash flows to and from the organization, and again, a net cash flow to the firm of $380 is obtained. In other words, depreciation contributes to cash flow because *less* taxes are paid out in cash to the federal government.

The other part of the cash-flow concept is to make comparison with another firm that is similar in all respects except that it does not depreciate its fixed assets. In the third column of Exhibit 1-4, the no depreciation firm has higher earnings of $300. But because no depreciation is charged, cash flow is also $300 and hence is lower than that for the firm that does charge depreciation. The added cash flow is equal to the depreciation charge multiplied by the federal tax rate. For the example, we obtain

Depreciation charge $200
× Federal tax rate   ×.40
Added cash flow $ 80

which is the difference between cash-flow values of $380 (depreciation) and $300 (no depreciation).

The second and a more general definition of cash flow focuses on the corporate checkbook. That is, cash flow deals with all of the various flows of cash into and out of the firm. Exhibit 1-5 shows cash flow in this context.[1] The schematic diagram in Exhibit 1-5 is closely patterned after the balance sheet of the firm. One difference is that leased assets are included. Another difference is in the way the various sources of financing to the firm are identified. The heavy arrows in Exhibit 1-5 signify the flow of values other than cash toward the assets of the organization. The other solid arrows pointing toward cash represent cash inflows while the dotted arrows pointing away from cash represent cash outflows. We also see that cash flow involves both working capital management (top part of the balance sheet) and long-term financial management (bottom part of the balance sheet). The large circle representing cash in Exhibit 1-5 is intended to emphasize the importance of cash within the firm, rather than its dollar size relative to other assets.

In addition to these important definitions involving working capital, a

---

[1]This diagram first appeared in K. V. Smith (ed.), *Readings on the Management of Working Capital* (St. Paul, Minn.: West Publishing Company, 1974), p. 6.

EXHIBIT 1-4

EXAMPLE OF CASH FLOW CALCULATION

	Depreciation: accounting basis	Depreciation: cash basis	No depreciation
Sales	$2,400	$2,400	$2,400
− Cost of goods sold	1,600	1,600	1,600
	$ 800	$ 800	$ 800
− Cash fixed expenses	300	300	300
	$ 500	$ 500	$ 500
− Depreciation	200	0	0
	$ 300	$ 500	$ 500
− Federal income taxes (40%)	120	120	200
Earnings	$ 180	$ 380	$ 300
+ Depreciation	200	0	0
Cash flow	$ 380	$ 380	$ 300

distinction can be made between permanent and temporary levels of working capital. *Permanent levels* of working capital are those amounts of various current assets and current liabilities that persist year after year and are not influenced by week-to-week or month-to-month fluctuations in the business activity of the firm. *Temporary levels* of working capital are the week-to-week and month-to-month fluctuations. For example, a historical review of Crescent Corporation revealed the following breakdown:

Component	Accounts receivable	Inventory	Accounts payable
Permanent level	$400,000	$300,000	$100,000
Temporary level (Dec. 31, 1977)	104,000	230,560	26,400
Total	$504,000	$530,560	$126,400

EXHIBIT 1-5

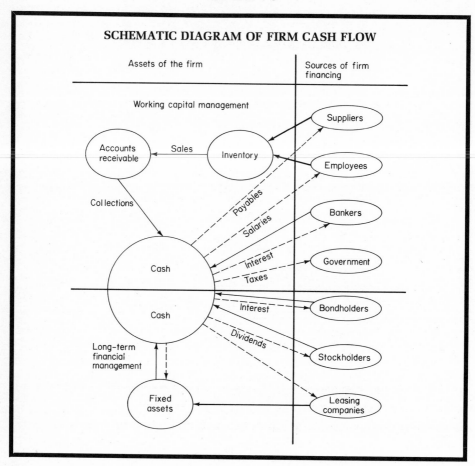

SCHEMATIC DIAGRAM OF FIRM CASH FLOW

Another, related way to break down working capital is into stocks and flows. A *stock* is a level of a working capital account at a point in time. A *flow* is a change in level of working capital during a period of time. In Exhibit 1-5, stocks are the amounts in the various balance sheet accounts, while flows are the movements of value between accounts. We will see later that an operational goal for working capital management includes consideration of both stocks and flows.

SOME STATISTICS

The scope of working capital management is described in the next four exhibits. The exhibits are based on three well-known but different sources of information. An aggregate portrayal of working capital in nonfinancial United States firms for selected years over the past two decades is presented in Exhibit 1-6. All of the current asset accounts increased steadily over the decade and totaled $731.6 billion at the end of 1975. Cash and equivalents include cash and various marketable securities. Accounts receivable and inventory constituted by far the largest dollar investment in working capital by business firms. It is also noted that cash and equivalents exhibited the slowest growth over the two decades, while the "other assets" (e.g., prepaid expenses) grew the fastest. On the other side of the balance sheet, current liabilities grew to $457.5 billion by the end of 1975, and hence there was aggregate net working capital of $274.1 billion. Among the current liabilities, accounts payable were by far the largest single item, but "other accruals" (e.g., salaries payable and prepaid revenues) exhibited the largest annual growth.

In contrast to these aggregate values, the scope of working capital management for individual firms is presented in Exhibit 1-7. Average values of individual working capital accounts as a percentage of total firm assets are presented for every other year over the past two decades. The sample of firms reflected in the average values ranged from 753 in 1957 to 2,563 in 1973. The clearest trend among the various accounts is the almost 50 percent reduction in cash and equivalents. Accounts receivable increased slightly, while inventory held remarkably constant at just over 20 percent of total assets. Current assets in total remained quite constant at just under 50 percent of assets. On the liability side of the balance sheet, current liabilities increased as a percentage of total financing. Unfortunately, the data source for Exhibit 1-7 does not include a breakdown of current liabilities into its component accounts. Overall, net working capital decreased from about 30 percent of total assets and financing in earlier years down to 24.8 percent at the end of 1975.

A somewhat different picture emerges if working capital accounts are expressed in terms of days sales outstanding. *Days sales outstanding* for a given account is defined as follows:

$$\text{Days sales outstanding in working capital account} = \frac{(365 \text{ days per year}) (\text{average account level})}{\text{annual firm sales}}$$

We notice that the definition includes both a balance sheet level (stock) for the working capital account and annual firm sales (flow) from the income statement. Using days sales outstanding to examine trends, we see in Exhibit 1-8 that accounts receivable increased over the two decades, while inventory remained relatively constant. The average number of days outstanding in cash increased significantly in the early 1960s and then decreased in the first half of the 1970s. And even though the number of days sales in current liabilities increased during the two decades, net working capital again decreased over time.

EXHIBIT 1-6

AGGREGATE WORKING CAPITAL POSITION OF NONFINANCIAL CORPORATIONS, SELECTED YEARS, 1957–1975
(All values are in billions of dollars)

Year	Cash and equivalents	Accounts receivable	Inventory	Other	Current assets	Accounts payable	Taxes payable	Other accruals	Current liabilities	Net working capital
1957	53.5	102.2	82.2	6.7	244.7	86.6	15.4	31.1	133.1	111.6
1960	57.3	129.2	91.8	10.6	289.0	106.8	13.5	40.1	160.4	128.6
1963	66.7	160.4	107.0	17.8	351.7	133.0	16.5	38.7	188.2	163.5
1965	66.9	194.1	126.9	22.3	410.2	163.5	19.1	46.9	229.6	180.7
1967	63.6	219.7	152.3	27.6	463.1	192.2	14.6	57.4	264.3	198.2
1969	58.5	197.0	186.4	31.6	473.3	204.2	12.6	76.0	287.9	185.7
1971	65.7	211.0	203.1	36.8	516.7	207.7	14.5	89.7	311.8	204.9
1973	72.4	269.6	246.0	54.4	643.2	265.9	18.1	117.0	401.0	242.3
1975	87.5	298.2	285.0	60.9	731.6	288.0	20.7	148.8	457.5	274.1
Annual increase	2.8%	6.1%	7.1%	13.0%	6.3%	6.9%	1.7%	9.1%	7.1%	5.1%

Source: Federal Reserve Bulletin, selected issues.

EXHIBIT 1-7

WORKING CAPITAL ACCOUNTS AS PERCENTAGE OF TOTAL ASSETS OF INDUSTRIAL CORPORATIONS, SELECTED YEARS, 1957–1975

Year	Number of firms	Cash and equivalents	Accounts receivable	Inventory	Other	Current assets	Current liabilities	Net working capital
1957	753	12.2%	14.4%	22.8%	1.0%	49.6%	19.0%	30.6%
1959	879	12.3	13.7	19.4	(0.4)	45.0	17.0	28.1
1961	1,484	12.1	16.4	21.3	1.1	50.9	20.7	30.2
1963	1,770	11.5	16.4	21.3	0.7	49.9	20.7	29.2
1965	1,933	10.4	17.5	21.5	0.8	50.2	22.5	27.7
1967	2,152	9.9	17.8	21.5	0.7	49.9	22.2	27.6
1969	2,333	8.8	18.1	21.2	1.0	49.1	23.6	25.5
1971	2,475	8.7	17.5	20.8	1.0	48.0	23.1	24.9
1973	2,563	7.8	18.2	21.8	1.1	48.9	24.7	24.2
1975	2,135	8.4	17.4	21.0	1.2	48.0	23.2	24.8

Source: Standard & Poor's Compustat Services, Inc.

As a starting point for a study of the working capital position of Crescent Corporation, the following calculations are made:

	Percentage of total assets	Days sales outstanding
Cash	4.5	4.4
Accounts and installment notes receivable	31.9	31.7
Inventory (raw material and finished goals)	24.0	23.9
Current assets	62.4	62.1
Accounts payable	5.7	5.7
Notes payable	9.0	9.0
Current liabilities	27.8	27.6
Net working capital	34.6	34.5

These values for Crescent can be compared with the average data in Exhibits 1-7 and 1-8.

A sharper comparison can be made, however, by using selected industry data in Exhibit 1-9. Average percentages (year-end 1975) are shown for firms in three industries within each of four economic sectors (manufacturing, wholesaling, retailing, and services). Sample sizes are seen to vary considerably for the selected industries. The percentage breakdowns of working capital accounts in Exhibit 1-9 reveal diversity between and within the four sectors. Again the relative importance of accounts receivable and inventory is noted, with the exception of the services sector where firms typically have smaller investment in those two working capital accounts. Some of the industries selected in Exhibit 1-9 for both the wholesaling and retailing sectors were deliberately chosen as the nearest comparison standard for Crescent Corporation. Inventory and accounts payable appear to be the particular working capital accounts where Crescent seems most unlike other firms in similar lines of business.

SOME GOALS

Because of the extent and importance of working capital management as portrayed in these statistics, it is well to consider the goals of the organization relative to its working capital. In doing this, we review the goals of the organization, of its overall managers, and finally of financial managers responsible for working capital. An understanding of these goals will enable us to focus more sharply on the management of working capital.

With respect to the business firm, a number of different goals have received attention. There are goals that have to do with the firm as an

EXHIBIT 1-8

WORKING CAPITAL ACCOUNTS IN DAYS SALES OUTSTANDING FOR INDUSTRIAL CORPORATIONS, SELECTED YEARS, 1957–1975

Year	Number of firms	Cash and equivalents	Accounts receivable	Inventory	Current assets	Current liabilities	Net working capital
1957	753	37 days	59 days	59 days	158 days	60 days	98 days
1959	879	144	56	52	146	55	91
1961	1,484	119	64	57	184	81	103
1963	1,770	153	70	57	202	85	117
1965	1,933	119	92	57	202	111	91
1967	2,152	118	89	58	204	106	98
1969	2,333	153	88	59	253	116	136
1971	2,475	93	84	61	196	125	71
1973	2,563	75	83	59	184	128	56
1975	2,135	76	76	58	178	120	58

Source: Standard & Poor's Compustat Services, Inc.

ongoing business. Goals often mentioned as foremost are producing quality products or generating useful services at appropriate prices. Other goals of a firm discussed by students of management are to provide job opportunities for individuals and to allocate resources in some effective manner. Attention has also been given to certain society-oriented goals—such as protecting the environment or conserving the natural resources of a region.

While such diverse goals may or may not receive prime attention, profitability is almost always mentioned by managers. One difficulty with profitability as a firm's goal is that is can be measured in a number of different ways. For example, profitability may be taken in an absolute sense as earnings after taxes from the income statement ($352,400 for Crescent in 1977), it can be earnings as a percentage of sales (4.3 percent for Crescent), it can be earnings as a percentage of total assets (15.9 percent), or earnings as a percentage of equity (22.0 percent).* Many writers assert that maximizing

*These and other measures of profitability will be defined and illustrated in Chapter 9.

EXHIBIT 1-9

WORKING CAPITAL ACCOUNTS AS PERCENTAGE OF TOTAL ASSETS OF SELECTED SECTORS AND INDUSTRIES, 1975

Sector and industry	Number of firms	Cash and equiv.	Accts. receiv.	Inven.	Other	Current assets	Accts. payable	Notes payable	Other accruals	Current liab.	Net working capital
Manufacturing:											
Soap & detergent	45	12.5%	24.5%	30.3%	1.3%	68.6%	13.1%	1.2%	14.9%	29.2%	39.4%
Meat packing	126	8.0	26.6	23.4	1.8	59.8	12.1	10.4	10.7	33.2	26.6
Aircraft parts	63	5.9	24.0	40.5	1.9	72.3	12.5	5.8	16.3	34.7	37.6
Wholesaling:											
Electrical appliances	147	7.0	30.9	44.4	1.2	83.5	26.7	9.8	9.1	45.6	37.9
Laundry and dry cleaning	36	4.8	31.9	33.7	1.4	71.9	13.7	12.1	13.6	39.4	32.5
Drugs	116	5.7	31.4	42.2	1.2	81.6	26.1	8.3	8.8	43.3	38.3
Retailing:											
Household appliances	167	9.8	16.1	49.7	2.6	78.3	24.4	8.8	15.9	49.0	29.3
Hardware	200	5.9	10.4	54.0	0.5	70.8	17.8	4.2	10.5	32.4	38.4
Furniture	519	5.1	37.5	34.8	1.4	78.8	12.2	9.3	14.5	35.9	42.9
Services:											
Bowling alleys	63	6.1	2.2	2.4	0.5	11.2	4.9	2.5	14.9	22.4	(11.2)
Data processing	61	8.4	25.7	13.9	3.6	51.5	14.2	7.5	12.5	34.2	17.3
Motels and hotels	131	4.8	4.4	2.4	1.3	12.9	4.3	2.3	9.9	16.5	(3.6)

Source: Robert Morris Associates Annual Statement Studies, 1976.

the total return (income plus appreciation) per share of common stock ownership is the single most important goal of the firm.

These various measures of profitability for a firm may not be the same as the goals of its managers. Many managers will perhaps admit that their major personal goal within the organization is simply to survive, or possibly to attain some higher level of responsibility or status within the organization. Increased attention given to stock options, profit-sharing plans, and executive bonuses in recent years reflects recognition that the goals of management can be made more consistent with the overall goals of the organization itself. Reducing any gap between the expressed goals of the organization and the perceived goals of its managers becomes a relevant goal of the organization. We shall assume that this is accomplished and managers of the firm do make decisions in order to enhance the profitability of the organization on behalf of its owners.

Financial management consists of one or more individuals within the organization who are responsible for financial decision-making. The chief financial officer is often the treasurer or the vice president of finance.[2] The controller has also become an influential member of the financial management team.[3] A finance committee often has important power within the managerial hierarchy. The managers of purchasing, production, credit, and marketing also make decisions having significant financial implications. For a small firm, the president may handle much of the financial decision-making. Regardless of size, financial management tends to be conducted at a high level within the organization, and much top-level control is financial control.

In the case of Crescent Corporation, Mr. Arthur Hanson, the newly appointed vice president of finance, is identified as the chief financial officer. He has been asked to take a careful look at the management of working capital within his firm. In this and subsequent chapters, we shall follow Hanson as he goes about this important assignment.

When we speak of the goals of financial management, we are specifically referring to the goals of the organization that pertain to the management of its financial resources. As such, those goals ought to be consistent with the firm's overall goals. Most discussions of financial management ultimately boil down to two major goals: profitability and liquidity. Some measures of profitability have already been identified. Liquidity has to do with ensuring that the firm is able to satisfy all of its financial obligations so that it continues in business and hopefully generates some level of profitability for its owners. Putting it another way, liquidity is a lower threshold on organi-

[2]The perspective of one treasurer toward working capital is found in C. H. Ludlow, "Managing Working Capital," reprinted in J. F. Weston and M. B. Goudzwaard (eds.), *Treasurer's Handbook* (Homewood, Ill.: Dow Jones-Irwin, 1977), Chapter 19.

[3]"The Controller: Inflation Gives Him More Clout with Management," *Business Week*, Aug. 15, 1977.

zational profitability. A familiar measure of liquidity is the *current ratio*, defined as current assets divided by current liabilities. For Crescent Corporation, the current ratio at the end of 1977 would be calculated as follows:

$$\frac{\text{Current assets}}{\text{Current liabilities}} = \frac{\$1,381,018}{\$614,400} = 2.25$$

Other measures of liquidity include expressing each working capital account in terms of days sales outstanding. We saw earlier that net working capital for Crescent amounted to 34.5 days of sales at the end of 1977.

Working capital decisions are a subset of financial decisions. As such, profitability and liquidity become appropriate goals for those managers assigned responsibility for the management of the working capital accounts of the firm. A few of the decisions made by those managers, such as increasing the firm's gross profit margin, can be shown to improve both the profitability and liquidity positions of the firm. But for most decisions, there is a trade-off between the profitability goal and the liquidity goal of the firm.

This is illustrated in Exhibit 1-10 for Crescent Corporation. The middle column replicates its financial statements from Exhibits 1-1 and 1-2. The first column of Exhibit 1-10 shows a similar firm in all respects except that its management takes a more cautious view toward the management of its working capital, which shows up in a larger cash balance, larger inventory, and smaller notes payable to the bank. Conversely, the third column shows a firm that takes a more aggressive view toward working capital as reflected in smaller cash, smaller inventory, but larger notes payable. The implications of these differences are summarized in measures of profitability (earnings as percentage of equity) and liquidity (current ratio) at the bottom of the exhibit. In moving from cautious to aggressive management of working capital, profitability increases from 18 percent to 28.4 percent, while liquidity drops from 3.2 to 1.5. It is not clear in this example that either cautious management or aggressive management would be preferred to existing management. It is clear, however, that Arthur Hanson and other relevant managers of Crescent Corporation should be aware of how their credit, inventory, and other policies are likely to impact the profitability and liquidity goals of the firm.

SOME PERSPECTIVE

At the outset, "working capital" was used as an adjective rather than as a noun. That was because this *Guide* is really about management—including the planning, executing, and controlling—of the firm's financial affairs, and especially of its working capital. In other words, it is really a *Guide to Working Capital Management*. To provide perspective for our study, we have reviewed in this introductory chapter some important definitions, we have examined the scope and importance of working capital within the firm

EXHIBIT 1-10

CRESCENT CORPORATION
ALTERNATIVE APPROACHES TO WORKING CAPITAL MANAGEMENT

	Cautious management	Existing management	Aggressive management
Balance Sheet			
Current assets	$1,673,608	$1,381,018	$1,102,084
Net fixed assets	831,600	831,600	831,600
Total assets	$2,505,208	$2,212,618	$1,933,684
Current liabilities	$ 514,400	$ 614,400	$ 714,400
Equity	1,990,808	1,598,218	1.219,284
Total financing	$2,505,208	$2,212,608	$1,933,684
Income Statement			
Net sales	$8,110,900	$8,110,900	$8,110,900
Cost of goods sold	4,216,700	4,216,700	4,216,700
Selling and administrative expenses	3,233,300	3,233,300	3,233,300
Earnings before interest and taxes	$ 660,900	$ 660,900	$ 660,900
Interest	10,500	20,500	30,500
Earnings before taxes	$ 650,400	$ 640,400	$ 630,400
Federal taxes	292,700	288,000	283,700
Earnings after taxes	$ 357,700	$ 352,400	$ 346,700
Earnings as percentage of equity	18.0%	22.0%	28.4%
Current ratio	3.2	2.2	1.5

and within the economy, and we have considered the goals that pertain to working capital management.

Based on that introduction, it is well to pinpoint the dual focus which will be reflected in successive chapters.

Managing working capital involves:
  1. *planning and controlling* the flow of dollars and value between various working capital and other balance sheet accounts so as to ensure adequate liquidity for the firm,
and
  2. *establishing and monitoring* appropriate levels in each working capital account so as to enhance firm profitability.

The reader should note that the first part of the dual focus is dynamic, involves flows of value, and leads to firm liquidity. The second part of the dual focus is static, involves levels of value, and leads to firm profitability. Management must necessarily make a trade-off between liquidity and profitability that is perceived to be in the best interest of the owners of the firm.

As was noted earlier, the subject of working capital management has become more complex, has received greater attention within the firm, and has led to improvement in managerial techniques. Still, it would appear that the subject of working capital has not received as much attention as have other areas of finance—particularly longer-term financial management. In addition, the subject of working capital management tends to be more a hodgepodge of individual topics, rather than a comprehensive subject in itself. Indeed, much of what has been written about the management of working capital has dealt with individual current assets and current liabilities.[4]

While progress has been made on how to manage individual working capital accounts, there has been less progress in terms of tying working capital together as a whole. Our approach will parallel past treatment by considering each of the major working capital accounts. Chapters 3 to 6 treat the respective current assets of the firm, while Chapters 7 and 8 deal with current liabilities. For each working capital account, liquidity and profitability will be seen to follow from a consideration of stocks and flows, respectively.

Overall continuity will be provided in two ways. First, our discussion of individual working capital accounts is included between two integrating

---

[4]A representative sampling of articles on working capital—both theoretical and applied—are found in K. V. Smith (ed.), *Readings on the Management of Working Capital* (St. Paul, Minn.: West Publishing Company, 1974).

chapters: Chapter 2 deals with the planning of working capital, while Chapter 9 treats the controlling of working capital. Second, repeated mention will be made of important linkages between various working capital accounts. We will see that there are important linkages between cash and marketable securities, accounts receivable and inventory, inventory and accounts payable, notes payable and cash, and so forth.

Just as each working capital account cannot be examined alone, the working capital of the firm cannot be considered in isolation from other financial decisions. Clearly, there are implications of working capital decisions to both the capital structure and capital budgeting decisions of the firm. Working capital has an impact on the firm's overall capital structure through the cost structure of the firm's current liabilities. And projections of working capital should be included for projects that are considered for the firm's capital budget. The scope of this *Guide* will not allow us to pursue those implications in depth. Still, we will continually be reminded that financial managers must have a broad perspective so that their working capital decisions are well understood and consistent with other financial decisions made within the firm.

Problem 1-1

Following the procedure in Exhibit 1-10, calculate measures of profitability and liquidity for Crescent Corporation which would result if management decided to double its raw material inventory. Assume that the offsetting balance sheet adjustment was increased retained earnings.

SOLUTION: Beginning with the balance sheet in Exhibit 1-2, doubling raw material inventory ($347,600) to $695,200 would lead to the following financial statements at the end of 1977:

Balance Sheet

Current assets	$1,728,618
Fixed assets	831,600
Total assets	$2,560,218
Current liabilities	$ 614,400
Equity	1,945,818
Total financing	$2,560,218

Income Statement

(Same as in Exhibit 1-1 or 1-10)

For profitability, we calculate

$$\text{Earnings as percentage of equity } \frac{\$352,400}{\$1,945,818} = 18.1\%$$

while for liquidity, we calculate

$$\text{Current ratio } \frac{\$1,728,618}{\$614,400} = 2.81$$

Thus, a doubling of raw material inventory for Crescent would lead to an improved measure of liquidity, but a lower measure for firm profitability.

Problem 1-2

Following the same procedure, calculate measures of profitability and liquidity for Crescent Corporation if short-term notes payable were doubled. Assume that the offsetting balance sheet adjustment was a reduced retained earnings.

Problem 1-3

Suppose that just before the end of 1977, Crescent Corporation sold additional shares of common stock for $200,000. What effect would that have on its measures of profitability and liquidity?

SUGGESTED READINGS

Beranek, W.: WORKING CAPITAL MANAGEMENT (Belmont, Calif.: Wadsworth Publishing Company, Inc., 1966).

"The Controller: Inflation Gives Him More Clout with Management," BUSINESS WEEK, Aug. 15, 1977.

Mehta, D. R.: WORKING CAPITAL MANAGEMENT (Englewood Cliffs, N.J.: Prentice-Hall, Inc., 1974).

Ramamoorthy, V. E.: WORKING CAPITAL MANAGEMENT (Madras, India: Institute for Financial Management and Research, 1976).

Smith, K. V. (ed.): READINGS ON THE MANAGEMENT OF WORKING CAPITAL (St. Paul, Minn.: West Publishing Company, 1974).

Stancill, J. McN., Jr.: THE MANAGEMENT OF WORKING CAPITAL (Los Angeles: University of Southern California Press, 1970).

Weston, J. F. and M. B. Goudzwaard (eds.): TREASURER'S HANDBOOK (Homewood, Ill.: Dow Jones-Irwin, 1977), Part VI.

Weston, J. F. and B. W. Sorge: GUIDE TO INTERNATIONAL FINANCIAL MANAGEMENT (New York: McGraw-Hill Book Company, 1977), Chapter 11.

2

PLANNING WORKING CAPITAL

Financial planning provides a logical starting point for many of the decisions which are made by financial managers. It is thus appropriate to begin our treatment of working capital management with a chapter on working capital planning. As will be our format throughout the *Guide*, we first discuss rationale and responsibility for working capital, and then various considerations and methods that may be useful to financial managers. In this chapter, we will also provide illustrations of how working capital planning is a key part of overall financial planning.

RATIONALE FOR PLANNING

Planning is really at the heart of management. At the level of an individual business, effective planning provides a starting point for management to direct and guide the firm toward its purposes and goals. Planning also provides a benchmark for ensuring a steady course toward accomplishment of those purposes and goals. At the level of the entire economy, effective planning by many firms should lead to appropriate allocations of resources—both human and capital.

It is unreasonable to discuss the management of working capital without an understanding of how it relates both to financial planning and to overall planning by managers at all levels within the organization. Exhibit 2-1 provides one possible perspective that permits us to identify several dimensions of planning.

A *first* dimension of planning is the level of abstraction. Typically, broad plans which are formulated at the top of the organization set the stage for detailed plans which are devised at lower levels in the hierarchy. Proper conceptualizing of the firm is shown in Exhibit 2-1 as the beginning step. This is where the founders and/or top management of the firm decide just what the business is to be about. With respect to Peter Drucker's useful distinction between efficiency (doing things right) and effectiveness (doing the right things),[1] conceptual planning clearly deals with effectiveness. Conceptual planning is where the major directions and goals of the firm are identified. Strategic business planning, the next step, is the identification and evaluation of broad alternatives—products, markets, processes, structures, and strategies—toward accomplishing the major directions and goals of the organization. This, in turn, leads to operational plans for each unit and component of the business.

A *second* dimension of planning within the firm is by function. Financial planning is shown in Exhibit 2-1 alongside of product planning, marketing planning, personnel planning, and so forth. Even if the firm is organized into product lines, divisions, or geographical areas, it is likely that planning is handled at least in part on a functional basis. A functional breakdown is seldom complete, however, as financial considerations are likely to be involved in all types and levels of planning.

A *third* dimension has to do with the purpose of the planning. Focusing on financial planning, we see that there are two broad purposes. The first purpose is planning financial feasibility for new products and ventures, while the second purpose is financial planning for ongoing operations. Some planning tools may be useful for new and existing operations (e.g., cash budgeting), while other tools may be more useful for one or the other. For example, break-even analysis, which frequently is mentioned and illustrated as a tool for financial planning, really is more apropos of planning the feasibility of new products.

A *fourth* dimension deals with time, and Exhibit 2-1 identifies short-term, medium-term, and long-term planning as being part of financial planning. Likely outputs of financial planning also are identified, and it is here that perspective for working capital planning is provided. Cash budgeting is included with pro-forma income statements as part of short-term planning. Working capital planning, especially the determination of appropriate levels of current assets and current liabilities, is viewed as part of medium-term planning. Long-term planning, which results in projected payouts and returns to common stockholders, also reflects the decisions which are made about the firm's working capital.

A *fifth* dimension of planning—though it does not show up in Exhibit 2-1—is the distinction between levels and flows. It was asserted in Chapter 1 that the job of managing working capital involves planning and controlling for liquidity (flows) and establishing and monitoring for profitability (levels). Cash budgets and pro-forma income statements are financial statements used in planning flows, while pro-forma balance sheets are the result of planning the levels of working capital accounts.

---

[1]P. F. Drucker, *Management: Tasks, Responsibilities, Practices.* (New York: Harper & Row, Publishers, Incorporated, 1974), Chapter 4.

EXHIBIT 2-1

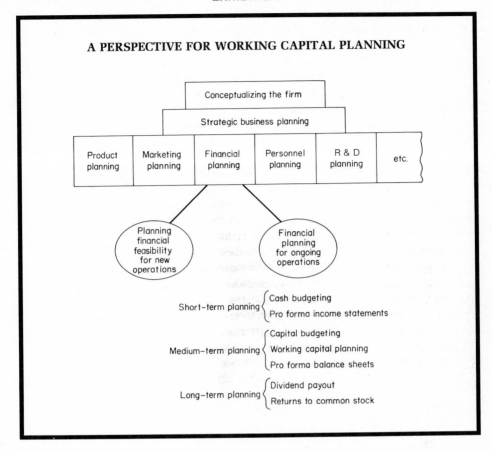

A PERSPECTIVE FOR WORKING CAPITAL PLANNING

In summary, working capital planning is part of financial planning, which, in turn, is one type of functional planning that builds upon strategic business planning. Other dimensions are the nature of what is being planned (flows or levels), the purpose of the planning (new or ongoing activity), and the future horizon (short-, medium-, or long-term).

RESPONSIBILITY FOR PLANNING

Planning, organizing, directing, and controlling are basic functions of the management process. While planning should logically begin at the top of the organizational hierarchy, responsibility for planning exists at all levels within the organization. Financial planning has been identified as one of the key functional areas of planning within the organization, while working capital planning is a part of financial planning that deals mainly with the shorter-term financial affairs of the business.[2] The responsibility for various working capital accounts often is given to different managers within the organization, and hence working capital plannng may be a shared responsibility in many instances.

Planning for individual working capital components normally would be conducted by the treasurer, the controller, the credit manager, various managers concerned with inventory, and perhaps higher management levels within the firm. The overall responsibility for coordinating the planning of working capital typically resides with the highest-level financial manager. For Crescent Corporation, Mr. Arthur Hanson is charged with the responsibility for planning and controlling working capital, and with the interface between working capital and long-term financing decisions.

It was stated earlier that planning should begin at the top of the organizational hierarchy. At the same time, the planning process should involve all levels of managers and supervisors that ultimately are affected by the plans that result. What this really means operationally is that higher levels of management "plan the planning process," while lower levels of management provide inputs from their areas of specialty. Those inputs are reviewed and coordinated into an overall plan for working capital and long-term financing at successively higher levels within the organization. The planning for working capital is thus a two-way process—with coordination and responsibility for the planning being conducted from the top down through the organization, but with forecasts and planning inputs being provided from the bottom up through the hierarchy.

FORECASTING PROCEDURES

Plans and budgets are the result of a planning process conducted by management. Output of the financial planning process is a series of financial statements including cash budgets, capital budgets, projected income statements, projected balance sheets, and projected statements of change in financial position. Excepting the possible use of such statements in negotiating loans from commercial banks, the output of financial planning is used internally by management in organizing and controlling financial activities of the business.

Inputs to the financial planning process are forecasts of sales, expenses, parameters (e.g., tax rates), and policies (e.g., disbursement procedures) that impact on cash flows and levels of assets and liabilities. There are different types of forecasting procedures that can be used by managers in preparing inputs to the planning process. Before proceding to discussions and illustrations of working capital planning, it is appropriate to review forecasting procedures.

[2]For an organizational review of responsibilities for financial planning, see R. C. Davis, *Industrial Organization and Management*, 3d ed. (New York: Harper & Brothers, 1957), Chapter 29.

Suppose that you were asked to forecast the 1978 annual sales for a certain business unit. Four years of prior sales data are available:

Year	Sales
1974	$100,000
1975	150,000
1976	200,000
1977	250,000

What would be your forecast? One procedure would be to calculate the *dollar increase* in sales for each year as the basis for your forecast. That would give:

Year	Sales	$ increase
1974	$100,000	—
1975	150,000	50,000
1976	200,000	50,000
1977	250,000	50,000
1978	($300,000) ⟵	50,000

The annual dollar increase in sales was constant at $50,000 for the past three years. A continuation of that trend for another year would lead, as shown, to a forecasted sales of $300,000 for the business unit.

An alternative procedure would be to calculate the *percentage increase* in sales for each year as the basis for your forecast. The calculation would be:

Year	Sales	% increase
1974	$100,000	—
1975	150,000	50.0
1976	200,000	33.3
1977	250,000	25.0
1978	($292,500) ⟵	17.0

Because the percentage increase became smaller in recent years, you might decide on a 17 percent increase as a reasonable estimate for 1978. As shown, that would lead to forecasted sales of $292,500.

A graphical procedure is useful in forecasting if several years of past data are available. The simplest graphical procedure is to draw freehand a straight line through past data plotted against time, extend the line for future years, and take points along the line as forecasts for those years.

To illustrate, suppose that you had ten years of historical sales data for another business unit.

Year	Sales	Year	Sales
1968	$11,000	1973	$15,000
1969	16,000	1974	12,000
1970	18,000	1975	18,000
1971	19,000	1976	26,000
1972	13,000	1977	23,000

Your task is to make sales forecasts for 1978 to 1980. These data are plotted in Exhibit 2-2. The solid line is drawn freehand so that about half of the points are above the line and about half of the points are below the line. Sales forecasts for the next three years are identified (with triangles) along an extension of the straight line. The forecasts are as follows:

Year	Forecast
1978	$21,000
1979	22,000
1980	23,000

Note that all three forecasts using this procedure are lower than the sales achieved in 1976 and 1977.

Suppose that there had been a change in management for the business unit in late 1972. As a result, you believe that it would be more appropriate to use only the five most recent years as the basis for your forecasts. The dashed line in Exhibit 2-2 is drawn freehand through the sales values for 1973 to 1977, and the following forecasts are obtained.

Year	Forecast
1978	$26,000
1979	29,000
1980	32,000

The graphical forecasting procedure is easy to use. The problem is in deciding what past period is most indicative of the future.

One disadvantage of the graphical procedure is that drawing a line freehand through plotted points is somewhat arbitrary. Three managers might well draw three different lines through the same set of plotted points. *Least squares* is a statistical method that enables one to determine (i.e., to "fit") the "best" line through the points—in the sense that the sum of the squared deviations from the points to the line is minimized. The reason for squaring is so that deviations of points above the line do not effectively cancel deviations of points below the line. Once the least squares line is determined, it can be used to forecast just as was done for the freehand procedure.

EXHIBIT 2-2

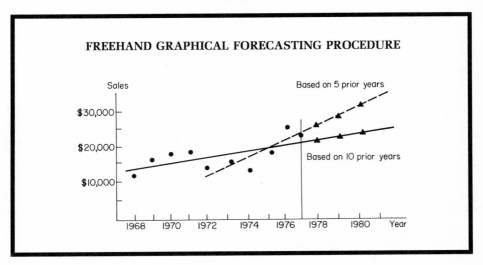

FREEHAND GRAPHICAL FORECASTING PROCEDURE

EXHIBIT 2-3

LEAST SQUARES FORECASTING PROCEDURE

Year	X	Sales	Y	X²	XY
1968	1	$11,000	11	1	11
1969	2	16,000	16	4	32
1970	3	18,000	18	9	54
1971	4	19,000	19	16	76
1972	5	13,000	13	25	65
1973	6	15,000	15	36	90
1974	7	12,000	12	49	84
1975	8	18,000	18	64	144
1976	9	26,000	26	81	234
1977	10	23,000	23	100	230
Totals	55		171	556	1,020

Calculating equations:

$$a = \frac{\Sigma Y \Sigma X^2 - \Sigma X \Sigma XY}{N \Sigma X^2 - \Sigma X \Sigma Y} = \frac{(171)(556) - (55)(1020)}{(10)(556) - (55)(55)} = 15.4$$

$$b = \frac{N \Sigma XY - \Sigma X \Sigma Y}{N \Sigma X^2 - \Sigma X \Sigma Y} = \frac{(10)(1020) - (55)(171)}{(10)(556) - (55)(55)} = 0.31$$

where Σ designates summation over all observations, and N designates 10 observations.

Exhibit 2-3 shows how the least squares method would be applied to sales data for the ten years from 1968 to 1977. The equation of a straight line that relates one variable Y to another variable X is given by

$$Y = a + bX$$

where Y = firm sales
X = time in years
a = intercept of the line
b = slope of the line

To simplify calculations, the values for X and Y are coded as shown in Exhibit 2-3. The values of X and Y are used to estimate the best straight line. Based on ten annual observations of sales, the least squares line for the illustration is estimated to be

$$Y = 15.4 + .31X$$

This relationship would then be used to forecast future sales as follows:

Year	X	Y = 15.4 + .31X	Forecast
1978	11	18.8	$18,800
1979	12	19.1	19,100
1980	13	19.4	19,400

Again, the forecasts for the period 1978–1980 are lower than the 1976 and 1977 values of sales. Higher forecasts would be obtained if the least squares method was applied to only the more recent observations.

If a plot of sales over time does not appear to follow a straight-line trend, then more complicated forecasting procedures may be used. For example, the least squares method can be used to fit a curvilinear relationship such as

$$Y = a + bX + cX^2$$

where the "squared" value of a variable is added to the equation. Least squares also can be used to fit a multivariate relationship of the form

$$Y = a + bX + cW + dZ$$

where W and Z are additional variables that influence sales Y. For example, W might represent a macrolevel economic variable (such as gross national product or disposable income) while Z might represent an apropos industry variable (such as housing starts or regulatory changes). Typically, more variables are added to the forecasting equation to try and explain the deviations of sales observations from simpler relationships having fewer variables.[3]

Since sales is just one input into financial planning, mention should also be made of how other variables are forecasted. Consider, for example, the inventory level for a firm or product. One possibility is to utilize one of the procedures already discussed for sales to forecast inventory directly. Another possibility, and one that is frequently used in practice, is to relate variables such as inventory to sales. In other words, a forecast of inventory is made indirectly through a forecast of sales. This might take the form of a simple "percentage-of-sales" relationship. Historical experience would be used to estimate the percentage relationships of inventory to sales. Note that the percentage-of-sales procedure is similar to the linear relationship already discussed, except that there is no intercept term and the percentage relationship is equivalent to the slope term. This procedure has the dual advantage of being easy to use, and also relatively accurate, especially for short-term forecasts. Moreover, many firms actually establish inventory levels on a percentage basis to sales.

Another aspect of forecasting has to do with the treatment of uncertainty. One possibility is to reflect uncertainty only in the sales forecast. Financial forecasts of flows and levels would be made for a range of different sales forecasts, and the range of outcomes (e.g., needed borrowing or excess funds) would be examined. If management assigns a numerical probability to each sales forecast, then "expected outcomes" can be calculated. Suppose, for example, that three sales forecasts are made for a particular product: optimistic, likely, and pessimistic. For each sales forecast, a probability is assigned, and a projection of needed borrowing is estimated. The values are as follows:

Type	Sales forecast	Probability	Needed borrowing
Optimistic	$800,000	.10	$50,000
Likely	700,000	.70	20,000
Pessimistic	500,000	.20	0

Expected sales for the product is found by multiplying each sales forecast by the associated probability and summing up all three forecasts

---

[3]It is not within the scope of this *Guide* to discuss and illustrate the more sophisticated procedures for forecasting. There are many excellent references on the method of least squares and other statistical techniques. Two, in particular, are R. Ferber, *Statistical Techniques in Market Research* (New York: McGraw-Hill Book Company, 1949), and R. G. Brown, *Smoothing Forecasting and Prediction of Discrete Time Series* (Englewood Cliffs, N.J.: Prentice-Hall, Inc., 1963).

Sales forecast		Probability		Weighted forecast
$800,000	×	.10	=	$ 80,000
700,000	×	.70	=	490,000
500,000	×	.20	=	100,000
		Expected sales		$670,000

In a similar manner, expected borrowing would be found

Needed borrowing	Probability	Weighted borrowing
$50,000	.10	$ 5,000
20,000	.70	14,000
0	.20	0
	Expected borrowing	$19,000

Probabilities and expected outcomes will be used frequently in this *Guide*.

Another possibility, albeit a much more complex procedure, is to allow each variable in the financial plan to vary. Simulation is a technique for systematically handling the uncertainty of many inputs to financial planning. We will not illustrate the use of simulation here. But in a later section of this chapter, computerized systems for financial planning will be discussed.

Much financial planning has to do with forecasting of flows—such as revenues, expenses, and cash inputs and outputs—toward better understanding the overall profitability and liquidity of the firm. Another part of financial planning is determining appropriate levels of various balance sheet accounts. Working capital planning focuses specifically on levels of current assets and current liabilities. The forecasting that is needed for this type of planning is of the various costs that are involved. Exhibit 2-4 is a typical pattern. As the level of the working capital account increases, "costs of too much" tend to increase, while "costs of too little" tend to decrease. Consider the costs associated with increasing the inventory level for a particular product. Warehousing and the value of funds invested in inventory are the costs of too much inventory. Foregone sales and profits are the costs of too little inventory. Based on a careful forecast of such costs, the financial manager for each working capital account should try to determine the

EXHIBIT 2-4

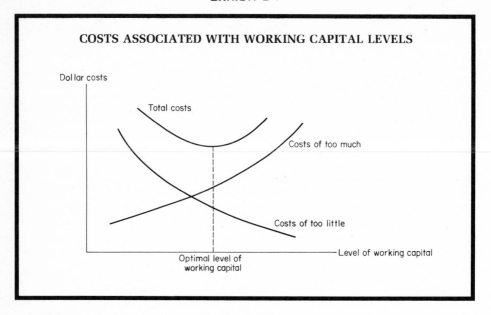

COSTS ASSOCIATED WITH WORKING CAPITAL LEVELS

particular level that minimizes the total of all relevant costs, and thus enhances firm profitability. In subsequent chapters, we will discuss the costs of too little and the costs of too much for many of the components of working capital.

One may question whether forecasting as an input to financial and working capital planning, be it for levels or flows, is an art or a science. Although graphical or statistical procedures may be used to extrapolate past experience, forecasting is still considered to be an art for two reasons. First, the financial manager must decide which of several available forecasting procedures is most appropriate in a given context. And second, the financial manager must decide when to temper the results of forecasting procedures with subjective judgment. Changes in technology, inflation, competition, top-level management, and government regulation could all cause a financial manager to alter a forecast based solely on historical experience. Furthermore, economic forecasts are seldom correct for long, and thus financial managers should always be prepared to revise their forecasts as new information becomes available.

PLANNING FINANCIAL FEASIBILITY

In Exhibit 2-1, it was suggested that financial planning can be divided into planning financial feasibility for new operations and financial planning for ongoing operations. This and the next sections of the chapter are devoted to further discussion and illustration of those two types of financial planning, but with special attention to the working capital implications. We begin here with planning financial feasibility. Our illustration is of a small and relatively simple new business, but the ideas and techniques would be just as applicable to a financial feasibility study for a new product or venture for an existing organization.

Suppose that you and a close friend have decided to start a retail bookstore business near the university campus where you were roommates. You plan to begin your business in January of 1978. Your friend is continuing graduate studies, but you plan to devote full time to the management of the bookstore. Your major competition is the university bookstore but that is located across the campus. By being much nearer the college dormitories, and by not specializing in just textbooks, you believe that there is good potential for growth of your business. Your forecast of book sales for the first several months of operation is as follows:

January 1978	100	July 1978	400	January 1979	600
February	200	August	600	February	600
March	300	September	500	March	500
April	300	October	600	April	700
May	400	November	700	May	400
June	500	December	1,400	June	500

Your average cost per book is estimated to be $6.50, and you plan an average sales price of $10.00 per book.

Your combined savings of $7,000 are supplemented by a $3,000 loan from the local bank to give you initial capital of $10,000. It is used to purchase $3,500 of fixtures for the store (1 percent depreciation per month), $5,850 of initial inventory (the cost of your first four months of forecasted book sales), and a beginning cash balance of $650. Your beginning balance sheet is as follows:

Assets		Liabilities and equity	
Cash	$ 650	Bank borrowing	$ 3,000
Inventory	5,850	Partnership equity	7,000
Fixtures	3,500	Total	$10,000
Total	$10,000		

You estimate that rent, advertising, utilities, depreciation, and other nonpersonnel fixed charges will be $545 per month. During the first year or so, you plan to pay yourself a salary of $500 per month, and you plan to hire part-time help for $250 per month.

In this illustration, as well as others in the chapters which follow, we will have occasion to discuss both variable and fixed costs. A *variable cost* is one which varies with the level of output or activity of an organization. Material and direct labor used in production are examples of variable costs. In contrast, a *fixed cost* is one which does *not* vary with level of output or activity. Rent, depreciation, and salaries of management are examples of fixed costs. Unfortunately, not all costs fit neatly into the variable and fixed categories. The total compensation to a salesman, for example, might consist of a base salary (a fixed cost to the firm) and a commission based on sales volume (a variable cost to the firm). In the retail bookstore illustration, the cost of books purchased for resale is a variable cost, while the other costs mentioned are fixed costs.

A first step in planning financial feasibility is to see if the forecasted level of book sales is sufficient to cover all forecasted expenses. Break-even analysis is a useful tool for doing so. The *regular break-even point* for a product or business is defined as that level of sales per period for which sales revenue just equals the total costs associated with the product or business. The break-even point is determined by setting up and solving the following equation:

$$\text{Sales revenue} = \text{variable costs} + \text{fixed costs}$$

In the illustration, it is convenient to treat a period as one month. The appropriate calculation is

Let X_r = regular break-even level of book sales
Set up the equation:

$$\underbrace{\$10.00X_r}_{\substack{\text{sales} \\ \text{revenue}}} = \underbrace{\$6.50\ X_r}_{\substack{\text{variable} \\ \text{cost}}} + \underbrace{\$545 + \$500 + \$250}_{\substack{\text{fixed} \\ \text{costs}}}$$

Rearrange and solve the equation:

$$(\$10.00 - 6.50)X_r = (\$545 + 500 + 250)$$
$$\$3.50X_r = \$1,295$$
$$X_r = \frac{\$1,295}{\$3.50}$$
$$X_r = 370 \text{ books per month}$$

Panel A of Exhibit 2-5 is a *regular break-even chart* for the illustration, and includes the regular break-even point. Note that fixed costs are added to variable costs to obtain total costs. The sales revenue line intersects the total

EXHIBIT 2-5

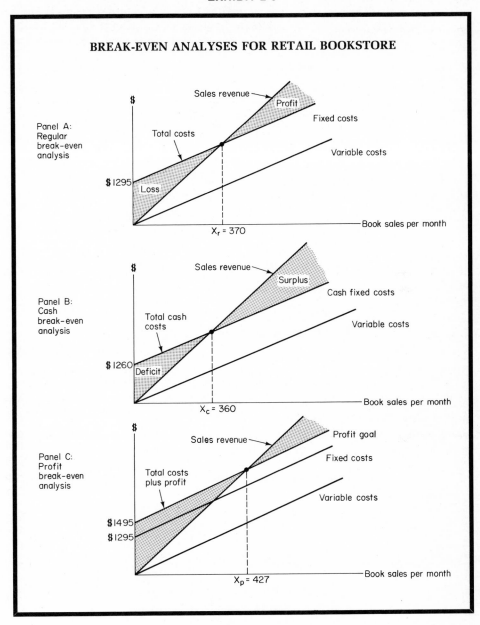

BREAK-EVEN ANALYSES FOR RETAIL BOOKSTORE

Panel A:
Regular
break-even
analysis

Sales revenue
Profit
Fixed costs
Total costs
Variable costs
$ 1295
Loss
$
Book sales per month
$X_r = 370$

Panel B:
Cash
break-even
analysis

Sales revenue
Surplus
Cash fixed costs
Total cash
costs
Variable costs
$ 1260
Deficit
$
Book sales per month
$X_c = 360$

Panel C:
Profit
break-even
analysis

Sales revenue
Profit goal
Fixed costs
Total costs
plus profit
Variable costs
$1495
$1295
$
Book sales per month
$X_p = 427$

cost line at the break-even point. The shaded area for sales *less* than 370 books per month designates an accounting loss. The shaded area for sales *greater* than 370 books per month designates an accounting profit. Using the chart, the monthly profit or loss at any level of forecasted sales can easily be determined.

Break-even analysis can be extended to focus more closely on the liquidity and profitability goals of the firm. We begin with liquidity. The *cash break-even point* is defined as that level of sales per period for which sales revenue just equals the cash outlays associated with the product or business. For the bookstore, depreciation ($35 per month) is the only noncash cost, and hence

Let X_c = cash break-even level of book sales
Set up the equation:

$$\underbrace{\$10.00X_c}_{\substack{\text{sales} \\ \text{revenue}}} = \underbrace{\$6.50X_c}_{\substack{\text{variable} \\ \text{costs}}} + \underbrace{\$510 + \$500 + \$250}_{\text{cash fixed costs}}$$

Rearrange and solve the equation:

$$\$3.50X_c = \$1,260$$
$$X_c = 360 \text{ books per month}$$

The cash break-even point is always lower than (or equal to) the regular break-even point because total fixed costs are always greater than (or equal to) cash fixed costs. Panel B of Exhibit 2-5 is a *cash break-even chart*. At sales above the cash break-even point, the shaded area represents a cash surplus, while at sales below the cash break-even point, the shaded area represents a cash deficit.

For the profitability goal, the *profit break-even point* is defined as that level of sales per period for which sales revenue just equals total costs plus a designated profit goal. Suppose that you set a first-year profit goal of $200 per month. The calculation would be as follows

Let X_p = profit break-even level of book sales
Set up the equation:

$$\underbrace{\$10.00X_p}_{\substack{\text{sales} \\ \text{revenue}}} = \underbrace{\$6.50X_p}_{\substack{\text{variable} \\ \text{costs}}} + \underbrace{\$1,295}_{\substack{\text{fixed} \\ \text{costs}}} + \underbrace{\$200}_{\substack{\text{profit} \\ \text{goal}}}$$

Rearrange and solve the equation:

$$\$3.50X_p = \$1,495$$
$$X_p = 427 \text{ books per month}$$

Panel C of Exhibit 2-5 is a profit break-even chart for the retail bookstore. The profit break-even point is higher than the other two break-even points because sales revenue must now cover costs plus profit. The shaded area for sales greater than 427 books per month represents additional profit to the business beyond the $200 per month goal which you set for your bookstore.

Recalling your sales forecast for the bookstore, it is apparent from the calculations that liquidity will be achieved by May 1978. Your profit goal will first be realized in June, and then again in August 1978. Remember, of course, that if your forecasts of sales and costs are not correct, then the dates for achieving liquidity and profitability may be different. It would be well to repeat the calculations for alternative forecasts of variable and fixed costs in order to check their impact on the respective break-even points. Break-even analysis also could be used to determine the effect of changing the price of the books being sold. These additional steps in testing the sensitivity of the break-even points may prove to be helpful in deciding whether or not to proceed with the bookstore venture.

Two subtle implications of working capital to break-even analysis should also be mentioned. First, regular break-even analysis (panel A in Exhibit 2-5) assumes that all books purchased are sold in the same month, or that inventory is held constant. Second, cash break-even analysis (panel B) assumes that all sales revenue is cash revenue, or that accounts receivable are held constant. In most cases, neither inventory nor accounts receivable would be expected to stay constant. As a result, the break-even points should be viewed as but rough estimates about the likely prospects for a proposed business.

The cash break-even point, in particular, should be viewed as but a preliminary check on firm liquidity. It is *not* a substitute for careful cash budgeting. A *cash budget* is a financial statement that compares cash inflows with cash outflows for each period during a planning horizon, and thereby determines when additional cash is needed or when excess cash is available. For the retail bookstore illustration, Exhibit 2-6 includes the details that are necessary in a cash budget for just the first three months of 1978. The month-by-month comparison is relatively straightforward once cash receipts and cash disbursements are determined. Care must be taken, however, in projecting cash receipts and cash disbursements. We see that a distinction must be made between cash sales (75 percent of total sales assumed in the illustration) and credit sales (25 percent, to be collected the following month). A distinction also must be made between purchases paid in cash (67 percent) or on credit from the supplier (33 percent, to be paid the next month). Necessary borrowing (interest rate 1 percent monthly) is projected in increments of $200. It is desirable to have a cash balance of about $1,000 at the beginning of each month. The "cumulative borrowing" row in the cash budget clearly depicts the liquidity needs of the business. For your bookstore, $9,600 of borrowed funds will be needed in March 1978 in order to sustain the projected growth of your bookstore volume.

The working capital implications are clear. Growth in sales is accompanied by an increase in your cash balance (from $650 to $969), accounts receivable (0 to $750), and especially in inventory ($5,850 to $10,400). Only

EXHIBIT 2-6

CASH BUDGETING FOR RETAIL BOOKSTORE

	January	February	March
Sales forecast	$1,000	$2,000	$3,000
Cash sales	750	1,500	2,250
Credit sales collected	0	250	500
Cash receipts	750	1,750	2,750
Cost of sales	650	1,300	1,950
+ Ending inventory	7,800	9,750	10,400
− Beginning inventory	5,850	7,800	9,750
Purchases	2,600	3,250	2,600
Credit payment	0	867	1,083
Cash payment	1,733	2,167	1,733
Other cash expenses	1,260	1,260	1,260
Cash disbursements	2,993	4,294	4,076
Beginning cash balance	650	977	977
+ Cash receipts	750	1,750	2,750
− Cash disbursements	2,993	4,294	4,076
− Interest on borrowing	30	56	82
Cash balance before borrowing	(1,623)	(1,623)	(431)
Additional borrowing	2,600	2,600	1,400
Cumulative borrowing	5,600	8,200	9,600
Cash balance after borrowing	977	977	969

a part of this is made available by suppliers, and there are no profits during the first quarter of 1978. Working capital requirements, in fact, cause you to almost double the total capital invested in the retail bookstore during just the first quarter of 1978.*

The bookstore example illustrates well what might be termed the

*Further analysis of the bookstore business will be found in the problems at the end of the chapter.

"dilemma of prosperity." Namely, that capital requirements, largely a result of working capital, are frequently severe for firms that contemplate rapid growth. The extent of the dilemma is readily seen with a month-by-month projection, and comparison of cumulative required borrowing (from the cash budget) with before-tax profitability (from the income statement). The clear advantage of such projections and comparisons is that the financial manager recognizes the problem enough in advance so as to try and secure the needed financing. If that financing is not available, then a decision should be made not to continue with the project, at least at the present time.

ONGOING FINANCIAL PLANNING

The retail bookstore illustration was appropriate for discussing break-even analysis and cash budgeting as tools for planning financial feasibility. However, the bookstore illustration is too simplistic for discussing the financial planning of an ongoing business firm. It also does not provide a very good picture of how cash budgeting and working capital planning fit into overall financial planning. Because of sheer size and the international scope of their operations, General Motors, Gillette, and Eastman Kodak likewise would not provide very useful examples of financial planning for purposes of this book. As a workable compromise, we choose to continue the illustration of Crescent Corporation.

Arthur Hanson, as vice president of finance, spearheads financial planning for Crescent. He also coordinates with planning in other functional areas of the business. His organization of financial planning for Crescent is depicted in the schematic diagram of Exhibit 2-7. It shows the interrelationships between various pieces of the total financial plan, but with special emphasis on the cash budget, which as previously mentioned, is a key part of working capital planning. A series of nineteen figures which comprise the total financial plan will be briefly reviewed.*

Figure 1 is not a plan or financial statement, but rather a summary of parameters and other information that is needed in constructing an overall financial plan. Included is the average price per unit, a cost breakdown for each unit sold, credit terms to customers and from suppliers, and certain other data that is needed in the projections. Mr. Hanson does not generate all that information himself, as it should reflect the collective thinking of several relevant Crescent managers. Figure 2 is a balance sheet as of the beginning of 1978, the calendar year for which the financial plan is to be prepared. Most likely, it is also a preliminary statement since Hanson and others on the Crescent management team certainly cannot wait until New Year's Eve 1977 in order to begin planning for 1978!

---

*In order to show how information from one statement is used in successive statements, it is convenient here to temporarily discontinue the numbering system for exhibits that is used in this chapter and throughout the book.

EXHIBIT 2-7

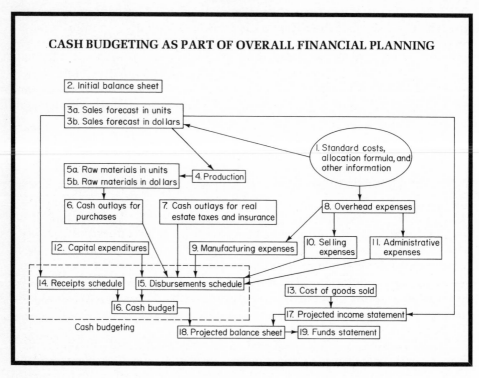

CASH BUDGETING AS PART OF OVERALL FINANCIAL PLANNING

The next components of the plan do not originate with financial managers, but rather are input to mainstream financial planning. Figure 3a is a sales forecast in units, while Figure 3b is dollar sales. The particular format, which is maintained throughout the illustration, includes a monthly projection for the first three months of 1978, and then quarterly projections for the rest of the year. Data are shown both for sales through distributors and sales through the Speedy Cleaners subsidiary. The highest sales volume is projected for the third quarter of 1978. Figure 4 is a production schedule, and Figures 5a (units) and 5b (dollars) are raw materials budgets. These schedules support the sales forecast.

The next series of projections have to do with expenses and cash flows that result from and are consistent with prior exhibits. Figure 6 projects the cash outlays associated with purchases, while Figure 7 shows the incidental cash outlays for real estate taxes and insurance. Overhead expenses for Crescent are projected in Figure 8, and then allocated to manufacturing expenses (Figure 9), selling expenses (Figure 10), and administrative expenses (Figure 11). This allocation is based on the particular cost accounting system used by Crescent. Capital expenditures are shown in Figure 12. The cost-of-goods-sold calculation for Crescent is presented in Figure 13.

FIGURE 1

CRESCENT CORPORATION
FINANCIAL PLANNING INFORMATION

- Retail price per unit $80.00
- Cost breakdown, per unit:

Raw materials	7.90
Direct labor	10.00
Misc. mfg. expense	0.75
Electrical power	1.10
Other direct costs	3.12
Total cost	$22.87

- Terms of purchase (from suppliers)
  2%/30 days, net 60 days
- Overhead allocation:

Manufacturing expenses	80%
Selling expenses	10%
Administrative expenses	10%

- Selling expenses:

Commissions	4% net sales to distributors
	20% net sales to Speedy
Advertising	10% net sales
Miscellaneous	3% net sales

- Cash dividends $80,000 ($20,000 quarterly)
- Interest 8%
- Federal tax rate 45%

- Terms of sale (allowed to customer):

  Speedy Cleaners

  50% on cash basis (7% discount)
  50% on institutional basis
  (30% down + 7 equal payments)

  Distributors

  50% cash discount (30 days net)

FIGURE 2

CRESCENT CORPORATION
BALANCE SHEET, DECEMBER 31, 1977

Assets			**Liabilities**	
Cash		$ 98,836	Accounts payable	$ 126,400
Accounts receivable		504,000	Notes payable	200,000
Installment notes receivable		201,600	Federal taxes payable	288,000
Inventory			Common stock and surplus	400,000
Raw materials		347,600	Retained earnings	1,198,218
Finished goods		182,960	Total	$2,212,618
Prepaid expenses		46,022		
Land		91,600		
Buildings	$800,000			
Acc. depr.	360,000	440,000		
Machinery	$672,000			
Acc. depr.	372,000	300,000		
Total		$2,212,618		

FIGURE 3a

SALES FORECAST (IN UNITS)

Item	January	February	March	1st quarter	2d quarter	3d quarter	4th quarter	Year
Speedy Cleaners	1,800	1,800	1,800	5,400	6,400	7,000	6,600	25,400
Distributors	12,600	12,600	12,600	37,800	43,600	52,400	43,400	177,200
Total	14,400	14,400	14,400	43,200	50,000	59,400	50,000	202,600

FIGURE 3b

SALES FORECAST

Item	January	February	March	1st quarter	2d quarter	3d quarter	4th quarter	Year
Speedy Cleaners—cash	$ 72,000	$ 72,000	$ 72,000	$ 216,000	$ 256,000	$ 280,000	$ 264,000	$1,016,000
Less 7% discount	5,040	5,040	5,040	15,120	17,920	19,600	18,480	71,120
Net cash sales	$ 66,960	$ 66,960	$ 66,960	$ 200,880	$ 238,080	$ 260,400	$ 245,520	$ 944,880
Speedy Cleaners—installment	72,000	72,000	72,000	216,000	256,000	280,000	264,000	1,016,000
Distributors	504,000	504,000	504,000	1,512,000	1,744,000	2,096,000	1,736,000	7,088,000
Total net sales	$642,960	$642,960	642,960	$1,928,880	$2,238,080	$2,636,400	$2,245,520	$9,048,880

FIGURE 4

PRODUCTION (IN UNITS)

Item	January	February	March	1st quarter	2d quarter	3d quarter	4th quarter	Year
Sales forecast (3a)	14,400	14,400	14,400	43,200	50,000	59,400	50,000	202,600
Desired ending inventory	8,000	8,000	8,000	8,000	12,000	6,600	10,600	10,600
Subtotal	22,400	22,400	22,400	51,200	62,000	66,000	60,600	213,200
Beginning inventory	8,000	8,000	8,000	8,000	8,000	12,000	6,600	8,000
Required production	14,400	14,400	14,400	43,200	54,000	54,000	54,000	205,200

RAW MATERIALS (IN UNITS)

Item	January	February	March	1st quarter	2d quarter	3d quarter	4th quarter	Year
Used in production (4)	14,400	14,400	14,400	43,200	54,000	54,000	54,000	205,200
Desired ending inventory	45,600	47,200	48,800	48,800	50,800	52,800	46,800	46,800
Subtotal	60,000	61,600	63,200	92,000	104,800	106,800	100,800	252,000
Beginning inventory	44,000	45,600	47,200	44,000	48,800	50,800	52,800	44,000
Required purchases	16,000	16,000	16,000	48,000	56,000	56,000	48,000	208,000

RAW MATERIALS

Item	January	February	March	1st quarter	2d quarter	3d quarter	4th quarter	Year
Used in production	$113,760	$113,760	$113,760	$341,280	$426,600	$426,600	$426,600	$1,621,080
Desired ending inventory	360,240	372,880	385,520	385,520	401,320	417,120	369,720	369,720
Subtotal	$474,000	$486,640	$499,280	$726,800	$827,920	$843,720	$796,320	$1,990,800
Beginning inventory	347,600	360,240	372,880	347,600	385,520	401,320	417,120	347,600
Required purchases	$126,400	$126,400	$126,400	$379,200	$442,400	$442,400	$379,200	$1,643,200

FIGURE 6

CASH OUTLAYS FOR PURCHASES

Item	January	February	March	1st quarter	2d quarter	3d quarter	4th quarter	Year
Beginning accounts payable	$126,400	$126,400	$126,400	$126,400	$126,400	$126,400	$126,400	$ 126,400
Required purchases (5b)	126,400	126,400	126,400	379,200	442,400	442,400	379,200	1,643,200
Subtotal	$252,800	$252,800	$252,800	$505,600	$568,800	$568,800	$505,600	$1,769,600
– Cash discounts taken	2,528	2,528	2,528	7,584	8,848	8,848	8,848	34,128
– Cash payment	123,872	123,872	123,872	371,616	433,552	433,552	433,552	1,672,272
Ending accounts payable	$126,400	$126,400	$126,400	$126,400	$126,400	$126,400	$ 63,200	$ 63,200

FIGURE 7

CASH LAYOUTS FOR REAL ESTATE TAXES AND INSURANCE

Item	January	February	March	1st quarter	2d quarter	3d quarter	4th quarter	Year
Real estate taxes	0	0	0	0	0	$12,900	0	$12,900
Insurance, buildings	0	0	0	0	$1,800	0	0	1,800
Insurance, machinery	0	0	0	0	2,400	0	0	2,400
Total	0	0	0	0	$4,200	$12,900	0	$17,100

FIGURE 8

OVERHEAD EXPENSES

Item	January	February	March	1st quarter	2d quarter	3d quarter	4th quarter	Year
Heat	0	0	0	0	$16,000	$33,000	$18,000	$ 67,000
Light	$ 2,000	$ 2,000	$ 2,000	6,000	6,600	7,200	6,600	26,400
Repairs	1,500	1,500	1,500	4,500	4,500	4,500	4,500	18,000
Total cash outlay	$ 3,500	$ 3,500	$ 3,500	$10,500	$27,100	$44,700	$29,100	$111,400
Depreciation—buildings	2,000	2,000	2,000	6,000	6,750	6,750	6,750	26,250
Insurance—buildings	260	260	260	780	930	930	930	3,570
Real estate taxes	1,000	1,000	1,000	3,000	3,300	3,300	3,300	12,900
Total overhead	$ 6,760	$ 6,760	$ 6,760	$20,280	$38,080	$55,680	$40,080	$154,120
Allocated to:								
Manufacturing expense (80%)	$10,274	$10,274	$10,276	$30,824	$30,824	$30,824	$30,824	$123,296
Selling expense (10%)	1,284	1,284	1,284	3,852	3,854	3,854	3,852	15,412
Administrative expense (10%)	1,284	1,284	1,284	3,852	3,854	3,854	3,852	15,412

FIGURE 9

MANUFACTURING EXPENSES

Item	January	February	March	1st quarter	2d quarter	3d quarter	4th quarter	Year
Direct labor	$144,000	$144,000	$144,000	$432,000	$540,000	$540,000	$540,000	$2,052,000
Misc. mfg.	10,800	10,800	10,800	32,400	40,500	40,500	40,500	153,900
Electrical power	15,840	15,840	15,840	47,520	59,400	59,400	59,400	225,720
Indirect labor	20,160	20,160	20,160	60,480	70,800	70,800	70,800	272,880
Maintenance—equipment	5,600	5,600	5,600	16,800	20,580	20,580	20,580	78,540
Total cash outlay	$196,400	$196,400	$196,400	$589,200	$731,280	$731,280	$731,280	$2,783,040
Allocated overhead (8)	10,274	10,274	10,276	30,824	30,824	30,824	30,824	123,296
Depreciation—machinery	8,000	8,000	8,000	24,000	29,400	29,400	29,400	112,200
Insurance—machinery	1,000	1,000	1,000	3,000	3,600	3,600	3,600	13,800
Total	$215,674	$215,674	$215,676	$647,024	$795,104	$795,104	$795,104	$3,032,336

FIGURE 10

SELLING EXPENSES

Item	January	February	March	1st quarter	2d quarter	3d quarter	4th quarter	Year
Commissions:								
Installment sales—Speedy	$ 14,400	$ 14,400	$ 14,400	$ 43,200	$ 51,200	$ 56,000	$ 52,800	$ 203,200
Cash sales— Speedy	13,392	13,392	13,392	40,176	47,616	52,080	49,104	188,976
Distributor sales	20,160	20,160	20,160	60,480	71,760	83,840	69,440	283,520
Advertising	64,296	64,296	64,296	192,888	223,808	263,640	224,552	904,888
Miscellaneous	19,289	19,288	19,289	57,866	67,142	79,092	67,366	271,466
Salaries	48,880	48,880	48,880	146,640	168,656	168,656	168,656	652,548
Total cash outlay	$180,417	$180,416	$180,417	$541,250	$628,162	$703,288	$631,896	$2,504,598
Allocated overhead (8)	1,284	1,284	1,284	3,852	3,854	3,854	3,852	15,412
Total	$181,701	$181,700	$181,701	$545,102	$632,016	$707,142	$635,748	$2,520,010

FIGURE 11

ADMINISTRATIVE EXPENSES

Item	January	February	March	1st quarter	2d quarter	3d quarter	4th quarter	Year
Supplies	$19,289	$19,288	$19,289	$ 57,866	$ 67,142	$ 79,092	$ 67,366	$271,466
Salaries	50,000	50,000	50,000	150,000	150,000	150,000	150,000	600,000
Total cash outlay	$69,289	$69,288	$69,289	$207,866	$217,142	$229,092	$217,366	$871,466
Allocated overhead (8)	1,284	1,284	1,284	3,852	3,854	3,854	3,852	15,412
Total	$70,573	$70,572	$70,573	$211,718	$220,996	$232,946	$221,218	$886,878

FIGURE 12

CAPITAL EXPENDITURES

Item	January	February	March	1st quarter	2d quarter	3d quarter	4th quarter	Year
Building addition	$30,000	$30,000	$ 40,000	$100,000	0	0	0	$100,000
New machinery	0	0	151,200	151,200	0	0	0	151,200
Total cash outlay	$30,000	$30,000	$191,200	$251,200	0	0	0	$251,200

FIGURE 13

COST OF GOODS SOLD

Item	January	February	March	1st quarter	2d quarter	3d quarter	4th quarter	Year
Raw materials (5b)	$113,760	$113,760	$113,760	$ 341,280	$ 426,600	$ 426,600	$ 426,600	$1,621,080
− Cash discounts taken (6)	2,528	2,528	2,528	7,584	8,848	8,848	8,848	34,128
Subtotal	$111,232	$111,232	$111,232	$ 333,696	$ 417,752	$ 417,752	$ 417,752	$1,586,52
Manufacturing expenses (9)	215,674	215,674	215,676	647,024	795,104	795,104	795,104	3,032,336
Total production cost	$326,906	$326,906	$326,908	$ 980,720	$1,212,856	$1,212,856	$1,212,856	$4,619,288
Beginning inventory	182,960	182,960	182,960	182,960	182,960	272,440	150,292	182,960
Subtotal	$509,866	$509,866	$509,868	$1,163,680	$1,395,816	$1,485,296	$1,363,148	$4,802,248
− Ending inventory	182,960	182,960	182,960	182,960	272,440	150,292	240,772	240,772
Cost of goods sold	$326,906	$326,906	$326,908	$ 980,720	$1,123,376	$1,335,004	$1,122,376	$4,561,476

Figures 14 to 16 comprise the cash budget for Crescent. Cash receipts are summarized in Figure 14 and cash disbursements are totaled in Figure 15. Cash receipts and cash disbursements then are brought together in Figure 16, and the required borrowing for Crescent Corporation is determined. We see that total borrowing of $150,000 is necessary during the first quarter of 1978, but that it is repaid during the last half of that year. Interest on the required borrowing also is reflected as a disbursement in the cash budget.

Paralleling the portrayal of firm liquidity in the cash budget, firm profitability is portrayed in the income statement of Figure 17. We see that profitability of Crescent increases until the fourth quarter. Figure 17 also reveals that portion of after-tax earnings that is paid to common shareholders, and that portion that is retained in the business. Retained earnings is projected to grow to $1,701,137 by the end of 1978.

The last two exhibits complete the financial planning. Figure 18 is a projected balance sheet as of the end of the year 1978. When compared with the beginning balance sheet (Figure 2), it is easy to see the changes that are projected for the year. Total assets for Crescent must increase by over 22 percent in order to support the growing sales volume of the firm. The statement of changes in financial position for 1978 (Figure 19) shows that cash flow (earnings plus depreciation) is used to pay cash dividends, add to the production capacity of the firm, and finally to increase Crescent's net working capital. A further breakdown of working capital reveals how each current asset and current liability changes during 1978. Once again, working capital is seen to be an important part of firm growth.

Relationships between the cash budget, projected income statement, and projected balance sheet should be apparent to the reader who diligently follows through the series of figures for Crescent Corporation. Working capital planning cannot be separated from overall financial planning. Projected values for one are used in the other, and conversely. The financial planning process allows Arthur Hanson and other managers of Crescent Corporation to see how liquidity and profitability are interrelated. It also allows those managers, though it is not done so here, to explore the sensitivity of liquidity and profitability to different parameters and forecasts, as well as to other sales forecasts which trigger the entire set of financial projections. Finally, the output of financial planning provides a starting point for further investigating individual working capital accounts and policies—just as we shall do in subsequent chapters.

COMPUTERIZED FINANCIAL PLANNING SYSTEMS

Even for relatively small firms such as Crescent Corporation, financial planning turns out to be a rather complex task for management. With only two distinct sales forecasts (Speedy Cleaners and distributors), and with a simple planning format (monthly and quarterly), a one-year financial plan still involved a series of nineteen financial schedules and statements. Imagine

FIGURE 14

CASH RECEIPTS SCHEDULE

Item	January	February	March	1st quarter	2d quarter	3d quarter	4th quarter	Year
Cash sales—Speedy (3b)	$ 66,960	$ 66,960	$ 66,960	$ 200,880	$ 238,080	$ 260,400	$ 245,520	$ 944,880
Installment collections—Speedy	72,000	72,000	72,000	216,000	230,400	251,200	268,000	965,600
Distributor collections	504,000	504,000	504,000	1,512,000	1,688,000	1,976,000	1,856,000	7,032,000
Total	$642,960	$642,960	$642,960	$1,928,880	$2,156,480	$2,487,600	$2,369,520	$8,942,480

FIGURE 15

CASH DISBURSEMENTS SCHEDULE

Item	January	February	March	1st quarter	2d quarter	3d quarter	4th quarter	Year
Payment for purchases (6)	$123,872	$123,872	$123,872	$ 371,616	$ 433,552	$ 433,552	$ 433,552	$1,672,272
Real estate taxes and insurance (7)	0	0	0	0	4,200	12,900	0	17,100
Overhead expenses (8)	3,500	3,500	3,500	10,500	27,100	44,700	29,100	111,400
Manufacturing expenses (9)	196,400	196,400	196,400	589,200	731,280	731,280	731,280	2,783,040
Selling expenses (10)	180,417	180,416	180,417	541,250	628,162	703,288	631,896	2,504,596
Administrative expenses (11)	69,289	69,288	69,289	207,866	217,142	229,092	217,366	871,466
Capital expenditures (12)	30,000	30,000	191,200	251,200	0	0	0	251,200
Income tax payments	0	0	72,000	72,000	72,000	72,000	72,000	280,000
Dividends	0	0	20,000	20,000	20,000	20,000	20,000	80,000
Total	$603,478	$603,476	$856,678	$2,063,632	$2,133,436	$2,246,812	$2,135,194	$8,571,074

FIGURE 16

CASH BUDGET, CALENDAR YEAR 1978

Item	January	February	March	1st quarter	2d quarter	3d quarter	4th quarter	Year
Beginning cash balance	$ 98,836	$138,318	$277,802	$ 98,836	$ 109,418	$ 125,462	$ 109,250	$ 98,836
Cash receipts (14)	642,960	642,960	642,960	1,928,880	2,156,480	2,487,600	2,369,520	8,942,480
Total available cash	$741,796	$781,278	$920,762	$2,027,716	$2,265,898	$2,613,062	$2,478,770	$9,041,316
− Cash disbursements (15)	603,478	603,476	856,678	2,063,632	2,133,436	2,246,812	2,135,194	$8,579,074
− Interest on borrowing	0	0	4,666	4,666	7,000	7,000	2,000	20,666
Ending balance before borrowing	$138,318	$177,802	$ 59,418	$ (40,582)	$ 125,462	$ 359,250	$ 341,576	$ 441,576
+ Additional borrowing needed	0	100,000	50,000	150,000	0	0	0	0
− Repayment of borrowing	0	0	0	0	0	250,000	100,000	200,000
Ending balance after borrowing	$138,318	$277,802	$109,418	$ 109,418	$ 125,462	$ 109,250	$ 241,576	$ 241,576

FIGURE 17

PROJECTED INCOME STATEMENT, CALENDAR YEAR 1978

Item	January	February	March	1st quarter	2nd quarter	3rd quarter	4th quarter	Year
Net sales (3b)	$642,960	$642,960	$642,960	$1,928,880	$2,238,080	$2,636,400	$2,245,520	$9,048,880
Cost of goods sold (13)	326,906	326,906	326,908	980,720	1,123,376	1,335,004	1,122,376	4,561,476
Gross profit	$316,054	$316,054	$316,052	$948,160	$1,114,704	$1,301,396	$1,123,144	$4,487,404
Selling expense (10)	181,701	181,700	181,701	545,102	632,016	707,142	635,748	2,520,008
Administrative expense (11)	70,573	70,572	70,573	211,718	220,996	232,946	221,218	886,878
Earnings before interest and taxes	$63,780	$63,780	$63,778	$191,340	$261,692	$361,308	$266,178	$1,080,518*
Interest (16)	0	0	4,666	4,666	7,000	7,000	2,000	20,666

Earnings before taxes	$63,780	$63,780	$59,112	$186,674	$254,692	$354,308	$264,178	$1,059,852
Federal taxes payable	28,701	28,701	26,601	84,003	114,611	159,439	118,880	476,933
Earnings after taxes	$35,079	$35,079	$32,511	$102,671	$140,081	$194,869	$145,298	$582,919
Common stock dividends	0	0	20,000	20,000	20,000	20,000	20,000	80,000
Added to retained earnings	$35,079	$35,079	$12,511	$82,671	$120,081	$174,869	$125,298	$502,919

Retained earnings (Dec. 31, 1977)	$1,198,218
Added to retained earnings in 1978	502,919
Retained earnings (Dec. 31, 1978)	$1,701,137

*After deducting $138,450 of depreciation included in cost of goods sold, selling expenses, and administrative expenses.

FIGURE 18

CRESCENT CORPORATION
PROJECTED BALANCE SHEET, DECEMBER 31, 1978

Assets			Liabilities	
Cash (16)		$ 241,576	Accounts payable (6)	$ 63,200
Accounts receivable		560,000	Federal taxes payable (17)	476,933
Installment notes receivable (14)		252,000	Common stock and surplus	400,000
Inventory			Retained earnings	1,701,137
Raw materials (5b)		369,720	Total	$2,641,270
Finished goods (13)		240,772		
Prepaid expenses		32,852		
Land		91,600		
Buildings	$900,000			
Acc. depr.	386,250	513,750		
Machinery	$823,200			
Acc.depr.	484,200	339,000		
Total		$2,641,270		

FIGURE 19

CRESCENT CORPORATION
PROJECTED STATEMENT OF CHANGES IN FINANCIAL POSITION,
CALENDAR YEAR, 1978

Sources of Funds		Uses of Funds	
Earnings from operations	$582,919	Cash dividends	$ 80,000
Depreciation	138,450	Building addition	100,000
Total	$721,369	New machinery	151,200
		Increased net working capital	390,169
		Total	$721,369

Summary of Changes in Working Capital Position

Increased cash	$142,740
Increased accounts receivable	56,000
Increased notes receivable	50,400
Increased inventory	79,932
Decreased prepaid expenses	(13,170)
Decreased accounts payable	63,200
Decreased notes payable	200,000
Increased taxes payable	(188,933)
Increased net working capital	$390,169

the added complexity in financial planning if Crescent had ten products, or perhaps fifty—or if they required weekly projections for two months, and then monthly projections for the rest of a two-year planning horizon. Or if Crescent had twenty divisions located throughout the United States, plus five additional divisions in foreign countries. Imagine further the added complexity if Crescent's projections are repeated a number of times in order to reflect the uncertainty in the sales and other forecasts used in the process.

Fortunately, the task of financial and working capital planning can be greatly facilitated with the use of electronic computers. Almost all firms use computers in billing customers, preparing payroll, and maintaining inventory records. Computers are also used by firms in research, engineering, production scheduling, and other problem-solving. The computers used in these various applications are frequently leased and sometimes owned. Either way, it takes a relatively small amount of computer capacity in order to do a great deal of financial planning.

Computerized financial planning is essentially a simulation of the future financial activity of a firm, culminating in projected financial statements. Although the scope and format of financial planning varies considerably from firm to firm, the basic structure in most cases would resemble the series of figures for Crescent Corporation that have been reviewed. The advantage of using computers, of course, is that that structure can be repeated for many products and for many variations of the input forecasts.

Although there can be little argument as to the importance of financial planning by management, or of the potential advantage of using computers in so doing, there is one question that remains. Namely, should management acquire the capability for computerized financial planning from an external source, or should management develop the capability within their firm? The decision about internal-versus-external capability depends on the size and complexity of the organization, the scope of financial planning that is desired, and flexibility for future change. In those cases where management decides *not* to develop the capability internally, a variety of financial planning programs are available from computer software companies. These services feature different types of computers, both interactive and batch modes of processing, and different types of reports that can be generated for management. Costs of external financial planning services, which include charges for development, data storage, and processing time, range upward from a minimum monthly expense of about $100.

SUMMARY

Planning is the starting point for management action, with financial considerations heavily involved once the basic thrust of the firm is identified. Financial plans and budgets are the result of a planning process that ideally involves all relevant levels of management. Different methods of forecasting the various inputs needed in financial planning were reviewed and compared. The important role of working capital within financial planning was illustrated both for the financial feasibility of a new product or for the projected operations of an ongoing business. The usefulness of computerized financial planning by a firm was stressed.

Problem 2-1

Using the data in Exhibit 2-3, forecast sales for 1978 to 1980 with the method of least squares and using only the most recent five years. Compare your results with the forecasts based on a freehand fit in Exhibit 2-2.

SOLUTION: Summing values for the $N = 5$ years, 1973–1977, we obtain from Exhibit 2-3 the following:

$$\Sigma X = 40 \qquad \Sigma X^2 = 330$$
$$\Sigma Y = 94 \qquad \Sigma XY = 782$$

Repeating the calculations gives

$$a = \frac{(94)(330) - (40)(782)}{(5)(330) - (40)(40)} = \frac{-260}{50} = -5.2$$
$$b = \frac{(5)(782) - (40)(94)}{(5)(330) - (40)(40)} = \frac{150}{50} = 3.0$$

and thus the least squares line is $Y = -5.2 + 3.0X$.
  The forecast would be made as follows:

Year	X	$Y = -5.2 + 3.0X$	Forecast
1978	11	27.8	$27,800
1979	12	30.8	30,800
1980	13	33.8	33,800

and can then be compared with the forecast based on a freehand fit.

Year	Freehand forecast	Least squares forecast	Percentage difference
1978	$24,000	$27,800	15.8
1979	27,000	30,800	14.1
1980	30,000	33,800	12.7

Problem 2-2

Recall the retail bookstore illustration in the chapter. Suppose you are forced to change book suppliers, and in so doing the average cost per book is increased from $6.50 to $7.75. What effect does that have on the regular break-even point for the bookstore?

SOLUTION: Let X_r = regular break-even point

$$\$10.00X_r = \$7.25X_r + \$545 + \$500 + \$250$$
$$(\$10.00 - \$7.25)X_r = (\$545 + \$500 + \$250)$$
$$\$2.75X_r = \$1,295$$
$$X_r = \frac{\$1,295}{\$2.75} = 471 \text{ books per month}$$

which is an increase of $471 - 370 = 101$ books.

Problem 2-3

For the same retail bookstore, and with the average cost per book at $6.50 (as in the chapter), prepare a projected income statement for the first quarter of 1978, and a projected balance sheet at the end of the first quarter. Also prepare a statement of change in financial position for the first quarter of 1978.

Problem 2-4

Sales for the last eleven months of 1977 for the Wholesale Widget Company (in thousands of units) were as follows:

February	30	June	50	October	60
March	30	July	40	November	40
April	40	August	60	December	50
May	40	September	50		

Forecast widget sales for the first half of 1978.

Problem 2-5

Using the sales forecast from the previous problem, prepare a cash budget for the first four months of 1978. Here are some additional facts:

- In that month, 75 percent of sales are collected; the remaining 25 percent are collected the following month.

- Purchases of widgets for resale average 70 percent of sales price; begin each month with inventory equal to next three months of sales; 50 percent purchases paid in current month; remaining 50 percent the following month.

- Begin 1978 with cash balance of $12,000; additional borrowing obtained in increments of $500.

- Variable expenses are the costs of widgets sold; fixed costs amount to $8,000.

Problem 2-6

Suppose that a new product is being introduced by a leading toy company. Management believes that the first year of sales for the product will depend critically on the health of the economy for that year. Four different forecasts and associated probabilities are set forth:

Economy	Sales forecast	Probability
Large advance	$300,000	.10
Small advance	240,000	.60
Slight downturn	200,000	.25
Recession	100,000	.05

What is the expected value of sales for the product?

SUGGESTED READINGS

Bacon, J.: MANAGING THE BUDGET FUNCTION (New York: The Conference Board, Inc., 1970).

Beranek, W.: WORKING CAPITAL MANAGEMENT (Belmont, Calif.: Wadsworth Publishing Company, Inc., 1966), Chapter 2.

Brown, R. G.: SMOOTHING FORECASTING AND PREDICTION OF DISCRETE TIME SERIES (Englewood Cliffs, N.J.: Prentice-Hall, Inc., 1963).

Davis, R. C.: INDUSTRIAL ORGANIZATION AND MANAGEMENT, 3d ed. (New York: Harper & Brothers, 1957), Chapter 29.

Drucker, P. F.: MANAGEMENT: TASKS, RESPONSIBILITIES, PRACTICES (New York: Harper & Row, Publishers, Incorporated, 1974), Chapters 4–10.

Ferber, R.: STATISTICAL TECHNIQUES IN MARKET RESEARCH (New York: McGraw-Hill Book Company, 1949).

Helfert, E. A.: TECHNIQUES OF FINANCING ANALYSIS, 4th ed. (Homewood, Ill.: Richard D. Irwin, Inc., 1977), Chapter 3.

Smith, J. E.: CASH FLOW MANAGEMENT (Cambridge, England: Woodhead-Faulkner Limited, 1975), Chapters 1–5.

Stancill, J. McN., Jr.: THE MANAGEMENT OF WORKING CAPITAL (Los Angeles: University of Southern California Press, 1970), Chapter 7.

Steiner, G. A.: TOP MANAGEMENT PLANNING (New York: The Macmillan Company, 1969), Chapter 20.

Weston, J. F.: "Financial Analysis: Planning and Control," FINANCIAL EXECUTIVE, July 1965, pp. 40–48.

Weston, J. F. and M. B. Goudzwaard (eds.): TREASURER'S HANDBOOK (Homewood, Ill.: Richard D. Irwin, Inc., 1976), Chapters 10, 13, 14.

Wilson, F. C.: SHORT-TERM FINANCIAL MANAGEMENT (Homewood, Ill.: Dow Jones-Irwin, 1975), Section 1.

3

MANAGING CASH

Cash is a key asset of the business firm. Cash is the means of purchasing parts and materials, and the plant and equipment used in production. It pays for the labor services of employees, the marketing skills of salesmen, and the administrative abilities of all levels of management. Cash also provides for interest payments to bankers and bondholders, taxes to governments, and dividends to stockholders. Although the importance of cash was stressed in Chapter 1, it is by no means the largest asset on the balance sheet. In fact, Exhibit 1-2 revealed that cash and cash equivalents as a percentage of total assets for all industrial corporations is considerably smaller than either accounts receivable or inventory. Moreover, cash and cash equivalents as a percentage of total assets has decreased significantly during the past two decades.

RATIONALE FOR CASH

The importance of effective cash management cannot be ignored in today's economy. Higher costs of borrowing money, higher yields on new and old types of short-term investments, periodic slowdowns in the United States economy, increasing inflation, and intensified competition between business firms have all contributed to the importance of cash management. The availability of improved management techniques has led to most firms being able to operate with less cash on the balance sheet throughout the year.[1]

There are three reasons given as to why a firm needs to hold cash. First, and certainly most important, cash is needed for operating purposes. Specifically, cash is used to acquire various factors of production that are used by

[1]A useful review of techniques for managing cash, together with a survey of current cash management practices, appeared in L. J. Gitman, E. A. Moses, and I. T. White, "An Assessment of Theory, Practice and Future Trends in Cash Management," paper presented at annual meeting of the Financial Management Association, Seattle, October 1977.

the firm in generating its products and its services. Short of returning to a barter system in our economy, it is necessary to have cash available for the many transactions that allow a business to continue operating from day to day and week to week. Cash balances also are needed in order to provide for the lack of synchronization between cash inflows to the firm and cash outflows from the firm.

Second, cash is needed for precautionary purposes. As mentioned in the previous chapter, planning is extremely important to the effective management of working capital. But a plan is not a reality, and one would seldom expect all forecasts in the financial plan to materialize exactly. If Crescent Corporation plans to purchase materials from a particular supplier for $10,000 during 1978, it may be that increasing costs in the economy, or perhaps some other development, may cause that supplier to have to charge $10,800 instead. As a result of that possibility, Crescent must have more than just $10,000 available. Another example would be a $20,000 payment from a customer that arrives ten days later than anticipated and thus is not available to the firm until later in the month. Most firms have literally thousands of cash transactions in a given month, so it is not surprising that they must typically plan to have additional cash available as a precaution against such uncertainties.

The third rationale for cash is for speculative purposes. This means that the firm chooses to maintain additional cash balances in the event that some unforeseen opportunity, not included in the plans of the business, develops. One such opportunity is unexpected changes in price levels. For example, a firm might have a chance to purchase materials at a special discount, or to acquire a specialized piece of equipment at an attractive price. Alternately, a firm might deliberately accumulate cash for the future acquisition of other companies. Though it is not clear just how much cash a firm should keep on hand in order to take advantage of such opportunities, the speculative motive should be understood by management.

The three reasons for holding cash have been briefly reviewed in order of their importance. That is, operating purposes are considered to be the most important, precautionary purposes are next in importance, and possibly the firm might consider holding additional cash balances for speculative purposes. In this chapter, we will be concerned primarily about the first two rationales for holding cash.

RESPONSIBILITY FOR CASH

Because cash is a key asset of the organization, it is not surprising that the responsibility for cash is usually assigned to a high level within the organizational hierarchy. In the vast majority of cases, responsibility for cash lies with the chief financial officer—either the treasurer or the financial vice president. Even if some of the detail work of controlling cash is delegated to lower-level managers, the chief financial officer typically would be involved in the management of cash.

In the case of Crescent Corporation, Arthur Hanson includes the management of cash among several important responsibilities. In larger firms, however, the scope of finance in general and working capital in particular, coupled with the advantages of specialization, may result in several managers being involved, and with a single manager being assigned to coordinate all their activities involving cash. For large firms that do business in numerous states and foreign countries, cash management may involve the coordination of several managers at different geographical locations. It is not surprising, therefore, that "cash management" has recently emerged as a distinct career specialization. There are professional seminars that deal with various techniques of cash management. There is also a trade association, called the Cash Management Institute, devoted to the collection and dissemination of information concerning corporate working capital, and cash management in particular.

For many firms, *cash* is taken to include currency and coin on hand, such as in petty cash or in cash registers, plus the current balances in a firm's various checking accounts. For other firms, cash is also taken to include cash surpluses that are invested in short-term marketable securities. Chapter 4 deals with managing marketable securities, and thus we will not consider those investments here. Neither shall we consider here the question of how much cash should be held apart from the firm's checking accounts for investment in marketable securities.

SOME FURTHER PERSPECTIVE

Another perspective is afforded by Exhibit 3-1. There, funds flow is shown as analogous to liquid flowing through a piping system. Each of the major assets of the organization is shown as a reservoir for which there is a particular level at each point in time. Those levels may also be viewed as investments made by the firm. The system of pipes which connect the various reservoirs are analogous to the funds flowing within the organization.

Financial managers should be concerned with the *width* of the pipes since that has to do with the extent of funds flow within the business. Financial managers also should be concerned with the *length* of the pipes since that has to do with the length of time necessary for funds to flow from one reservoir to the next. At a point in time, the total investment of a firm reflects both the levels in the reservoirs and the funds flowing in the piping network. Finally, financial managers should be concerned with the various *valves* where they can have a direct influence on funds flow within the organization. Obvious examples of valves in a typical business include management issuing bonds and stocks, borrowing short-term funds, pur-

EXHIBIT 3-1

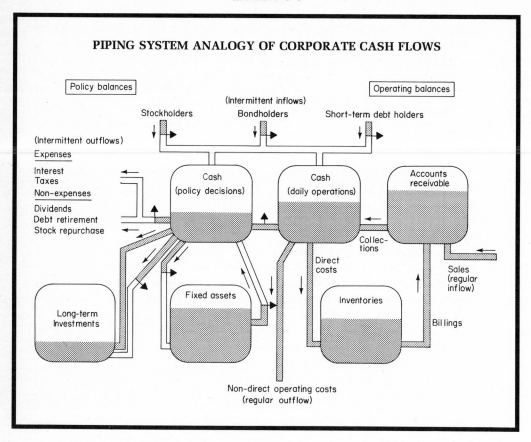

PIPING SYSTEM ANALOGY OF CORPORATE CASH FLOWS

chasing or selling fixed assets, and making dividend payments. Less obvious examples of valves are changes in credit policy, inventory safety stocks, and disbursement procedures.

The importance of cash flow and effective cash management should be apparent from Exhibit 3-1. Cash is shown as two separate reservoirs (i.e., balances)—though in reality there is just one cash account. Exhibit 3-1 includes a cash balance associated with policy decisions and also a cash balance associated with daily operations. The policy cash cycle (the left half of Exhibit 3-1) involves the network connecting fixed assets, long-term investments, and other cash flows which are not part of the mainstream activity of the firm. Inflows and outflows for the policy cash cycle tend to be intermittent rather than continuous or regular. They also tend to be difficult to forecast in many instances. It is important, though, that intermittent flows not be left out of the firm's cash budget.

   The operating cash cycle (the right half of Exhibit 3-1) is really the heart of cash management. It is a revolving, self-generating cycle that varies with the scope of business activity. The piping system analogy reminds us that a firm cannot begin without adequate investments in cash and inventory. Ultimately there must be an investment in accounts receivable as well. The operating cash cycle also includes two important cash flows of interest in this *Guide*. There are outflows as payment to suppliers for materials and parts purchased on credit, and there are inflows from credit customers as they pay their bills.

   Cash flows in connection with credit serve to introduce the concept of float, which is an important aspect of cash management. *Float* has to do with the time lag or delay between the moment of disbursement of funds on the part of the buyer and the moment of receipt of funds on the part of the seller.* Float consists of mail time, processing time, and clearing time within the banking system. Float has value in the sense that funds represent an earning opportunity to the firm. Suppose that your firm has investment opportunities on which the average return is 12 percent. This also can be viewed as the firm's *cost of capital*. The $20,000 payment from a credit customer that arrives ten days late represents a foregone opportunity as follows

$$\$20,000 \times 12\% \times \frac{20 \text{ days late}}{365 \text{ days in year}} = \$131.51$$

In other words, your firm could have expected to earn $131.51 on the $20,000 had it been received ten days earlier.

   Viewed in this fashion, float can be either negative or positive from the viewpoint of the firm's cash flow. On the one hand, *negative float* is the value of the length of time the firm must wait in order to be able to use the funds which ultimately are paid by the buyers of the firm's products and services. The value of negative float is a foregone investment opportunity just as in the example. On the other hand, *positive float* is the value of time during which the firm can continue to use the funds that are destined to be received by suppliers from whom the firm purchases raw materials and parts. The value of positive float is what the firm can expect to earn on the delayed payment. Even though most firms both sell and buy on credit, negative float and positive float do not necessarily cancel. The popular statement about a firm that "it lives on its float" really is concerned only with positive float. For most firms, there is negative float as well. The important comparison then is between the value of positive float and the value of negative float. Both negative and positive float will be considered further in the sections and chapters which follow.

   Given the added perspective of Exhibit 3-1, including the concept of float,

---

*More precise definitions of float are presented in a subsequent section.

we can specify an appropriate goal for the financial manager(s) responsible for cash.

> The *goal of cash management* is to reduce the amount of cash that is being used within the firm so as to increase organizational profitability, but without lessening business activity or exposing the firm to undue risk in meeting its financial obligations.

This statement reflects both the profitability and liquidity goals of working capital management, and thus it is consistent with the dual focus established for the *Guide* in Chapter 1. The observed fact that many managers have been able to substantially reduce the cash necessary to operate their business suggests that this cash management goal has been taken seriously by many firms.

Having already discussed and illustrated cash budgeting in the preceding chapter, it remains to consider the additional steps which are part of managing cash within the organization. Six important steps are: collecting cash, mobilizing cash, disbursing cash, establishing cash balances, investing cash surpluses, and covering cash shortages. The last two steps will be considered in Chapters 4 and 7, respectively, and thus we turn now to the first four.

COLLECTING CASH

Many firms would prefer to do much or all of their business for cash. However, our society and economy have moved more and more into credit as a way of conducting business. As a result, most business firms sell their products and services on credit rather than for cash. In Chapter 5, we will deal with how a firm establishes an appropriate credit policy and manages the accounts receivable that result. But from the perspective of managing cash, an important aspect is just how effectively the firm is able to collect the payments due from their customers. The intent of collecting cash is to reduce negative float. That is, the firm should try to collect cash from customers as quickly as possible, but without adversely reducing future sales and profits.

There are three ways that a firm can improve the collection of cash. The first is to change the paying behavior of its customers, the second is to improve the delivery system for those payments, and the third is to bypass the problem. The third possibility, which has to do with factoring of receivables, is considered in Chapters 5 and 8.

With respect to changing the behavior of the customers, one possibility is simply to request that customers pay sooner. This can be done with letters, telephone calls, or even personal visits. While this procedure may work on occasion, it is not likely to be a sustained improvement, especially given the credit practices of competitive firms in the industry. Another possibility, and one likely to be more effective, is to offer the customer an economic incentive for paying bills faster. This usually takes the form of a cash discount that is offered to credit customers.

For example, Crescent Corporation might offer its customers the following credit terms: 2/15, net 30. This means that if customers mail their checks by the fifteenth day following the receipt of the invoice for their purchases, the seller is willing to make a 2 percent price concession. In other words, Crescent is willing to lower the price to its customers by 2 percent, if the customers are willing to pay within two weeks. If the cash discount is not taken, then the full amount of the stated invoice is due from the buyer on the thirtieth day following receipt of invoice. As we shall see in Chapter 7, there is a high implicit cost of not taking cash discounts, and thus discounts are usually an effective way of inducing customers to pay quicker. The disadvantage, of course, is that the seller must reduce price, and hence profit, in order to affect the paying behavior of the customers.

The second major way that a firm can improve its collecting of cash is to somehow reduce the delay from the moment the customer mails the check until the moment the firm is able to actually use that cash in its operations. In other words, an attempt is made to reduce negative float. Methods designed to do this typically try to circumvent the usually slow mail system that prevails in the United States. One possibility is for the firm to engage in regional banking. That is, a firm establishes collection accounts at a series of commercial banks strategically located around the country. This causes the geographically dispersed credit customers of the firm to pay bills in their local region, rather than causing all payments to be sent to a central location in the United States. By so doing, the firm is able to get cash payments from customers into use more quickly because banks are able to transfer funds much more quickly than the U.S. Postal Service is able to do. A bank selected for collection purposes should either be a large bank that clears its own checks, or a small bank located in a city that also has a Federal Reserve bank. In addition, a bank selected for collection purposes should be one that processes checks and gives credit to the receiving firm as quickly as any competing bank in that region.

Another possibility is to utilize a lockbox collection system. A *lockbox* is a procedure whereby a firm rents a post office box in a particular city and entrusts its management to a commercial bank. The bank monitors the lockbox periodically, twenty-four hours per day. As soon as checks from customers arrive, they are microfilmed, checked for completeness, and deposited in the account of the receiving firm. Only then would the slower accounting process begin. The effect of a lockbox so managed is to reverse two important functions: the receipt and deposit of cash payments from credit customers, and the accounting for those payments by the seller firm.

A *lockbox collection system* is a series of lockboxes strategically placed in cities around the United States to reduce negative float. A lockbox collection system can be an effective means of improving the collection of cash, but improvement is not possible without additional costs to the firm.[2] The next section illustrates the type of analysis that would be necessary in exploring the possibility of a lockbox collection system.

LOCKBOX ANALYSIS

Suppose that a firm headquartered in Chicago, Illinois, sells a commercial product on credit in five large cities within the United States: Chicago, New York, Atlanta, Houston, and Los Angeles. Exhibit 3-2 reveals the average mail times between all pairs of cities.* The times range from 2.1 days between Atlanta and Houston to 5.9 days between Los Angeles and New York. Suppose further that the intracity mail time for all of the five cities is one day. We also assume that it takes one additional day to process checks within the home office.

Average daily sales volume in the five markets of the firm is as follows:

City	Daily volume
Atlanta	$ 5,000
Houston	4,000
Los Angeles	3,000
Chicago	2,000
New York	1,000
Total	$15,000

and totals $15,000 per day. Exhibit 3-3 is a calculation of negative float for the firm if there are no lockboxes, and all payments are sent to the home office in Chicago. When the daily sales volumes are multiplied by the mail times between each city and Chicago (including the intracity times), it is

[2]The 1977 survey paper by Gitman et al., op. cit., reported that lockboxes were the most frequently used method of speeding the collection of accounts receivable by the 97 Fortune 1000 firms that responded.

*The mail times used in the illustration are hypothetical. Average mail times between many United States cities are published by Phoenix Hecht Cash Management Services, Inc. (Chicago, Il 60601).

EXHIBIT 3-2

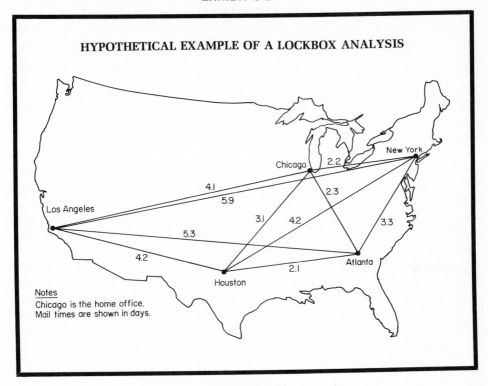

HYPOTHETICAL EXAMPLE OF A LOCKBOX ANALYSIS

Notes
Chicago is the home office.
Mail times are shown in days.

EXHIBIT 3-3

DAILY SALES VOLUMES AND COLLECTION TIMES WITHOUT LOCKBOX COLLECTION SYSTEM

City	Daily sales volume	Current collection times in Chicago
Chicago	$ 2,000	$2,000 × 2.0 days* = $ 4,000
New York	1,000	1,000 × 3.2 days = 3,200
Atlanta	5,000	5,000 × 3.3 days = 16,500
Houston	4,000	4,000 × 4.1 days = 16,400
Los Angeles	3,000	3,000 × 5.1 days = 15,300
Totals	$15,000	$55,400†

*Includes one-day processing delay in home office before deposit.
†Average negative float due to mailing and processing delays.

seen that the average sales volume in transit to Chicago is $55,400. In other words, if the firm causes all of its customers to pay their bills to the headquarters in Chicago, there will be on average approximately $55,400 in the mail at all times. We shall refer to this as "negative float" for the hypothetical firm, although only mailing and processing delays are considered.

Exhibit 3-4 includes sequential analyses of optimal lockbox locations. In each instance, the presence of a lockbox in a city is to reduce both mail and processing times, because the funds are deposited immediately when they are received at the lockbox. For the single-box analysis, it is seen that a lockbox in either Chicago, Atlanta, or Houston would be preferable to the existing system of no lockboxes. For example, if the lockbox were in Chicago, negative float would be reduced to $40,400. That value is obtained by multiplying the sales volume for each city by the indicated mail and processing time, and adding the products for all five cities. Note that the greatest reduction in negative float would occur if a single lockbox were placed in Atlanta. The reason for this is that the highest sales volume for the firm is in Atlanta, and thus the lockbox would have its greatest impact if placed there. For a system of two lockboxes, there are ten combinations of the five cities where they might be placed. It turns out that the best combination would be to place one lockbox in Atlanta and one lockbox in Los Angeles, with negative float being reduced to $24,300. Exhibit 3-5 also includes analyses of three, four, and five lockbox systems.

The optimal solution for the illustration is shown in Exhibit 3-5. The best combination for systems of one to five lockboxes is shown in terms of the gross improvement (i.e., reduction) in negative float. From that is subtracted an estimate of the required cash balance that a commercial bank would require for managing the collection system. In the illustration, the required balance for a commercial bank is estimated to be $1,000 as a fixed fee plus $5,000 for each lockbox that is managed by the commercial bank. The final column of Exhibit 3-5 shows the net improvement for each of the five systems. The optimal solution would be for the firm to implement lockboxes in just Atlanta and Los Angeles.

Interestingly, the optimal solution for the illustration does not include a lockbox in the headquarters city of Chicago. It is thus a different solution from what some managers might select without going through an analysis of mail and processing times, plus a comparison of float reductions with system costs. The illustration serves to emphasize a key point—namely, that just one aspect (i.e., lockbox location) of just one part (improving collection times) of just one current asset (cash) is likely to represent a complex decision for the manager assigned to cash. Lockbox analysis is a specialized skill that many financial managers might be reluctant to pursue without help. If lockboxes seemed to be an appropriate consideration for Crescent Corporation, it is likely that Arthur Hanson would depend at least in part on assistance from the cash management section of Crescent's commercial

EXHIBIT 3-4

SEQUENTIAL ANALYSES OF OPTIMAL LOCKBOX LOCATIONS

1-box analysis		Chicago		New York		Atlanta		Houston		Los Angeles	
Chicago	$2,000	1.0	$ 2,000	2.2	$ 4,400	2.3	$ 4,600	3.1	$ 6,200	4.1	$ 8,200
New York	1,000	2.2	2,200	1.0	1,000	3.3	3,300	4.2	4,200	5.9	5,900
Atlanta	5,000	2.3	11,500	3.3	16,500	1.0	5,000	2.1	10,500	5.3	26,500
Houston	4,000	3.1	12,400	4.2	16,800	2.1	8,400	1.0	4,000	4.2	16,800
Los Angeles	3,000	4.1	12,300	5.9	17,700	5.3	15,900	4.2	12,600	1.0	3,000
1-box summary		3d	$40,400		$56,400	1st	$37,200	2d	$37,500		$60,400

2-box analysis	1st: Atlanta and Los Angeles	Gross float = $24,300
3-box analysis	1st: Atlanta, Houston, and Los Angeles	Gross float = $19,900
4-box analysis	1st: Chicago, Atlanta, Houston, and Los Angeles	Gross float = $16,200
5-box analysis	1st: Lockboxes in all five cities	Gross float = $15,000

EXHIBIT 3-5

FINAL SOLUTION FOR HYPOTHETICAL EXAMPLE

System	Gross float	Gross improvement	Required balance*	Net improvement
Current status (no lockbox)	$55,400			
1 box (A)	37,200	$18,200	$ 6,000	$12,200
2 boxes (A-L)†	24,300	31,100	11,000	20,100‡
3 boxes (A-L-H)	19,900	35,500	16,000	19,500
4 boxes (A-L-H-C)	16,200	39,200	21,000	18,200
5 boxes (A-L-H-C-N)	15,000	40,400	26,000	14,400

*Required balance = $1,000 × $5,000 × no. of lockboxes.
† A = Atlanta, L = Los Angeles, H = Houston, C = Chicago, N = New York.
‡ Optimal solution.

banker. Some of the larger metropolitan commercial banks have sophisticated computer programs for determining the optimal location of lockboxes. Still, Mr. Hanson must understand the nature of a lockbox analysis well enough to judge whether he concurs with the conclusions of the analysis.

MOBILIZING CASH

Once a firm has collected cash from its cash and/or credit customers, the next step is to make effective use of those funds. Cash mobilization consists of an information system for cash, plus alternative methods of transferring cash between various points within the firm. If a firm did all its business in a single location and utilized a single bank account, then cash mobilization would be relatively straightforward. For firms that have many divisions, facilities, and bank accounts scattered all over a state, a region, the United States, or the world, cash mobilization is an important part of the job of managing cash. The intent of mobilizing cash is to have adequate cash available when it is needed, but without having excessive cash balances that do not contribute to the firm's profitability. The need for effective mobilization is created by the lack of national banking in the United States, or even of branch banking in many states, coupled with the relatively slow and inconsistent U.S. Postal Service.

The first part of mobilization is to know the locations of expected cash receipts, planned cash disbursements, and available cash balances at any point in time. Cash receipts and disbursements are identified as part of the firm's cash budgeting process. Available cash includes petty cash plus all bank account balances net of any compensating balances.* While the extent of information needed for effective cash mobilization varies greatly among firms, clearly the problem intensifies with the size of the firm and the scope of its operations.

An example may be helpful. A large firm in a technological industry has over forty divisions and facilities located all over the United States and portions of Canada. Operations are generally decentralized, but management believes it important for the firm to have centralized control of cash flow within the organization. To accomplish this, the firm developed a computerized information system that determines the most effective use of funds. At the close of each business day, each division (or facility) manager sends a brief telegram to Los Angeles. The message consists of a series of dollar amounts including cash inflows and cash outflows for that day, plus a forecast of net cash flows for the next five working days. The telegrams are sent to Los Angeles because it is at the extreme western end of the time zone in the continental United States. The data received from the divisions are fed into a computer programmed to analyze the current availability of cash as compared with cash requirements for the firm during the next few working days. The output of the computer analysis is a message wired back to each division or facility instructing management what action should be taken regarding cash. One message might be for a division to send $20,000 to another division. Another message might be that the division should expect to receive $15,000 from corporate headquarters. Note that this is not a system that implements the flow of funds between divisions, but rather an information system and decision analysis that results in appropriate actions for the relevant managers in all divisions. It is a highly sophisticated system that cost the firm several years and many thousands of dollars to develop fully.

Although a company the size of Crescent Corporation probably could not afford such a sophisticated system, it is clear that Arthur Hanson and his staff must develop an information system that helps recognize the coming needs for cash within their firm. Each bank used by Crescent can be helpful concerning its cash status with Crescent, but no single bank can do that for a firm that does business nationwide. One alternative is to make use of a commercial "for hire" system, such as is provided by the National Data

---

*Compensating balances are minimum average checking account balances which are often required by commercial banks as part of lending agreements. Compensating balances are mentioned later in this chapter and discussed further in Chapter 8.

Corporation (Atlanta, GA 30329). As funds are deposited at various points around the country, each unit manager makes a toll-free call to National Data and indicates the number of deposits made that day as well as the dollar amount deposited. This information is added to a central data file for that particular customer over a twenty-four-hour period. At the designated cut-off time each working day, the information is consolidated, and the appropriate amounts to be transferred from one account to another in order to avoid negative balances is indicated. The cost of this National Data service is a few cents per deposit input, subject to a minimum charge per month.

Having determined the appropriate actions to be taken, the next step is to consider ways of actually transferring funds between different geographical locations within the firm.[3] One procedure for transferring funds is through the Western Union Bank Wire. This is a private system to which over 240 commercial banks in seventy-five cities have access. Each subscriber has a teleprinter and point-to-point operation, thus allowing funds to be transferred almost instantaneously between two remote locations. There are five automated regional switching centers (San Francisco, Dallas, Atlanta, Chicago, and New York), and the system operates between 8 A.M. and 8 P.M. eastern time. The Western Union Bank Wire allows a firm to transfer funds rapidly from one part of the country to another. It allows payment to be made to third parties. The Western Union Bank Wire can be used to request credit information from subscribing banks. And it can be used to help implement other necessary activities such as security transactions. In terms of the cost effectiveness of this transfer procedure, it has been estimated that the Western Union Bank Wire is not appropriate unless a firm is transferring at least $3,000 to 4,000.

A second procedure is the Federal Reserve Wire System, which is available to all banks that are members of the system in the United States. Instructions for transfer are punched onto a paper tape and entered into a terminal. Each terminal is scanned every three minutes by each member bank, and thus there is almost continual contact between the terminals in all member banks.

A third procedure for transferring cash within a firm is through the use of depository transfer checks. These are preprinted checks made payable to the name of the organization. They are not negotiable and are not signed, and therefore there is no risk in using them. The advantage of using depository transfer checks is their low banking charge, which is estimated to be 5 to 10 cents per check. A disadvantage is that they must clear through the banking system, and funds may not be available for one or two business days.

A fourth procedure is to use personal couriers to transfer large amounts of checks from one location to another. It is a particularly useful procedure when the amount of funds involved is large. Suppose that a firm needed to

---

[3]For an excellent review of procedures for transferring funds, see F. W. Searby, "Using Your Hidden Cash Resources," *Harvard Business Review*, March–April 1968, pp. 71–80.

transfer $5 million from Atlanta to Chicago. If the opportunity value of money to the firm is 12 percent annually, then each day saved in delivering that amount would have a value to the firm of

$$\$5,000,000 \times 12\% \times \frac{1 \text{ day saved}}{365 \text{ days in year}} = \$1,643.84$$

The salaries and airfare for a personal courier to get from Atlanta to Chicago would certainly be less than that, and thus it would be financially feasible to transfer such an amount by courier. Courier services are provided by firms such as Brinks and International Courier Corporation.

DISBURSING CASH

Just as a firm should prefer to collect cash from its customers as quickly as possible, so too should it prefer to delay paying its suppliers and other creditors as long as possible. At the least, it should prefer to increase the delay between the time that cash payments are made and the time that cash actually clears out of the firm's checking account. In other words, the intent of disbursing cash is to increase positive float, but in a manner which does not adversely impair supplier relationships.[4]

One general procedure for increasing positive float is to centralize the disbursing function of the firm into a single headquarters account and thereby take advantage of mailing delays. This can be done even though cash collecting is decentralized. Arthur Hanson, for example, has examined this possibility, and now all disbursing for Crescent Corporation is done from the corporate headquarters.

A related procedure, so-called *remote point disbursing*, is to deliberately cause cash payments to be made from a distant location. This procedure can be used because the postmark date on a letter usually constitutes the date of legal payment. If, for example, payment is due to a supplier in Seattle for purchased materials or parts, the firm might issue the check from its bank account in Miami. On a company-wide basis, the reader may note that the problem of cash disbursement is just the opposite of that in an earlier section, when lockbox analysis was used to *minimize* negative float. Here, the idea would be to select a set of disbursement locations so as to *maximize* the total time (mail, processing, and clearing) between mailing payments to suppliers and the resultant decrease in the firm's cash account.[5] Such practices may add several days to the positive float of the firm, and thereby allow it to retain valuable funds for other investment opportunities. Wach-

[4]Surprisingly, the Gitman et al. survey, op. cit., found that many fewer firms use techniques designed to increase positive float than to decrease negative float.

[5]For an example of how the solution to optimal cash disbursement would be obtained, see L. J. Gitman, D. K. Forrester, and J. R. Forrester, Jr., "Maximizing Cash Disbursement Float," *Financial Management*, Summer 1976, pp. 15–24.

ovia Bank and Trust Company in Winston-Salem, for example, became a specialist in remote point disbursing, especially for payments due west of the Mississippi River.[6] It simply takes longer for checks clearing to North Carolina to work their way through the bank collection system, and for the checks to finally clear the disbursing firm's bank account. Clearly, procedures for slowing down cash payments should be evaluated with respect to their possible impact on foregone discounts. This aspect of disbursing cash will be further examined in Chapter 7.

Another procedure that can be used is to make payments by draft rather than by check. A bank draft is an order drawn by a corporation on itself and marked "payable through" a specific bank. It does not represent an order to a bank to pay the funds. Instead, the bank presents the draft one day later to the issuing firm and only then are the funds necessarily made available. This causes an additional one-day delay before the cash effectively leaves the firm's checking account. Many firms, including American Telephone and Telegraph, have utilized bank drafts for their extensive payrolls. Bank drafts also have been used for quarterly dividend payments.

BENEFITS VERSUS COSTS

It may be argued that collecting cash and disbursing cash are really mirror images. It cannot be argued, however, that the two steps simply offset each other. Indeed, many firms have been able both to collect faster and disburse slower. The aggregate of these improvements has been observed (Chapter 1) in a steady decrease over time of cash and equivalents as a percentage of total assets. Larger firms probably have effected larger improvements, because they have been able to allocate greater resources to the task. On balance, firms have been able to make improvements in managing cash because their financial managers have paid closer attention to the collecting, mobilizing, and disbursing of cash. While previous sections have identified some of the procedures which can be used by financial managers, our coverage did not address the question of how much those procedures ought to be employed. What needs to be considered for each cash management procedure is a comparison of its relevant benefits and costs to the firm.

To do this, a closer look at float is useful. Exhibit 3-6 is a timeline diagram for a single transaction (material ordered for production), viewed from the perspective of both the seller and the buyer. Key steps in the complete transaction, beginning with the placing of an order by the buyer and ending with cash actually removed from the buyer's bank account, are identified. Float is defined in terms of value received and value given. Negative float (for the seller) is the value of the material during the period between the time material is shipped and the time payment for that material is actually available. Positive float (for the buyer) is the value of the material during the

[6] "Making Millions by Stretching the Float," *Business Week*, Nov. 23, 1974.

EXHIBIT 3-6

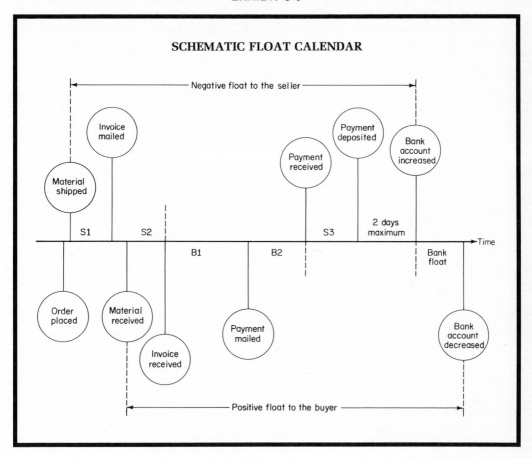

SCHEMATIC FLOAT CALENDAR

period between the receipt of material and the time funds actually leave the buyer's account. According to the float calendar, negative float and positive float for a given transaction are not necessarily the same length of time.

Exhibit 3-6 also identifies the specific actions that can affect float. Three actions are from the seller's perspective, while two actions are from the buyer's perspective. The seller can *reduce* negative float by prompt billing (S1) and by billing from a location near the buyer (S2). Using regional banking or a lockbox system, the seller also can reduce negative float by prompt deposit of a received payment (S3). Meanwhile, the buyer can *increase* positive float by delaying payment (B1) and by remote point disbursement (B2). The seller can influence buyer payment behavior (B1) with cash discounts. The seller also can influence somewhat the delivery time for the payment (B2). In contrast, the buyer has little influence on the seller's actions (S1, S2, and S3). The extent of float also is dependent on institutional features of the banking industry—including the maximum two days before a deposit by the payee is available to the seller, and the additional transit time until the buyer's checking account is reduced. Attention has been given in recent years to possible revisions by the Federal Reserve System in clearing time allowances among commercial banks.

For any of the specific actions identified in Exhibit 3-6, the financial manager can estimate the benefits and costs to his firm, as either a seller or as a buyer, toward deciding whether or not that action would represent an improvement. An important aspect of that decision would be the value of float to the firm as discussed earlier in the chapter.

To illustrate, suppose that you were considering the replacement of your firm's manual billing procedure with an automated system. The estimated cost of implementing the automated system is $4,500. From the perspective of the seller, the automated system would reduce by two days the length of time (S1) between shipment of material sold, and the mailing of an invoice for the sale to the buyer. If total billings during the year are estimated to be $6 million, then the two-day reduction in negative float would have value to the firm of

$$\$6,000,000 \times 12\% \times \frac{2 \text{ days sooner}}{365 \text{ days in year}} = \$3,945.21$$

where the earnings opportunity to the firm is estimated to be 12 percent. Since the expected benefit ($3,945) is less than the cost ($4,500) of the new system, the replacement would *not* be expected to add to the profitability of your firm.

The same procedure of comparing costs and benefits can be applied to any specified action designed to decrease negative float or to increase positive float. The lockbox analysis presented earlier in the chapter was another example in which estimated benefits exceeded the estimated costs of the change. The responsible financial managers thus can make those changes in the cash management system of their firm that are consistent with the profitability goal of the organization. A similar theme will be suggested in Chapter 9 for evaluating all proposed changes in the working capital management of the firm.

ESTABLISHING CASH BALANCES

The three steps of collecting, mobilizing, and disbursing cash all have to do with the dynamic flow of dollars toward, within, and from the organization. The other step of managing cash to be discussed has to do with a stock or level problem—namely the establishment of an appropriate cash balance for the firm. This problem is complicated because of the three rationales for holding cash that were identified at the outset of this chapter. It is also complicated because most firms have cash balances at numerous locations around the country. In addition, the problem of an appropriate cash balance is complicated because commercial banks frequently charge for various services rendered to a firm with required (i.e., compensating) balances. The purpose of establishing cash balances is to have enough for operating purposes, but otherwise not more than is needed to pay banks for services received. Some aspects that a financial manager ought to consider in trying to determine appropriate levels of cash will be mentioned.

A primary aspect of the problem is to decide how large a cash balance is needed to ensure continuity of operations over time for a single business unit. It should be recognized that a cash balance is needed because inflows and outflows of cash are not the same each day. Since cash budgeting for most firms is done on a week-to-week and month-to-month basis, a cash balance is really needed to match the intraweek and intramonth cash flows.

For a business unit (division or facility) that has been in existence for some time and is not contemplating major changes in operation, historical data can be used to determine an appropriate cash balance. Otherwise, it is strictly a subjective estimation. If average cash inflows and average cash outflows, based on historical experience, are calculated for each day of the month over the past few years, the pattern of average daily cash needs for the business unit can be identified. Arthur Hanson has done so for the manufacturing division of Crescent Corporation, and the resulting pattern is shown in Exhibit 3-7. We see that cash inflows build to a peak on the tenth or eleventh day, probably reflecting the response of credit customers to a cash discount that is offered by Crescent. Cash outflows are more steady throughout the month, with periodic peaks due to the weekly payroll for the division. Between the ninth and eighteenth days, cash inflows exceed cash outflows, so there really is no need for a cash balance.

But for the other days of the month, cash outflows exceed cash inflows and a cash balance is needed for operations. An estimate of the required balance for the Crescent division can be obtained by adding the average daily shortages beginning with the nineteenth day through the end of the month and continuing through the eighth day of the next month. The calculation is shown in Exhibit 3-8. A minimum cash balance of approximately $81,000 would be needed, on average, on the eighteenth day to ensure operations from one month to the next.

Since that estimate of a needed cash balance reflects only planned operations, it is necessary to consider another aspect of the problem—the precautionary and speculative motives for holding cash. For the speculative motive, it is difficult to provide guidelines, except that balances held for such purposes obviously detract from the main and hopefully profitable operations of the firm. As for the precautionary motive, the financial manager can calculate the variability (e.g., the standard deviation) in historical daily cash inflows and outflows. The greater the variability in daily net cash flows, the greater is the need for an added component in the recommended cash balance for the unit.

EXHIBIT 3-7

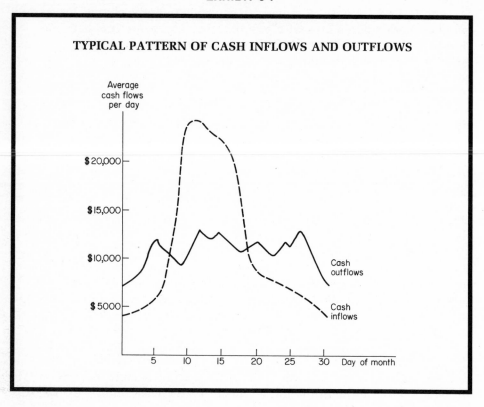

TYPICAL PATTERN OF CASH INFLOWS AND OUTFLOWS

The final aspect of the problem is to coordinate the respective cash balances of all units of the business. This is not an easy task since the firm may have numerous balances for different purposes, such as deposit accounts, disbursement accounts for payroll and federal taxes, and operating accounts. If financial managers are not careful in coordinating these various accounts, the aggregate cash balance for the firm can become excessive.

One way to avoid an excessive cash balance in a complex organization is to utilize *zero-balance accounts*. This is a procedure whereby a bank account is deliberately managed to have a zero balance each day. For cash inflows, the aggregate of all deposits into a given lockbox or regional bank are transferred out daily to another corporate account in the same bank. For cash outflows, the funds necessary to cover all disbursements from a given account are transferred in daily from another corporate account in the same bank. The advantage of zero-balance accounts is that the uncertainty of clearing times for cash payments is centralized, and thus the funds needed to assure coverage are reduced. For zero-balance accounts, the commercial bank cannot be compensated by the existing balance, and thus the firm must pay for those accounts either in fees or through balances in other accounts.

EXHIBIT 3-8

CALCULATING THE MINIMUM CASH BALANCE

Day	Outflow	Inflow	Net outflow	Cumulative
19	$11,500	$ 9,500	$2,000	$ 2,000
20	12,000	8,500	3,500	5,500
21	11,000	8,000	3,000	8,500
22	10,500	7,500	3,000	11,500
23	11,000	7,500	3,500	15,000
24	12,000	7,000	5,000	20,000
25	11,000	7,000	4,000	24,000
26	12,000	6,500	5,500	29,500
27	12,500	6,000	6,500	36,000
28	10,500	5,500	5,000	41,000
29	9,000	5,000	4,000	45,000
30	8,000	4,500	3,500	48,500
31	7,500	4,000	3,500	52,000
1	7,000	4,000	3,000	55,000
2	8,000	4,000	4,000	59,000
3	8,500	5,000	3,500	62,500
4	10,000	5,500	4,500	67,000
5	12,000	6,000	6,000	73,000
6	11,500	6,500	5,000	78,000
7	11,000	8,000	3,000	81,000
8	10,500	10,500	—	81,000

Note: Based on cash inflows and outflows as depicted in Exhibit 3-7.

Chapter 8 includes more detail on how commercial banks are paid for the various services they render to a firm.

Exhibit 3-9 is a schematic diagram of how zero-balance accounts might be used in conjunction with other corporate accounts. The illustrative firm consists of a centrally located corporate headquarters, an East Division, and

EXHIBIT 3-9

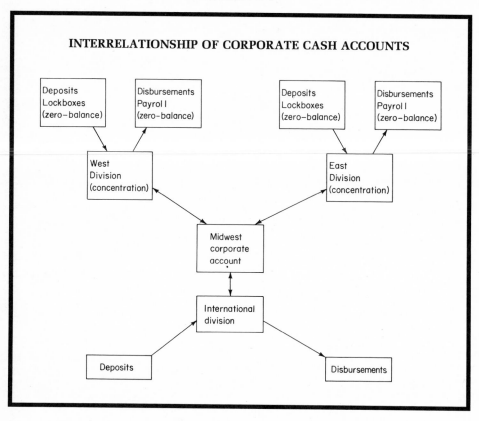

INTERRELATIONSHIP OF CORPORATE CASH ACCOUNTS

a West Division. Each division has both deposit accounts and disbursement accounts in the same bank that are maintained at a zero balance. For East Division, its deposit account is used for collecting cash from customers in the eastern United States, while its disbursement account is used for paying suppliers in the western United States. A *concentration account* is a bank account that is used to effect zero-balance accounts, and also to compensate the commercial bank. In Exhibit 3-9, there is one concentration account for the East Division and another concentration account for the West Division. There also is a corporate account which is used to coordinate the divisional flows and balances. Investment of surplus cash—to be discussed in the following chapter—typically is done in conjunction with the corporate cash account of the firm. While the illustration in Exhibit 3-9 is greatly oversimplified, it does emphasize the importance of an overall perspective and management of the firm's cash balance.

Exhibit 3-9 also indicates the added complexity that exists when a firm has international operations. If the relationship between foreign currencies was constant over time, then international business could be viewed as just one additional division of the firm. But the variability of exchange rates over time adds a whole new dimension to the problem of managing cash, as exchange rate risk and international tax consequences are added to the existing uncertainty in cash collections and disbursements. In making decisions about the various steps of managing cash, the financial manager must decide on that part of the additional risk exposure that the firm is willing to face, and that part for which hedging actions are appropriate. As before, these decisions by financial managers should be based on a careful evaluation of the relative benefits and costs to the firm.

It is at the point of coordination of bank accounts—both nationally and internationally—that the several steps of managing cash are seen in conjunction. Decisions about collecting cash, mobilizing cash, disbursing cash, and establishing cash balances should be made with respect to the needs of the total firm and not from the limited perspective of individual units. While commercial bankers can provide help on each step and at various locations, only the financial manager, and appropriately only at the corporate level, really has the overall perspective to properly manage the levels and flows of cash for the organization.

ELECTRONIC FUNDS TRANSFER SYSTEM

Despite the considerable progress that has been made in cash management, many managers and economists predict that further improvements are likely to come in the years ahead. Their predictions have to do with an emerging technology that promises to significantly reduce float and to change the ways in which business transactions are implemented. The new technology is commonly referred to as *electronic funds transfer system* (EFTS). In this final section, we briefly explore the nature of EFTS and its possible implications to corporate cash management.

Electronic funds transfer means different things to different people, mainly because it is more than just a single system. Instead, it is a series of systems that are linked electronically in a vast telecommunications network. One part of EFTS is the system whereby the plastic credit cards of consumers are validated—when presented at supermarkets, gasoline stations, department stores, and other retail establishments—and the resulting purchases are automatically debited to their individual accounts. Another part of EFTS is the system whereby corporations and governments transmit payroll on magnetic tape to depository institutions for automatic crediting to employee accounts. The wire system that connects banks and other financial institutions and allows for automatic clearing of transactions is yet another part of EFTS. Another part is for periodic and automatic payments on behalf of individuals and families for their utility bills and their consumer and mortgage loans.

Individuals, corporations, financial institutions, and all levels of government will be impacted in a society where payments by check are replaced by electronic payments. While arguments in favor of EFTS typically focus on relative efficiencies to all concerned, there are substantial costs of further development and of the hardware necessary to implement various parts of EFTS. Many uncertainties also remain about ultimate design, ownership of facilities, and, as always, responsibility for control and regulation.[7]

Corporate management cannot ignore the present and future implications of EFTS to their firm. The question is not one of whether EFTS is a reality or not, but just how soon and in what format EFTS will impact the organization. Financial managers responsible for cash, in particular, should remain informed about the latest developments of EFTS, and how those developments ultimately may impact on both negative and positive float, and on the overall management of working capital within the organization.

SUMMARY

Cash is the first item encountered on the balance sheet of the firm. It is the smallest of the working capital components, and it is the current asset for which the greatest improvement in management has occurred over the past few years. Managing cash involves several steps in the flow of cash toward, within, and from the organization, and also includes the overall level of cash that is held. For each step, a comparison of benefits and costs to the firm should be conducted by the responsible financial manager. Electronic funds transfer systems will most likely continue to improve the management of cash in the years ahead.

Problem 3-1

Recall the lockbox analysis in the chapter. What would be the optimal solution if the required balance to manage the lockbox collection system were changed to a $5,000 fixed fee, plus $3,000 for each lockbox managed?

SOLUTION: Only the final step in the analysis would be altered. Following the procedure in Exhibit 3-5, we obtain

System*	Gross improvement	Required balance	Net improvement
1 box	$18,200	$ 8,000	$10,200
2 boxes	31,100	11,000	20,100
3 boxes	35,500	14,000	21,500
4 boxes	39,200	17,000	22,200
5 boxes	40,400	20,000	20,400

[7]For further discussion, see J. B. Benton, "Electronic Funds Transfer: Pitfalls and Payoffs," *Harvard Business Review*, July–August, 1977, pp. 16–22.
*A system of four lockboxes would be optimal.

Problem 3-2

If a firm's opportunity rate is 10 percent, what would be the value of changing to a system of meeting the $1 million monthly payroll by bank draft and thereby increasing positive float by five days?

SOLUTION: The calculation follows the procedure used in the chapter. Namely, the value would be

$$\$1{,}000{,}000 \times 10\% \times \frac{5 \text{ days increased}}{365 \text{ days in year}} = \$1{,}369.86$$

to the firm each month, or a total annual value of $16,438.32.

Problem 3-3

What would be the maximum amount that a firm should be willing to pay for a cash mobilization system that was expected to reduce the total average cash balance of the firm by $250,000? Assume that the firm's cost of capital is 11.5 percent.

Problem 3-4

Use the cash-flow pattern in Exhibit 3-7 to estimate the net cash inflow to the firm during the middle part of the month when cash inflows exceed cash outflows. What is the net cash flow, on average, for the entire month?

Problem 3-5

Recall again the lockbox analysis in the chapter. What would be the optimal solution if the firm decided to discontinue its operation in New York City? Assume that the lost sales from New York are not made up in any of the other four cities.

SUGGESTED READINGS

Benton, J. B.: "Electronic Funds Transfer: Pitfalls and Payoffs," HARVARD BUSINESS REVIEW, July–August 1977, pp. 16–22.

"Cash Management: The New Art of Wringing More Profit from Corporate Funds," BUSINESS WEEK, March 13, 1978, pp. 62–68.

Fisher, D. I.: CASH MANAGEMENT (New York: The Conference Board, Inc., 1973).

Gitman, L. J., D. K. Forrester, and J. R. Forrester, Jr.: "Maximizing Cash Disbursement Float," FINANCIAL MANAGEMENT, Summer 1976, pp. 15–24.

Gitman, L. J., E. A. Moses, and I. T. White: "An Assessment of Theory, Practice and Future Trends in Cash Management," paper presented at annual meeting of the Financial Management Association, Seattle, October 1977.

Lordan, J. F.: THE BANKING SIDE OF CORPORATE CASH MANAGEMENT (Boston: Financial Publishing Company, 1973).

"Making Millions by Stretching the Float," BUSINESS WEEK, Nov. 23, 1974.

Orgler, Y. E.: CASH MANAGEMENT: METHODS AND MODELS (Belmont, Calif.: Wadsworth Publishing Company, Inc., 1970).

Searby, F. W.: "Use Your Hidden Cash Resources," HARVARD BUSINESS REVIEW, March–April 1968, pp. 71–80.

Slater, S. D.: THE STRATEGY OF CASH (New York: John Wiley & Sons, Inc., 1974).

Smith, J. E.: CASH FLOW MANAGEMENT (Cambridge, England: Woodhead-Faulkner Limited, 1975).

Smith, K. V. (ed.): READINGS ON THE MANAGEMENT OF WORKING CAPITAL (St. Paul, Minn.: West Publishing Company, 1974), Section II.

4

MANAGING MARKETABLE SECURITIES

Investment in marketable securities is an opportunity for those firms having excess cash for relatively short periods of time. That opportunity consists of a series of short-term investment alternatives that have unique characteristics, including varying maturities, and different yields. We will discuss marketable securities from the perspective of adding to firm profitability while maintaining adequate firm liquidity.

RATIONALE FOR MARKETABLE SECURITIES

In the previous chapter, it was argued that cash is a key asset of the business firm. Although much of the discussion focused on the flow of cash toward, within, and from the organization, cash can also be viewed as an investment by the firm, or alternatively, as one of its short-term or temporary uses of funds. Indeed, cash is the first current asset listed on the balance sheet of the firm. However, the first asset sometimes encountered is not just cash, but rather "cash and cash-equivalents," or just "cash and equivalents." In these instances, "cash-equivalents" refers to marketable securities. In other instances, marketable securities are listed just below cash as a separate current asset. All of the exhibits in Chapter 1 used to portray the scope of working capital management included cash and equivalents as a single component of working capital.

Exhibit 4-1 depicts graphically how marketable securities are used over time to help balance the firm's longer-term uses and sources of funds with its shorter-term needs and sources. A representative pattern over a two-year horizon is shown. Panel A of Exhibit 4-1 depicts how the fixed assets and current assets might vary. Fixed assets are increased only once at the beginning of the second year, while current assets exhibit a definite seasonal pattern. Panel B of Exhibit 4-1 shows the gradual increase of long-term financing as a result of retained earnings. It also shows a slightly different

EXHIBIT 4-1

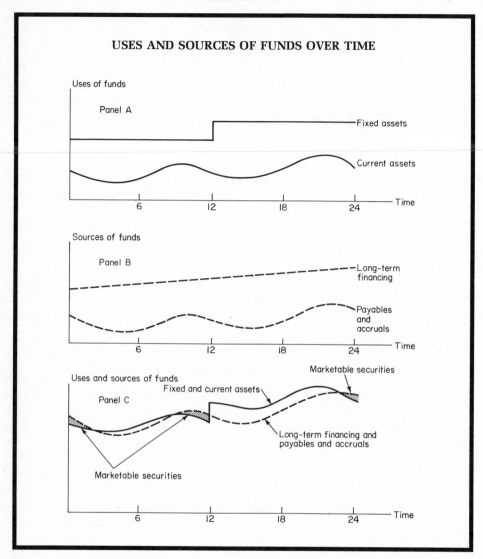

USES AND SOURCES OF FUNDS OVER TIME

seasonal pattern for the short-term financing available from accounts payables and other accruals such as taxes payable, interest payable, and prepaid revenues. Sources and uses are brought together in panel C. For two periods of several months, total uses of funds exceed total sources of funds, and firm management must seek short-term borrowing. That is the subject of Chapter 8.

During the other parts of the two-year horizon, the opposite situation occurs, where sources of funds exceed uses of funds. One possible response by management is to do nothing, and simply let the excess funds accumulate as additional cash in the firm's checking account. While that response would add to firm liquidity, it does not contribute to firm profitability since a checking account earns no interest. Another possible response by management is to invest excess funds in assets that earn a return and thus add to firm profitability. Assets that can be quickly converted to cash, such as securities, are particularly useful for investing excess funds, since firm liquidity can be maintained at the same time that additional returns are being earned. Since most firms are not in the business of managing investment portfolios over time, the usual practice is to restrict investment of excess funds to securities that reach maturity within a year. Otherwise, the firm has converted a short-term asset (cash) to a long-term investment (common stock, corporate bonds, etc.) that would properly be placed among the firm's long-term assets.

Marketable securities refer to securities that have a short maturity, or securities that management intends to liquidate within one year. They include a number of short-term instruments that are issued by the United States government, government agencies, and various organizations within the private sector. Those investment opportunities comprise the subject matter of this chapter.

RESPONSIBILITY FOR MARKETABLE SECURITIES

Marketable securities result from investment decisions that really are not the main part of the firm's business. But marketable securities cannot be ignored as they constitute a part of the value of the firm that is entrusted to management. For some firms, that investment extends to millions or even billions of dollars.

Exhibit 4-2 includes data on the marketable securities held by five well-known United States firms at the end of 1972 and 1976. The five firms were chosen because of their familiarity and also because of the differences between them. Of the five firms, the largest portfolio of marketable securities for both years was held by IBM. Exxon exhibited a significant increase in proportional holdings from 1972 to 1976, while Ford exhibited a significant decrease. Northrop had no holdings of marketable securities at the end of 1972, but held a substantial portfolio four years later. Although the marketable securities held by Du Pont increased from $150 million in 1972 to $175 million in 1976, the value of Du Pont's holdings as a percentage of current assets decreased from 8.2 percent to 6 percent during that period.

We will not consider possible reasons for these occurences, except to note that the five firms did not follow the same policy. Investment in marketable securities by a firm is likely to vary with the nature of the business, and the

EXHIBIT 4-2

MARKETABLE SECURITIES HELD BY SELECTED UNITED STATES FIRMS, YEAR-END 1972 AND 1976

Firm	Year-end 1972			Year-end 1976		
	Holdings	% current assets	% total assets	Holdings	% current assets	% total assets
IBM	$2.4 billion	50.1	22.4	$5.9 billion	60.0	33.6
Exxon	1.2 billion	17.1	5.6	3.8 billion	25.2	10.5
Ford	1.1 billion	19.9	9.5	909 million	11.0	5.8
Du Pont	150 million	8.2	3.4	175 million	6.0	2.5
Northrop	0	0	0	84 million	23.7	15.7

Source: Annual reports.

time when its balance sheet is prepared. Investment may also depend on whether the firm chooses to show its marketable securities at cost (the historically accepted procedure), or the lower of cost or market value (a procedure which may be used). Investment in marketable securities by a given firm is also likely to vary with the aggressiveness that financial managers adopt with respect to profitability vis-à-vis liquidity.

The chief financial officer of a firm typically would be charged with the responsibility for marketable securities. For some firms, this is only an occasional responsibility. Crescent Corporation, for example, does not show marketable securities on its balance sheet at the end of 1977 (Exhibit 1-2). If and when Crescent were to find itself with excess funds for a period of time, Mr. Arthur Hanson would be responsible for ensuring that those funds earned as high a rate as possible.* But other firms, particularly those whose activities are subject to extreme seasonal variations, may make investments in marketable securities on a more or less regular basis. The extent of activity in marketable securities is so great in some firms as to occupy the full time of one or more managers.

Based upon the perspective of Exhibit 4-1, we can specify an appropriate goal for the financial manager responsible for marketable securities.

---

*If the financial plans for Crescent in 1978 materialize as shown in Chapter 2, the projected cash balance of $241,576 at the end of 1978 would represent almost 10 percent of Crescent's total assets (see Figure 18), and it might then be appropriate to invest part of the cash in marketable securities.

> The *goal of marketable securities management* is to invest the tempo-
> rary excess funds of a firm in order to add to organizational
> profitability.

In this and successive chapters, the suggested goal for management focuses
on firm profitability. Although the liquidity goal is not mentioned, the
implication of management decisions to the liquidity position of the organization should be explored via careful cash budgeting.

The task of financial managers who become involved with marketable
securities, either full-time or part-time, consists of three issues. First, managers must understand the detailed characteristics of different short-term
investment opportunities. Second, managers must understand the markets
in which those investment opportunities are bought and sold. Third, managers must develop a strategy for deciding when to buy or sell marketable
securities, which securities to hold, and how much to buy or sell in each
transaction. The remainder of this chapter examines these issues in some
detail.

CHARACTERISTICS OF MARKETABLE SECURITIES

Six types of marketable securities will be discussed. They are U.S. Treasury
bills, federal agency issues, commercial paper, certificates of deposit, bankers' acceptances, and repurchase agreements. There are other types that are
occasionally held by firms, but the six mentioned are the instruments most
frequently held by business firms.[1] Important attributes of marketable securities—maturities, denominations, marketability, and yield determination—
are summarized in Exhibit 4-3. *Maturity* is defined as the length of time
until the principal amount of a marketable security is returned to the
investor. *Denomination* is the unit of transaction for buying or selling a
marketable security. *Marketability* is the ability of an investor to sell a short-
term issue to another investor. *Yield determination* is the way in which an
owner of a marketable security earns a return on the investment.

The U.S. Treasury issues Treasury bills with maturities ranging from
ninety-one days to six months and nine months to one year. The shorter
maturities are sold weekly, while the longer maturities are sold monthly by
the Treasury. Denominations range from $10,000 to $1 million. A business

---

[1]Of ninety-eight large firms that responded to a recent survey on managing cash and equivalents, seventy-six occasionally hold commercial paper, seventy-three hold repurchase agreements, seventy-one hold U.S. Treasury securities, sixty-eight hold certificates of deposit, fifty-
seven hold bankers acceptances, and forty-five hold federal agency issues. See L. J. Gitman, E.
A. Moses, and I. T. White, "An Assessment of Theory, Practice and Future Trends in Cash
Management," paper presented at annual meeting of the Financial Management Association,
Seattle, October 1977.

EXHIBIT 4-3

SELECTED CHARACTERISTICS OF MARKETABLE SECURITIES

Type	Maturities	Denominations	Marketability	Yield determination
U.S. Treasury bills	91 days to 1 year	$10,000 to $1 million	Active secondary market	Appreciation due to discount
Federal agency issues	Few months to several years	$1,000 to $1 million	Active secondary market	Interest paid at maturity
Commercial paper	3 to 270 days	$1,000 to $5 million	Inactive secondary market	Appreciation due to discount
Certificates of deposit	Few months to one year	$100,000 to $1 million	Active secondary market	Interest paid at maturity
Banker acceptances	Few weeks to 180 days	$25,000 to $1 million	Active secondary market	Appreciation due to discount
Repurchase agreements	Few days	$10,000 to $1 million	Active secondary market	Appreciation due to discount

firm can purchase bills directly from the U.S. Treasury (the so-called *primary market*), through the firm's commercial bank, or from dealer firms that specialize in government securities. Because the dealer firms constitute a secondary market for these securities, it is also possible for a business firm to invest for short periods of time in U.S. Treasury certificates and notes that have maturities of a year or longer. For example, a firm might purchase five-year Treasury notes that have only six months remaining until maturity.

Securities issued by the U.S. Treasury are considered to be the safest investments a firm, or any investor for that matter, can make. The reason is that U.S. Treasury issues are backed by the vast resources of the United States government. There is no interest paid on Treasury bills. Treasury bills are sold at a discount from their face amount, and thus the yield to an investor is solely the appreciation that is earned at maturity. The yield on U.S. Treasury bills, in particular, is generally taken as a measure of the "riskless" rate of return that exists in the economy at a point in time. The yield on United States government securities is subject to federal income taxes but is exempt from state income taxes.

Securities issued by various agencies of the federal government are another investment opportunity for firms having excess funds. They include the issues of government-sponsored corporations such as Federal National Mortgage Association (FNMA), Banks for Cooperatives, Federal Home Loan Bank, Federal Intermediate Credit Bank, and Federal Land Banks. They also include the issues of government-guaranteed agencies such as Export-Import Bank, Federal Housing Administration, Farmers Home Administration, Government National Mortgage Association (GNMA), and the Tennessee Valley Authority.

Maturities on the various federal agency issues range from a few months to several years, while denominations vary from $1,000 to $1 million. While the method of issuance by the agency varies from one type of security to another, there is an active *secondary market* wherein a firm can buy and sell these securities. Interest, typically paid at maturity, is subject to federal income taxes, and for certain issues to state income taxes as well. Yields on federal agency issues are higher than on U.S. Treasury bills, reflecting a belief by investors that they are somewhat more risky.[2]

The remaining categories of marketable securities are issued by corporations in the private sector. *Commercial paper* is the name given the promissory notes sold by commercial banks, finance companies, and industrial firms. It is unsecured except for the overall financial strength and reputation of the issuing firm. Commercial paper can be bought from finance companies in maturities of 3 to 270 days, in denominations of $1,000 to $5 million, but usually with a $25,000 minimum purchase. Commercial paper of finance

[2]For detailed specifications of all attributes of U.S. Treasury securities and federal agency issues, see *Handbook of Securities of the United States Government and Federal Agencies* (New York: First Boston Corporation, annually).

companies and industrial firms also can be purchased from dealers, though the denominations are usually higher. There is a limited secondary market for commercial paper, and thus firms typically plan to hold until maturity.

Commercial paper does not carry an interest payment, but rather is purchased on a discount basis, like U.S. Treasury bills. Yields on paper are higher than on U.S. Treasury bills, again reflecting the higher risk that is associated with firms in the private sector. The generally safe image of commercial paper was severely tarnished in 1970 when the Penn Central Railroad announced bankruptcy and about $75 million in its commercial paper could not be redeemed.

In the early 1960s, commercial banks began to issue certificates for the time deposits placed by corporations in their banks. Often referred to as just "CD's," *certificates of deposit* are negotiable and thus can be bought and sold prior to maturity. Denominations are large, as seen in Exhibit 4-3. There is an active secondary market through securities dealers, and thus firms can invest excess funds for short periods of time. Yields, which include interest paid at maturity, are similar to those on commercial paper. As with all securities issued in the private sector, yields on commercial paper are subject to federal income taxes.

Bankers' acceptances are instruments used for delayed payments in certain types of domestic and international business. They are actually drafts drawn against deposits in commercial banks, but with payment at maturity guaranteed by the bank. Bankers' acceptances are negotiable instruments that are traded at a discount (from the maturity payment value) in an active secondary market. Yields on bankers' acceptances are roughly comparable to the yields on commercial paper and certificates of deposit.

For investing excess funds over a period of a few days, over a weekend, or just overnight, it is possible for a firm to purchase U.S. Treasury bills from a securities dealer subject to an agreement that the dealer will buy back the Treasury bills at a specified price and time. This arrangement, which is known as a *repurchase agreement*, offers great flexibility to a firm for earning added return once its precise cash-flow requirements are determined. There is also an active secondary market for repurchase agreements. Yields are comparable to those of U.S. Treasury bills.

CHARACTERISTICS OF THE MONEY MARKET

Excepting commercial paper, we see in Exhibit 4-3 that the different types of marketable securities are traded in an active secondary market. It is an over-the-counter market in contrast to the organized securities exchanges on which corporate stocks and bonds are traded. The *money market* as it is commonly called, is a system of telephones and teletypes that interconnect a network of twenty to thirty firms specializing in high-quality, short-term marketable securities such as have been described. These firms buy and sell marketable securities, either for their own account as dealers, or as agents for commercial banks or other securities firms. The communication network allows a business firm to easily compare alternative prices and yields for each type of marketable security. Transactions consummated via the telephone and teletype network are then confirmed in writing.

The procedures used by a firm's financial manager to buy and sell marketable securities depend on the type of financial instrument involved. In some instances, the manager may interact directly with the issuing government or institution, while in others, the manager may interact with money-market dealers or agents. If commercial banks are used to buy and sell marketable securities, they represent another entry to the money market. Obviously all middlemen, including commercial banks, that help to effect securities transactions for a business firm will charge for their intermediation service. Typically that charge, which ranges from .10 percent to .25 percent, is effected via a higher price paid (i.e., the *asked* price) or a lower price received (i.e., the *bid* price) for the particular marketable security.

Not unlike the situation in other financial and capital markets, the prices of marketable securities in the money market reflect the interacting forces of demand and supply, as well as the relative risk that is associated with those securities. The yield on a marketable security reflects supply, demand, and relative risk. The calculation of yield to a firm that invests in a marketable security is facilitated by the following formula.

$$Y = \frac{P_2 - P_1 + I}{P_1} \times \frac{365}{n}$$

where Y = yield to the firm
   P_1 = purchase price of the marketable security
   P_2 = sales price of the marketable security
   I = interest paid on the marketable security
   n = number of days the security is held

Prices are net of any transaction costs paid to financial intermediaries. If the marketable security is held to maturity (M), then $P_2 = M$, and Y is referred to as the *yield to maturity*.

To illustrate the use of this formula, it is convenient to use certain of the marketable securities that have been described. Consider an investment by Crescent Corporation in $10,000 worth of ninety-one-day U.S. Treasury bills for $9,850. In terms of the above notation, the calculation of yield to maturity would be as follows:

$$P_1 = \$9,850 \qquad\qquad I = 0$$
$$P_2 = M = \$10,000 \qquad n = 91 \text{ days}$$
$$Y = \frac{\$10,000 - \$9,850 + 0}{\$9,850} \times \frac{365 \text{ days}}{91 \text{ days}} = 6.11\%$$

Alternatively, Crescent could purchase $10,000 worth of a certain federal agency issue that pays $400 interest at maturity in 210 days. The purchase price is $10,000—the face amount of the particular issue. Following the same procedure, we obtain

$$P_1 = \$10,000 \qquad\qquad I = \$400$$
$$P_2 = M = \$10,000 \qquad n = 210 \text{ days}$$
$$Y = \frac{\$10,000 - \$10,000 + \$400}{\$10,000} \times \frac{365 \text{ days}}{210 \text{ days}} = 6.95\%$$

As expected, the yield to maturity for the federal agency issue is higher than that on the Treasury bill because of higher risk, and possibly because of the longer maturity.

In both of the examples, the marketable security is held until maturity. If Crescent sells a marketable security prior to maturity, the realized yield will reflect changes in interest rates within the economy. Consider another example of a security held for one month during which interest rates increase significantly, with prices of marketable securities falling. The price of the particular marketable security falls from $9,900 to $9,850 in one month. The appropriate calculation is

$$P_1 = \$9,900 \qquad\quad I = 0$$
$$P_2 = \$9,850 \qquad\quad n = 30 \text{ days}$$
$$Y = \frac{\$9,850 - \$9,900 + 0}{\$9,900} \times \frac{365 \text{ days}}{30 \text{ days}} = -6.14\%$$

This calculation illustrates possible loss to a firm that sells marketable securities prior to maturity.

Rearranging the yield equation, and letting $P_2 = M = \$100$, we obtain another useful formula

$$P_1 = \frac{365 \, (I + \$100)}{Yn + 365}$$

This formula expresses the current price (per $100 of maturity value) of a marketable security in terms of its yield to maturity and the length of time until maturity. The current price of a sixty-day Treasury bill that yields 7.0 percent would be calculated as follows:

$$Y = 7\% \qquad\qquad I = 0$$
$$P_2 = M = \$100 \qquad n = 60 \text{ days}$$
$$P_1 = \frac{365 \, (\$100 + 0)}{(.07)(60) + 365} = \$98.86$$

Selling price was set at $100 because prices of marketable securities are quoted in those units. Each issue of the *Wall Street Journal* includes bid prices (for sellers), asked prices (for buyers), and values of yield to maturity for longer-term United States government securities and for federal agency issues. Bid and ask quotations for U.S. Treasury bills are in terms of yields rather than prices. Occasionally, the *Wall Street Journal* also includes current yields on commercial paper and certificates of deposit. Prices and yields shown in the financial pages are indicative of general trends, and do not represent actual transactions in the money market.

Exhibit 4-4 presents annual yields on certain types of marketable securities during the past decade. Values shown are average yields for the year and do not reflect the variability in prices of marketable securities during each year. For comparative purposes, the *prime rate*—the interest rate on bank loans to large, financially strong corporations—is included in Exhibit 4-4. The reader can observe variations over time for each type of marketable security, as well as variations between the different types available to the firm that has excess funds.

A *basis point* is defined as .01 percent of yield. In other words, 100 basis points of yield equals 1 percent of yield. Fifty basis points equals 0.5 percent of yield. Basis points frequently are used to discuss differences in yields over

EXHIBIT 4-4

ANNUAL YIELDS ON MARKETABLE SECURITIES, 1965–1976

Year	U.S. Treasury bills (3 mo.)	Federal agencies*	Commercial paper	Certificates of deposit	Bankers' acceptances	Prime rate
1965	3.95%	5.81%	4.38%	4.83%	4.22%	5.00%
1966	4.88	6.25	5.55	6.22	5.36	5.75
1967	4.32	6.46	5.10	6.06	4.75	5.75
1968	5.34	6.97	5.90	6.65	5.75	6.38
1969	6.78	7.81	7.83	8.28	7.61	7.68
1970	6.46	8.44	7.72	8.93	7.31	7.25
1971	4.35	7.74	5.11	6.46	4.85	5.68
1972	4.07	7.60	4.69	4.90	4.47	5.25
1973	7.04	7.95	8.15	8.42	8.08	8.00
1974	7.89	8.92	9.87	10.25	9.92	10.50
1975	5.84	9.01	6.33	6.77	6.30	7.75
1976	4.99	8.99	5.35	5.24	5.19	6.75

Source: Federal Reserve Bulletin.
*Based on Federal Home Loan Bank Board (new mortgage series).

time for a security, or between the yields of two or more marketable securities. Exhibit 4-5 shows the yields on the more risky marketable securities measured in basis points *relative* to the yields on ninety-one-day U.S. Treasury bills. Values in Exhibit 4-5 also may be viewed as *excess yields* available on different types of marketable securities. One clear observation from Exhibit 4-5 is that excess yields vary considerably over time and also among the different types of marketable securities. The range of excess yields is from a high of 400 basis points to a low of 20 basis points, both values occurring in 1976. The highest excess yields over the past decade have been for federal agency issues—here measured by yields on Federal Home Loan Bank Board issues. Federal agency yields also exceeded the prime rate in every year but 1973. The lowest excess yields usually were for bankers' acceptances. Another observation is that the highest excess yields for three of the types occurred during the credit crunch of 1974.

EXHIBIT 4-5

ANNUAL EXCESS YIELDS ON MARKETABLE SECURITIES, IN BASIS POINTS, 1965–1976

Year	Federal agencies	Commercial paper	Certificates of deposit	Bankers' acceptances	Prime rate
1965	186	43	88	27	105
1966	137	67	134	48	87
1967	214	78	174	43	143
1968	163	56	131	41	104
1969	103	105	150	83	90
1970	198	126	247	85	69
1971	339	76	211	50	133
1972	353	62	83	40	118
1973	91	111	138	104	96
1974	103	198	236	203	261
1975	317	49	93	46	191
1976	400	36	25	20	176

Source: Calculations based on Exhibit 4-3.
Note: Excess yield on each type of marketable security is measured relative to the yield on ninety-one day U.S. Treasury bills.

We have examined yield in some detail because it is a visible and measurable characteristic of a marketable security. Before proceeding, it should be noted that yield is *not* the only characteristic of a marketable security that is considered by a financial manager. As part of the survey of large United States corporations (discussed in footnote 1), the authors reported how financial managers ranked various characteristics in order of importance. The first choices of ninety-nine respondents were as follows:

Characteristic	Number of first choices
Market price stability	46
Marketability	27
Yield	13
Maturity	12
Other	1
Total	99

Yield was of highest importance for only thirteen financial managers in the sample.[3]

COST-BALANCING MODELS

A good deal of attention in the finance literature has been given to the question of how the firm's portfolio of marketable securities ought to be managed. Much of that attention has focused on analytical models which attempt to balance the various costs associated with the firm's cash balance, and the firm's portfolio of marketable securities. Most of the analytical models are special cases of the general cost framework depicted in Exhibit 2-4 as part of our discussion of financial forecasting. The analytical models, or "cost-balancing models" as they are sometimes called, differ in their formulation of the problem, especially in how future cash needs are assumed to occur. Toward better understanding how assumptions of future cash needs impact the costs to the firm, we will review four particular cost-balancing models that have been proposed.

One cost-balancing approach is concerned with the optimal amount of financing to be obtained from long-term capital markets.[4] The firm's desired cash balance is subtracted from that optimal amount, with the difference

---

[3]Gitman et al., op. cit.

[4]See H. Bierman, Jr. and A. K. McAdams, *Management Decisions for Cash and Marketable Securities* (Ithaca, N.Y.: Cornell University Press, 1962), Chapter 6.

representing the appropriate investment in marketable securities. The optimal financing from the capital markets Q is given by the square-root formula

$$Q = \sqrt{\frac{2\,F\,D}{i - Y}}$$

where F = the fixed flotation cost of obtaining new financing
$\quad\quad D$ = the firm's total net outlay of cash for the next period
$\quad\quad i$ = the percentage interest rate on new financing
$\quad\quad Y$ = the percentage yield on marketable securities

The formula is obtained by minimizing the total cost to the firm, which includes the costs of obtaining additional funds from the capital market (the costs of too little) plus the opportunity cost of the funds held in cash or cash equivalents (the costs of too much).

To illustrate, suppose that net cash outlay for the next year D = $800,000. Suppose further that F = $50,000, i = 8%, and Y = 6%. Using the formula, we obtain

$$Q = \sqrt{\frac{(2)(\$50,000)(\$800,000)}{.08 - .06}} = \$2,000,000$$

as the optimal financing each time new external funds are obtained. If the firm's desired cash balance is estimated to be $600,000, then this model would suggest

$$\$2,000,000 - \$600,000 = \$1,400,000$$

as the amount to be invested in marketable securities.

The first analytical model gets at the investment in marketable securities indirectly. The other three models focus instead on how financial management should *switch* funds between the firm's cash account and its portfolio of marketable securities. The models differ in how the firm is assumed to obtain and utilize cash. Exhibit 4-6 is a timeline comparison of the assumptions that underlie each of the three cost-balancing models.

The second model to be discussed was proposed by William Baumol in 1952.[5] As seen in panel A of Exhibit 4-6, Professor Baumol assumed the firm's demand for cash (totaling D for the period) to be a steady net outflow. It is satisfied by periodic withdrawals of an equal amount C from the marketable securities portfolio. For each withdrawal during the period there

[5]W. J. Baumol, "The Transaction Demand for Cash: An Inventory Theoretic Approach," *Quarterly Journal of Economics*, November 1952, pp. 545–556. A useful comparison of this and the following two cost-balancing models is found in J. F. Weston and E. F. Brigham, *Managerial Finance*, 5th ed. (Hinsdale, Ill.: The Dryden Press, Inc., 1975), Appendix B to Chapter 7.

EXHIBIT 4-6

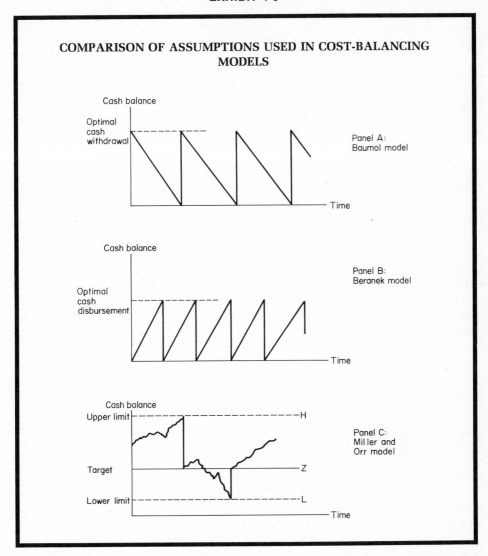

COMPARISON OF ASSUMPTIONS USED IN COST-BALANCING
MODELS

Panel A:
Baumol model

Panel B:
Beranek model

Panel C:
Miller and
Orr model

is a fixed transaction cost b. That cost component must be balanced against
the foregone yield Y on marketable securities. The optimal withdrawal to
minimize total costs was found to be

$$C = \sqrt{\frac{2Db}{Y}}$$

Note the similarity of this to the previous formula, since both formulations involve a balancing of two cost components. If $b = \$150$ per transaction, and D and Y are defined as before, then

$$C = \sqrt{\frac{(2)(\$800,000)(\$150)}{.06}} = \$63,300$$

is the optimal size of each transfer from the portfolio to the cash account of the firm. If the optimal solution is used by the financial manager, then there would be

$$\frac{\$800,000}{\$63,300} = 12.6$$

transfers during the year, or about once a month.

A third model was proposed by William Beranek in 1963.[6] His formulation, as shown in panel B of Exhibit 4-6, involves a steady accumulation of cash receipts during the year with periodic cash disbursements. The formulation is thus quite different from that of Professor Baumol. The rationale behind Professor Beranek's assumption is that the financial manager has much greater control over cash disbursements than over cash receipts. Beranek also associated a probability distribution with net cash flows. The financial manager's problem is to allocate available funds at the beginning of each period between the firm's cash account and its portfolio of marketable securities, so as to maximize expected return to the firm. Yields from marketable securities are balanced against transaction costs plus the costs of being short of cash when disbursements are due. The solution obtained by Professor Beranek is to set the cash balance at a level so that the cumulative probability of cash shortage is equal to the ratio $Y \div S$ where S is the firm's shortage cost (per unit per period). If the firm prefers to borrow additional funds rather than forego cash discounts from suppliers, then shortage cost could be taken as $S = i - Y$, which is the borrowing rate for the firm net of what can be earned (on average) on marketable securities.

The fourth model by Merton Miller and Daniel Orr in 1966 was a control limits approach to guiding the actions of the financial manager.[7] As seen in panel C of Exhibit 4-3, net cash flows (and hence the cash balance) are assumed to occur randomly over time. The upper and lower control limits are designed by H and L respectively, while Z designates the target cash level. If the cash balance reaches H then an amount $H - Z$ is invested in marketable securities. Conversely, if the cash balance drops to L then an amount of marketable securities $Z - L$ is sold. The decision problem is to determine Z and H so as to minimize the total cost of transferring funds to

[6]W. Beranek, *Analysis for Financing Decisions* (Homewood, Ill.: Richard D. Irwin, Inc., 1963), Chapter 11.

[7]M. H. Miller and D. Orr, "A Model of the Demand for Money by Firms," *Quarterly Journal of Economics*, August 1966, pp. 413–435.

and from the portfolio plus the opportunity cost of idle funds in the firm's checking account. The lower limit L on the cash balance is specified by management, depending on how much risk they are willing to accept. Miller and Orr solve the problem and derive the following formulas for determining the upper control limit and target cash level

$$Z = \sqrt[3]{\frac{3b\sigma^2}{4Y}} + L \text{ and } H = 3Z - 2L$$

where b = the fixed transaction cost per transfer

Y = the yield (daily) on marketable securities

σ = standard deviation of daily changes in the cash balance

This cube-root formula is based on a further assumption that increases and decreases in the firm's cash account are equally likely. Professors Miller and Orr tested their solution using actual data for the Union Tank Car Company. They were able to reduce the average daily cash balance of the firm by about 40 percent and to decrease the number of buy and sell transactions of marketable securities by over 30 percent.

We shall leave an illustration of this model to the problems at the end of the chapter. It is interesting to note from the solution equations that the firm's target level for cash increases with higher transaction costs, and also with greater variability in daily cash flows. As would be expected, the target level for cash decreases with higher yields on marketable securities.

Although the four cost-balancing models are similar in structure, they differ considerably in how the cash-flow profile of the firm is modeled. Three distinct profiles were shown in Exhibit 4-6. Some readers probably noticed that *none* of the four models provided any distinction between different types of marketable securities. In addition, the usefulness of any one of the cost-balancing models in managing marketable securities would depend on how realistic are the cash-flow assumptions for that model, as well as on how realistically the model is able to portray the associated costs to the firm.[8] Only in the fourth model did the authors devote much attention to the important problems of model implementation.

STRATEGIES FOR MANAGING MARKETABLE SECURITIES

In the preface to this *Guide*, an important gap that exists between the theory and practice of working capital was identified. In discussing the firm's investment in marketable securities, that gap is particularly apparent. The first sections of the chapter included institutional description of six types of

---

[8]An interesting study of the value of cost-balancing models using simulation is H. G. Daellenbach, "Are Cash Management Optimization Models Worthwhile?" *Journal of Financial and Quantitative Analysis*, September 1974, pp. 607–626. A conclusion of the study was that cost-balancing models have limited usefulness when the cash flow pattern of the firm is nonstationary, i.e., when it does not follow a predictable pattern over time.

marketable securities, and of the money market in which purchases and sales are transacted. In contrast, the previous section reviewed four cost-balancing models that have been proposed by academics for help in managing marketable securities. To stop here would be to leave a gap between the theory and practice of managing marketable securities. Instead, we shall consider a series of seven strategies that can be used by financial managers in handling the periodic excesses of cash for their firms. In action terms, the seven strategies are as follows:

1. Do nothing

2. Make investments ad hoc

3. Ride the yield curve

4. Develop guidelines

5. Utilize control limits

6. Manage with portfolio perspective

7. Follow a mechanical procedure

One alternative strategy, the first on the list, is to do nothing. In other words, the financial manager would simply let excess cash accumulate in the firm's checking account. No investments are made in marketable securities, and hence there is no attempt to add to the profitability of the firm. Such a strategy does enhance liquidity, but at the expense of additional profitability. It should be noted that many firms, especially small firms, do not take advantage of opportunities to invest in marketable securities. Whether or not that is an appropriate strategy depends on the extent of firm liquidity, as well as on the resources that may be devoted to the managing of that particular component of working capital.

The second strategy on the list above is to make occasional investments in marketable securities, but only on an ad hoc basis. This also appears to be a strategy used by many firms of all sizes, particularly those who cannot devote much time or resources to that aspect of the business. Decisions and implementation of this strategy are likely to be handled by the chief financial officer of the firm. The strategy reflects an attempt to add to firm profitability, but in a manner which does not significantly detract from firm liquidity, or to expose the firm to the risk of interest rate changes. This might be accomplished by purchasing securities where maturities coincide with projected cash disbursements by the firm.

The third strategy, frequently mentioned by financial managers, is to *ride the yield curve*. It is essentially a technique for trying to increase the yield from the portfolio of marketable securities by speculating on changes in interest rates. If a manager believes, for example, that interest rates will decline in the next few months, he purchases longer-term securities since their prices will rise more than the prices of shorter-term securities. Alternatively, a manager may sell longer term securities before their maturity in order to achieve a higher yield. A difficulty with this strategy is that it necessitates greater risk in order to try for greater yield and that may or may not be consistent with how firm liquidity ought to be managed. Riding the yield curve necessitates that a particular manager's expectation for future interest rates is somehow different from that of other managers who buy and sell marketable securities. There is, however, considerable evidence suggesting the futility of trying to somehow do better than average, and that the potential of greater return is almost always accompanied by greater risk to the firm.

At the other extreme, seventh on the list, a financial manager might transfer funds between marketable securities and the firm's cash account according to a mechanical procedure. The models developed by Professors Baumol and Beranek are examples of how a mechanized procedure could be used. The ultimate success of such a strategy is apt to depend on how well the firm's cash-flow pattern is coincident with that assumed in developing the procedure. There does not appear to be much evidence that such assumptions can be justified in practice. Nor does there appear to be much evidence that firms try to utilize mechanical procedures in practice. At best, the cost-balancing models might be useful in better understanding the costs associated with the firm's cash account and its portfolio of marketable securities.

The sixth strategy is to manage the firm's marketable securities according to the tenets of portfolio theory. That theory holds that a relevant goal is to maximize expected return for a given level of risk, or to minimize risk for a given level of expected return. Furthermore, portfolio theory holds that each member security should be valued in terms of its relative contributions to the return and risk of the total portfolio, and not just on its individual merits. Operationally, this approach might lead to a portfolio of marketable securities well diversified by types of security, by maturity, and by risk. Although portfolio theory has been developed in terms of explicit formulas for expected return and risk, it is viewed here more as an overall way of using the perceived interrelationships between marketable securities to help construct a portfolio that is consistent with the financial goals of the firm. Portfolio theory does not provide guidelines on how funds should be switched between the portfolio and the firm's cash account.

Utilizing a system of control limits, the fifth strategy, theory can be put into practice. As was shown in Exhibit 4-6, the strategy developed by Professors Miller and Orr is based on an assumption that cash inflows and outflows occur randomly over time. The control system triggers actions only when the cash balance reaches the upper or lower control limits. It provides no guidance as to which particular marketable securities ought to be added to or deleted from the portfolio. As such, the control limit system should probably be viewed as only a partial strategy for managing marketable securities.

The final strategy on the list, the fourth, is to develop explicit guidelines that help the financial manager in handling the firm's investments in marketable securities. The guidelines are viewed as a way of systematically reflecting management's viewpoint toward return and risk, as well as toward the proper role of the marketable securities portfolio within the firm. Examples of guidelines that might be followed are to (1) try where possible to hold marketable securities until their maturity, (2) avoid putting a major portion of the firm's excess funds in any single marketable security, or type of short-term investment, (3) not speculate on future changes in interest rates, and (4) minimize where possible the transaction costs associated with managing the portfolio of marketable securities.

There is no guarantee that using guidelines such as these will lead to an optimal solution. But if the guidelines are used in conjunction with a system of control limits—or at least with some explicit recognition of the costs of a cash balance that is too small or too large, this strategy represents a bridge between theory and practice. It is likely that many large firms have developed an overall strategy for managing marketable securities that features guidelines of the type suggested here. At the same time, it is likely that many smaller firms, which have not been able to devote many resources to this single aspect of working capital management, would do well to reevaluate their current strategies for handling the excess funds in the business.

SUMMARY

Marketable securities become a component of working capital when the firm temporarily finds itself with excess funds. Characteristics of six different types of marketable securities were discussed. We also compared a series of cost-balancing models that are frequently mentioned in connection with a firm's excess funds. A series of alternative strategies for managing a firm's portfolio of marketable securities was reviewed, with an eye toward arriving at a workable compromise between theory and practice.

Problem 4-1

What is the yield to maturity on a $10,000 Treasury bill that has a purchase price of $9,900 and a maturity of ten weeks?

SOLUTION: Using the formula explained in the chapter, we obtain

$$P_1 = \$9,900 \qquad\qquad I = 0$$
$$P_2 = M = \$10,000 \qquad n = 10 \text{ weeks} = 70 \text{ days}$$
$$Y = \frac{\$10,000 - \$9,900 + 0}{\$9,900} \times \frac{365 \text{ days}}{70 \text{ days}} = 5.27\%$$

Problem 4-2

Apply the Miller-Orr model to the following parameter values in order to construct a control system for managing the cash balance of a firm:

$$b = \$100; \ Y = 6\%; \ L = \$2,000; \ \sigma = \$1,400.$$

SOLUTION: Plugging into the solution formulas presented in the chapter gives

$$Z = \sqrt[3]{\frac{(3)(\$100)(\$1,400)^2}{(4)(.06)}} + \$2,000 = \$8,260$$
$$H = (3)(\$8,260) - (2)(\$2,000) = \$20,780$$

Based on these control limits, the following two actions would periodically be triggered:

1. When the cash balance reaches the upper control limit of $H = \$20,780$, the financial manager would purchase $H - Z = \$20,780 - \$8,260 = \$12,520$ worth of marketable securities.

2. When the cash balance reaches the lower control limit of $L = \$2,000$, the financial manager would sell $Z - L = \$8,260 - \$2,000 = \$6,260$ worth of marketable securities.

Problem 4-3

Assume that a firm's net cash needs are fairly constant from week to week and total $1,500,000 for the next quarter. Marketable securities yielding 7.5 percent are available. If each transfer of funds from the marketable securities portfolio to the firm's cash account costs $100, how many times will the firm sell securities during the quarter? What will be the firm's average cash balance?

SOLUTION: The scenario matches the second cost-balancing model discussed in the chapter. The calculation of the optimal transaction size is as follows:

$$D = \$1,500,000 \qquad Y = 7.5\% \qquad b = \$100$$
$$C = \sqrt{\frac{(2)(\$1,500,000)(\$100)}{.075}} = \$63,300$$

The number of transactions during the quarter would be

$$\frac{\$1,500,000}{\$63,300} = 23.7$$

or a transaction every three to four days. Since net cash needs are constant, the average cash balance would be

$$(1/2)(\$63,300) = \$31,650$$

throughout the quarter.

Problem 4-4

How much would a firm pay for a $5,000 federal agency issue that pays $200 at maturity in six months (180 days), and for which the yield to maturity is 8 percent?

SUGGESTED READINGS

Baumol, W. J.: "The Transaction Demand for Cash: An Inventory Theoretic Approach," QUARTERLY JOURNAL OF ECONOMICS, November 1952, pp. 545–556.

Beranek, W.: ANALYSIS FOR FINANCIAL DECISIONS (Homewood, Ill.: Richard D. Irwin, Inc., 1963), Chapter 11.

Bierman, H., Jr. and A. K. McAdams: MANAGEMENT DECISIONS FOR CASH AND MARKETABLE SECURITIES (Ithaca, N.Y.: Cornell University Press, 1962).

Daellenbach, H. G.: "Are Cash Management Optimization Models Worthwhile?" JOURNAL OF FINANCIAL AND QUANTITATIVE ANALYSIS, September 1974, pp. 607–626.

Dufey, G. and I. H. Giddy: THE INTERNATIONAL MONEY MARKET (Englewood Cliffs, N.J.: Prentice-Hall, Inc., 1978).

Fisher, D. I.: CASH MANAGEMENT (New York: The Conference Board, Inc., 1973), Chapter 5.

Gitman, L. J., E. A. Moses, and I. T. White: "An Assessment of Theory, Practice and Future Trends in Cash Management," paper presented at annual meeting of the Financial Management Association, Seattle, October 1977.

HANDBOOK OF SECURITIES OF THE UNITED STATES GOVERNMENT AND FEDERAL AGENCIES (New York: First Boston Corporation, annually).

Johnson, R. W.: FINANCIAL MANAGEMENT, 4th ed. (Boston: Allyn and Bacon, Inc., 1971), Chapter 5.

Miller, M. H. and D. Orr: "A Model of the Demand for Money by Firms," QUARTERLY JOURNAL OF ECONOMICS, August 1966, pp. 413–435.

Stancill, J. McN., Jr.: THE MANAGEMENT OF WORKING CAPITAL (Los Angeles: University of Southern California Press, 1970), Chapter 3.

Stone, B. K.: "The Uses of Forecast and Smoothing in Control-Limit Models for Cash Management," FINANCIAL MANAGEMENT, Spring 1972, pp. 72–84.

Weston, J. F. and E. F. Brigham: MANAGERIAL FINANCE, 5th ed. (Hinsdale, Ill.: The Dryden Press, Inc., 1975), Appendix B to Chapter 7.

5

MANAGING ACCOUNTS RECEIVABLE

Cash is a key asset in transacting the business of the organization, but it is not the only medium of exchange in our economic system. Increasingly, business is transacted on a credit basis. Virtually all balance sheets include accounts receivable among the current assets and accounts payable among the current liabilities. Accounts receivable and accounts payable reflect credit transactions by the firm. This chapter deals with the management of accounts receivable.

RATIONALE FOR RECEIVABLES

All things being equal, many corporate managers might prefer to do business on a cash basis. But all things are not equal, and competition has led many firms to do part or all of their business on a credit basis. Credit is the ability of a consumer or organization to obtain goods, services, real assets, and even cash in exchange for a promise to pay later. Credit is thus a medium of exchange, but of limited acceptance to the seller since not all promises to pay later are of equal quality. With respect to the piping system analogy in Chapter 3, credit sales by a firm amount to one type of delay in the operating cycle.

Since most firms are doing more and more business on a credit basis, the question arises as to just how credit—and in particular accounts receivable—ought to be managed. The answer is threefold. First, credit should be extended by the firm in so far as it enhances sales and the profitability from those sales. This, we have seen, is consistent with maximizing return to the owners of the business. Second, credit ought to be managed in such a way that the firm's investment in accounts receivable is protected, and is consistent with other investments which are made. Third, the credit and collection activities of the firm must be coordinated with the total cash flow of the firm in order to ensure a continuity in operations.

RESPONSIBILITY FOR RECEIVABLES

As with managing cash, the ultimate responsibility for managing accounts receivable typically resides with the chief financial officer of the firm. That responsibility includes an important role in developing the firm's overall credit policy. In many firms, the credit manager is assigned responsibility for managing credit operations on a day-to-day basis. Crescent Corporation has a credit manager, but Arthur Hanson has ultimate responsibility for managing accounts receivable. We will discuss the management of accounts receivable from the viewpoint of both the credit manager and the chief financial officer of the firm.

Responsibility for accounts receivable also is likely to depend upon the extent to which decision-making is centralized or decentralized within the organization. For small firms, the credit department may consist of only the credit manager and secretarial support. At the other extreme, credit departments for large firms may well include a hundred or more employees. Even if credit and collections activities are decentralized within the firm, there is likely to be a corporate credit manager who coordinates credit activities from an overall perspective. For reasons we will see later, managing accounts receivable is likely to take more time than managing accounts payable.

The responsibility for managing receivables includes four key steps: (1) establishing credit terms, (2) granting credit to specific customers, (3) monitoring payment patterns and performing necessary collections followup, and (4) ensuring that the firm's investment in accounts receivable is appropriate. The four steps are relevant both to the management of *consumer credit,* which involves sales to individuals and families, and to the management of *commercial credit,* which involves sales to other business firms. An important prerequisite of the four steps is an information system that includes accurate records of credit applications to the firm, as well as payment experience for those customers that are granted credit. The need for an accurate information system applies equally to all components of working capital discussed in this *Guide.*

The first two steps comprise the firm's credit policy. Specifically, a *credit policy* identifies the authority for making credit decisions, the exact terms of credit sales to all types of consumer and commercial customers, and guidelines for selecting credit customers. The credit policy of a centralized firm is usually established by the chief financial officer, the credit manager, and possibly other key managers in the organization. Even for decentralized firms, responsibility for the broad aspects of a credit policy is likely to reside at corporate headquarters.

ESTABLISHING CREDIT POLICY

The extent to which a business should and does grant credit to other firms varies greatly. On the one hand, there may be larger, financially sound firms that are granted as much credit as they want. On the other hand, there may be smaller, financially weak customers for whom the business is unwilling to grant any credit at all, with any sales done solely on a cash basis. In between these extremes is a large number of firms that have some potential for being granted credit, but certainly not an unlimited amount. The heart of an effective credit policy must be aimed at those firms.

Exhibt 5-1 is a simple framework for understanding the need for a sound credit policy. Credit customers are categorized (after the fact) as those that pay promptly, those that delay payment, and those that never pay. Possible actions by the firm are categorized into situations where credit is granted and those for which credit is rejected. This gives six possible outcomes for which an economic result can be measured. Four of the outcomes are clear-cut. Outcome 1 is where the firm makes a correct decision and grants credit to a customer that pays promptly. For this outcome, profitability to the firm is increased. For outcome 2, the firm loses sales and profitability when credit is rejected to a customer that would have paid promptly. For outcome 5, the firm incurs collection costs and bad debt expenses since the customer never pays. And outcome 6 is where the firm makes a correct decision and rejects credit to a customer that would never pay. Here the firm also enhances profitability by avoiding collection costs and bad debt expenses.

The other two outcomes are less clear-cut. Outcome 3 is where credit is granted to a customer that ultimately pays, though not promptly. For that possibility, profitability to the firm is reduced by collection expenses. If credit is not granted to the slow-paying customer, as in outcome 4, then foregone profits are offset by the collection expenses that are avoided. The credit policy of a firm should be designed to accurately identify (in advance)

EXHIBIT 5-1

SIX ALTERNATIVE OUTCOMES OF A CREDIT DECISION

	Action by firm	
Ultimate result	*Grant credit*	*Reject credit*
Customer pays promptly	1. Profitability increased	2. Lost sales and profitability
Customer delays payment	3. Collection expenses	4. Lost sales and profitability minus collection expenses avoided
Customer never pays	5. Collection and bad debt expenses	6. Collection and bad debt expenses avoided

outcomes 1 and 6, to avoid outcomes 2 and 5, and to minimize the costs associated with outcomes 3 and 4.

It should be noted that the framework in Exhibit 5-1 does not fully reflect the scope of the problem in managing accounts receivable. For example, what about the consumer that pays promptly for five or six years and then fails to pay for a large order? What about the company whose volatile business causes its management to exhibit an erratic payment pattern over time? And how do changes in overall economic conditions impact the benefits and costs of the different outcomes?

Also as part of establishing the firm's credit policy, there are other decisions which must be made. A system of forms, paperwork, and overall information flow must be developed within the credit department. A security agreement containing the main points of the buyer-seller relationship must be designed if it is to accompany a credit transaction. The possible use of credit insurance must be explored. Credit insurance is typically purchased by a selling firm to protect it against the financial failing of any of its major credit customers. Financial management must decide whether any part of the firm's accounts receivable will be factored—that is, sold to a third party (more on this in Chapter 8). All of these decisions must be carefully made and periodically reviewed within the context of the firm's overall credit policy.

Nevertheless, the framework in Exhibit 5-1 does help to specify an appropriate goal for the financial managers responsible for accounts receivable.

The *goal of accounts receivable management* is to set credit terms, grant credit to customers, monitor payment patterns, and apply necessary collection procedures so as to increase organizational profitability.

CREDIT TERMS

A starting point in credit policy is to decide on appropriate credit terms to offer potential customers. The terms may well differ from product to product and market to market. One determinant in setting terms for commercial credit is the length of time necessary for the customer's payment to be converted into cash. A first question is simply the due date for payment from a credit customer.

The added cost to the firm of making a sale on credit, rather than for cash, includes the value of the firm's investment in the sale (i.e., the cost of goods sold) during the period until the cash payment is received. In Chapter 3, we discussed and illustrated a procedure for using the firm's cost of capital to calculate the dollar value of the foregone opportunity if the firm must wait for the cash proceeds from a sale. In some sense, the added cost to the firm of a credit sale should reflect the expenses of maintaining a credit function within the organization. To simplify our discussion, that cost component will not be considered until later in the chapter and in Chapter 9 of the *Guide*.

Suppose that Crescent Corporation is considering the sale of one of its cleaning appliances to a retailer, but only on a credit basis. The production cost, including an appropriate allocation of overhead, is $90 per unit. Management plans to price the applicance at $120. It appears that the retailer will agree to purchase the appliance for $120 if given 60 days to pay. Such a credit arrangement would be referred to as "net 60 days." After careful study, Arthur Hanson has concluded that Crescent's opportunity cost—or cost of capital as it is often called—is 10 percent. The added credit cost for the sale of having to wait 60 days for payment is

$$\$90 \times 10\% \times \frac{60 \text{ days delay}}{365 \text{ days in year}} = \$1.48$$

This in turn would be added to the production cost to obtain the total cost of the sale

Production cost	$90.00
+ Credit cost	+ 1.48
Total cost	$91.48

The potential profit on the credit sale of one appliance would become

Sales price	$120.00
− Total cost	− 91.48
Profit	$ 28.52

Note that $90, rather than $120, was used in obtaining credit cost, since $90 is the investment which Crescent has in each unit at the time the credit terms are established.

Analysis of the credit decision is more complicated if the possibility of a cash discount exists. The reason is that two or more cost calculations must be made, and the likely responses of the buyer must be considered. Suppose that Crescent offers the retailer the terms "2/30, net 60" which means that the retailer also has the option of paying within 30 days and receiving a 2 percent discount, or an effective price of ($120)(98%) = $117.60. As we will see in Chapter 7, the cost to the buyer of *not* taking a cash discount is quite high, so that many buyers would rather pay in 30 days than wait the full 60 days. From the seller's perspective, the production cost is the same, while the added credit cost of waiting only 30 days is 74 cents, or just half of what it would be if payment is made in 60 days. The potential profit to the firm of two alternative payment patterns by the customer is as follows:

	30-day payment	60-day payment
Effective price	$117.60	$120.00
−Production cost	90.00	90.00
−Credit cost	0.74	1.48
Profit	$ 26.86	$ 28.52

Because the cash discount more than offsets the difference in credit costs, profit to the firm is higher if the customer pays in two months. If the customer never pays, the loss to the firm would amount to the $90 production cost plus the credit cost up to the point that the account is written off as a bad debt expense. For example, if Crescent writes off bad accounts after six months (182 days), the firm's loss would amont to $94.49 ($90.00 production + $4.49 credit).

The result of different payment patterns can be summarized with an expected-outcome calculation. Because Crescent Corporation has sold cleaning applicances to retailers for several years, management has accumulated considerable data on payment patterns. Based on that data, probabilities can be assigned to three distinct outcomes: payment in 30 days (70 percent), payment in 60 days (29 percent), and nonpayment (1 percent). Expected profit to Crescent would be calculated as follows:

Payment pattern	Profit or (loss)	Probability	Weighted profit
30 days	$26.86	.70	$18.80
60 days	28.52	.29	8.27
Bad debt	(94.49)	.10	(0.94)
Expected profit			$26.13

The expected profit calculation becomes even more complicated if additional outcomes—such as the retailer delaying payment for 90 days and *still* taking the discount—are considered. In any event, the final decision on appropriate credit terms depends on both the economic consequences of possible outcomes, together with the relative chances (or probabilities) that the outcomes will materialize. In a later section, we will see that a return-on-investment framework can also be used to evaluate alternative credit terms.

CREDIT ANALYSIS

The next step in managing receivables is to decide which customers should be granted credit. This and the following section discuss ways in which credit customers are selected. The traditional approach to credit analysis is to investigate the potential customer with respect to four factors, and then summarize the results in order to make a decision on whether or not to grant credit. If a decision is made to grant credit, then another decision must be made as to how much credit. The four factors are commonly referred to in the credit profession as the "four C's of credit"—character, capacity, capital, and conditions. We will consider each in turn.

Character has to do with honesty, integrity, fairness, and other human traits that cause a customer to want or intend to pay for a purchase by a designated due date. While an evaluation of character can be attained through personal interviews, or from data provided in a credit application, the most direct evidence of character is simply the customer's prior payment record. Evidence about character is also available from other creditors, or from firms that serve as credit intermediaries.

In contrast to intent to pay, *capacity* has to do with ability to pay by a designated due date. Evidence about capacity comes mainly from financial data on the potential customer, and in particular the customer's periodic incomes and expenditures. In other words, capacity to pay on schedule is related to the income statement of the customer. Also part of capacity is how a particular credit sale will be handled along with existing financial obligations and other credit purchases by the customer during the same period. Financial statements provided by the customer or by credit intermediaries are a primary source of information on capacity.

Capital also has to do with the financial resources of the customer, but in particular the financial backing of the customer if capacity proves inadequate. Capital is measured by the assets of the customer, or more precisely, by the customer's equity. In other words, capital is related to the balance sheet of the customer. For this factor of credit, an important distinction arises between consumer and commercial credit, since most consumers have relatively little equity that could be seized in settlement of an unpaid bill. Again, financial statements, either personal or corporate, are a primary source of information on capital.

The fourth factor of credit is *conditions,* which means the economic and political environment within which credit decisions are made. Conditions is a factor over which the potential customer has no control. Although conditions at the national level may provide some perspective, the credit manager probably would focus on the economic conditions in the local area. In the case of commercial credit, the credit manager probably would focus on current conditions in the particular industry of the potential customer. Information on conditions comes from different sources than those used for the first three C's of credit.

The credit analysis of a prospective customer thus includes a breadth of factors that should be considered. In addition to credit data requested from the customer directly, information can be obtained from trade references, bank references, credit bureaus, and from the company's own records if the customer has previously purchased from the selling firm. The extent of the credit analysis also depends on the amount of credit that is requested, and on any significant changes that are made by the firm in its overall credit policy.

Putting all the information on the four C's together to make a final credit decision is a necessary but difficult task. Difficulties arise in how each factor is measured, as well as in the subjective way that the factors are weighted and brought together for a final decision. Judgment by the credit analyst that results from on-the-job experience is clearly necessary. The relative importance of the four factors of credit is likely to vary from one credit analyst to another. Seldom is traditional credit analysis reduced to a formula or otherwise mechanical procedure—even though guidelines may routinely be applied in a mechanical way to disapprove clearly poor credit risks, or to approve clearly acceptable credit customers. Furthermore, the Equal Credit Opportunity Act mandates clear policy statements by the selling firm on the subjective type of decisions. That is, for any credit decisions made outside of an empirically validated, mechanical credit-scoring system (see next section), there must be written policy statements to avoid any possible discimination.

Exhibit 5-2 depicts a logic that might be used subjectively by a credit analyst in processing credit information. For simplicity, conditions is ignored as a credit factor, and attention is focused only on three credit factors: character, capacity, and capital. Measures of the three factors may be quantitative assessments (e.g., financial ratios) or qualitative judgments (e.g., "too much," " just right," etc.). Each measure of a credit factor is compared against a numerical or subjective standard, and the application is judged to be "strong" or "weak" for that factor. The result of the logic in Exhibit 5-2 is four categories of risk ranging from excellent to dangerous. The intent of the logic is not to suggest that each credit application is handled in the same mechanical fashion, but rather that each credit factor is somehow evaluated separately within the total credit analysis. Also note that two of the four categories ("excellent risk" and "fair risk") lead to the second important decision as to how much credit ought to be granted. Here, again, the decision of how much credit is largely subjective, and arbitrary guidelines often are used by credit analysts to reach a final decision.

EXHIBIT 5-2

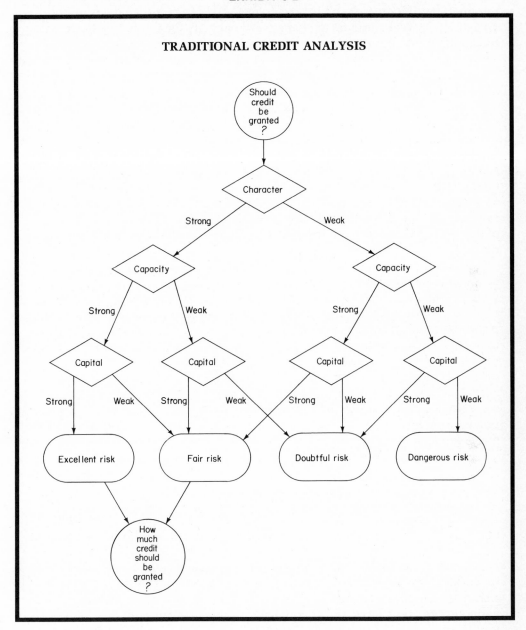

TRADITIONAL CREDIT ANALYSIS

Many readers may have noted that certain credit applications would not require the full logic in Exhibit 5-2. For example, if a credit analysis revealed an extremely weak measure of character or capacity for a potential customer, the application might well be rejected without further investigation of other credit factors. Another reason why the full logic might not be used in each instance is that the cost of information may outweigh the benefit of additional credit analysis.

Exhibit 5-3 outlines a three-stage, sequential procedure for credit analysis that explicitly reflects the cost of additional information. The first stage is a review of company files on past payments by the credit applicant. The second stage is an internal credit analysis based on information provided by the applicant. The third stage is an external credit analysis obtained from a credit agency. The cost per applicant increases with subsequent stages. The idea is not to to proceed to the next stage unless the expected benefit to the firm exceeds the cost of further information. Probable outcomes and the size of the credit request are important factors in deciding whether to proceed or not.

To illustrate, suppose that company files (Stage 1) indicate that an applicant has a "good history" of prompt payments. The question is whether to grant credit immediately, or to seek additional information (Stage 2)? In order to answer that question, one would need to know the following: (1) the past experience of customers that have a "good history," (2) the gross margin to the firm on the products being sold on credit, (3) collection costs incurred in the event of delinquent payment, (4) the timetable for writing off bad debts, (5) the firm's cost of capital, (6) the dollar size of the credit request, and (7) the cost of securing additional information. We will not pursue sequential credit analysis here,[1] except to point out that it is a complex procedure which leads to useful guidelines for helping the credit manager make decisions.

CREDIT-SCORING SYSTEMS

Many firms have used sophisticated statistical techniques in conducting their credit analyses. Multiple discriminant analysis employs a series of variables to categorize people or objects into two or more distinct groups. A *credit-scoring system* utilizes multiple discriminant analysis to categorize potential credit customers into two groups: good credit risks and bad credit risks. An important advantage of a credit-scoring system is that all of the variables are considered simultaneously, rather than individually as in the traditional logic of Exhibit 5-2. The plastic credit cards used by millions of citizens are the result of credit-scoring systems. In addition to widespread

[1] For further discussion and illustration, see D. Mehta, "The Formulation of Credit Policy Models," *Management Science*, October 1968, pp. B30–50.

EXHIBIT 5-3

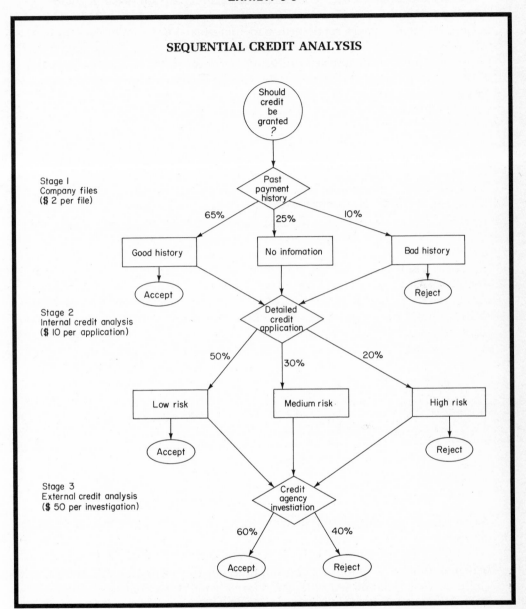

SEQUENTIAL CREDIT ANALYSIS

Should credit be granted ?

Stage 1
Company files
($ 2 per file)

Past payment history

65%   25%   10%

Good history   No infomation   Bad history

Accept   Reject

Stage 2
Internal credit analysis
($ 10 per application)

Detailed credit application

50%   30%   20%

Low risk   Medium risk   High risk

Accept   Reject

Stage 3
External credit analysis
($ 50 per investigation)

Credit agency investiation

60%   40%

Accept   Reject

usage in consumer credit, credit-scoring systems are increasingly used in commercial credit.

Suppose that a large retail firm had historical information on 200 customers who paid promptly and 200 customers who did not. Using data from those 400 credit applications, multiple discriminant analyses were made to determine the particular set of credit variables that best distinguishes the prompt group from the not-prompt group. The following profile of eight variables were identified:

Age (0.4)	Annual income (0.6)
Marital status (20.0)	Residence (4.6)
Occupation (4.3)	Home ownership (1.2)
Time on last job (0.9)	Telephone (15.0)

Multiple discriminant analysis also determined the numerical weightings which each of the variables should be given in calculating a total weighted credit score for each credit applicant. The relative weights of the eight variables are shown in parentheses. The discriminant procedure also provides information to management on how credit-score levels are related to likely payment patterns by customers. Suppose the following guidelines were developed:

Credit score	*Action*
Less than 60	Deny credit
60 to 80	Investigate further
Greater than 80	Grant credit

Notice that for credit scores between 60 and 80, the guidelines call for additional credit investigation.

Exhibit 5-4 shows how the credit score would be calculated for a hypothetical applicant. The middle column includes the particular values for the applicant. When combined with the relative weights, a total credit score of 104.1 is obtained. Since this easily exceeds the critical level of 80, the customer would be granted credit without further analysis.

One advantage of credit scoring, already mentioned, is that several variables are considered collectively. This captures interrelationships between variables that may be overlooked in a traditional credit analysis. Another advantage is that credit-scoring systems can be used to routinely accept or reject credit applications for which the final decision is relatively clear. This frees time for credit analysts to focus in greater detail on marginal applica-

EXHIBIT 5-4

ILLUSTRATION OF CREDIT-SCORING SYSTEM

Variable	*Measurement*	*Value*	*Weight*	*Weighted value*
Age	In years as reported	36	0.4	14.4
Marital status	Coded 1 (yes) or 0 (no)	1	20.0	20.0
Occupation	Coded 1 to 5 for different professions	4	4.3	17.2
Time on last job	In years as reported	6	0.9	5.4
Annual income	In thousands of dollars as reported	22.5	0.6	13.5
Residence	Coded 1 to 5 for different postal zones	3	4.6	13.8
Home ownership	Number of years owned as reported	4	1.2	4.8
Telephone	Coded 1 (yes) or 0 (no)	1	15.0	15.0
Total credit score				104.1

tions. In so doing, credit scoring does not substitute for sound human judgment, but rather serves to direct that judgment to more difficult credit decisions. A disadvantage of credit scoring is that expenses are incurred by the firm in developing a workable system. Care must be taken in constructing samples of good and bad customers. Managerial judgment is needed in selecting the best profile of credit variables. Management must also experiment with the resulting guidelines to ensure that the costs of wrong decisions are minimized.

MONITORING RECEIVABLES

Managing receivables does not end with the granting of credit. Indeed, considerable effort may be spent in monitoring the payment behavior of customers over time and taking corrective action on delinquent accounts. For firms that have many credit customers, it is essential that management develop a system of monitoring that is both timely and accurate. In this section, we review a series of monitoring techniques that are available to the credit manager. Our purpose is not to pursue all the details of the available technology, but rather to show that certain measures of credit status may be more informative than others. We will focus on aggregate measures of collection patterns for the firm, rather than on individual credit accounts. Whereas individual account monitoring is necessary for slow-paying customers, the monitoring of receivables begins with aggregate measures as a check on the firm's credit policy.

One way to monitor payment behavior is to relate receivables to firm assets or firm sales. Relating accounts receivables to firm assets takes the form of the ratio

$$\frac{\text{Accounts receivable}}{\text{Total assets}}$$

This indicates the percentage of the total resources of the firm that are invested in the delayed payments of credit customers. The ratio actually overstates the firm's investment since accounts receivable are recorded at the sales price rather than the firm's cost of the products or services sold on credit. The investment implications of accounts receivable will be further explored later in the chapter.

Receivables can be related to firm sales in different ways. To compare the alternatives, suppose you are the credit manager of a large firm. The monthly sales and month-end level of accounts receivable for one of your product lines during the past year was as follows:

Month	Sales	Receiv-ables	Month	Sales	Receiv-ables
January	$30,000	$61,200	July	$50,000	$ 88,000
February	29,000	60,900	August	56,000	104,400
March	31,000	58,800	September	65,000	125,200
April	30,000	59,300	October	75,000	144,200
May	35,000	64,300	November	84,000	157,100
June	42,000	74,100	December	98,000	175,000

By looking at the trends during the year, it would appear both sales and receivables were relatively level through April, but then increased steadily for the remainder of the year. These trends lend support to an important observation made in Chapter 2: a growing business will necessitate an increased investment in working capital.

A sharper focus on customer payment behavior is obtained by calculating the "collection period" for a product or business as follows:

$$\text{Collection period} = \frac{\text{accounts receivable}}{\text{credit sales per day}}$$

This is a particular application (to accounts receivable) of the "days sales outstanding" definition which appeared in Chapter 1. If collection period is calculated at the end of each quarter, then for the first quarter of the year, we would obtain

$$\text{Collection period} = \frac{\$58,800}{(\$30,000 + 29,000 + 31,000) \div (91 \text{ days})} = 59.5 \text{ days}$$

For the full year, the quarterly monitoring of accounts receivable would give

Quarter	Collection period
1st	59.5 days
2d	63.0
3d	66.6
4th	62.0

The trend in collection periods suggests that customers, on average, slowed down in their payments during the last three quarters of the year. A difficulty with looking just at collection period is that the ratio reflects sales growth and customer behavior.[2]

In order to disentangle sales trends and customer behavior, an *aging schedule* may be used. An aging schedule shows how long accounts receivable have been outstanding at a point in time. For the example, the aging schedule at the end of each quarter would be

Interval	Outstanding accounts receivable			
	1st quarter	*2d quarter*	*3d quarter*	*4th quarter*
0–30 days	$31,000	$42,000	$ 65,000	$ 98,000
31–60	20,600	24,500	42,500	58,800
61–90	6,000	6,000	16,000	14,300
91–120	1,200	1,600	1,700	3,900
121–150	0	0	0	0
Totals	$58,800	$74,100	$125,200	$175,000

Comparing aging schedules at periodic intervals, the credit manager may be able to spot changes in the payment behavior of the firm's customers.

[2]For further discussion, see W. G. Lewellen and R. W. Johnson, "Better Way to Monitor Accounts Receivable," *Harvard Business Review*, May–June 1972, pp. 101–109.

EXHIBIT 5-5

PERCENTAGE OF RECEIVABLES OUTSTANDING AT END OF MONTH

Percentage outstanding after	Jan.	Feb.	Mar.	Apr.	May	June	July	Aug.	Sept.	Oct.	Nov.	Dec.
Current month	100%	100%	100%	100%	100%	100%	100%	100%	100%	100%	100%	100%
1 month	72	71	71	72	70	71	77	76	71	72	70	71
2 months	20	20	21	20	19	21	32	34	19	19	20	19
3 months	5	4	5	5	3	4	8	12	6	5	5	5
4 months	0	0	0	0	0	0	0	0	0	0	0	0

Converting dollar values to percentages of the total for each interval helps to remove the influences of changing sales level.

But probably the best way to spot changes in customer behavior is to prepare a schedule of the percentage portions of each month's sales that are still outstanding at the end of successive months. Exhibit 5-5 illustrates that schedule for the same example. Comparing the relative percentages at month-end through the year, we see that no accounts were paid until the next month after the credit sales, and all unpaid accounts at the end of four months were written off as bad debt expenses. Despite the growth in sales throughout the year, the only change in behavior by credit customers was a slowing of payments during July and August. In September, customers reverted to their prior pattern. A subsidiary advantage of the monitoring technique in Exhibit 5-5 is that a historical record of payment percentages can be used in projecting the monthly collections that are needed in the firm's cash budget.[3]

COLLECTING RECEIVABLES

Collecting receivables begins with timely mailing of invoices. It includes the systematic monitoring and record-keeping for the many customers who pay promptly. Collecting receivables includes as well the additional steps that may be taken for those customers who do not pay promptly. There are several procedures available to a credit manager, who must judiciously decide when, where, and to what extent pressure should be applied to delinquent accounts. Management collection activity should be based on a careful comparison of likely benefits and costs.

One inexpensive procedure is to do nothing but hope that the customer will eventually pay. We already have seen that the added credit cost of delayed payments is the time value of the firm's investment in the product or materials sold to the delinquent buyer. There may also be a reluctance to wait because of a belief that the chances of collecting an overdue account may actually decrease with time. Another relatively inexpensive procedure is to periodically send duplicate copies of the original invoice to the buyer as a reminder that the bill has yet to be paid. Collection letters probably are the most frequently used procedure because of their lower cost and the flexibility with which the credit manager can deliver the message to the delinquent customer. Written followup on an overdue account is referred to as "dunning."

If these procedures are not successful, then the credit manager may resort to stronger, but more expensive procedures. Personal telephone calls can serve to get the attention of a slow payer. Telephone calls can consist of a routine reminder, or serve to initiate a constructive counseling of the customer by the selling firm. Wire messages or registered letters also serve to get

---

[3]See B. K. Stone, "The Payments-Pattern Approach to the Forecasting and Control of Accounts Receivable" *Financial Management*, Fall 1976, pp. 61–78.

attention. Another procedure is to inform the customer that unless payment is received by a certain date, a draft will be forwarded to the customer's bank. This serves to enlist a third party (i.e., the banker) in the collection process. Collection agencies are another procedure which can be effective, but at some cost (as much as 30 percent to 50 percent on all accounts) to the seller—both in terms of the delinquent payment and any future business with the same credit customer. Usually the last resort, also expensive, is a formal legal action through attorneys. It would not be uncommon for an attorney to charge 10 percent to 20 percent of the amount collected, and with a minimum charge on smaller accounts.

It is difficult to provide an exact prescription as to which and when these collection procedures should be employed. A credit manager should certainly not spend $500 to collect a $300 account receivable—unless somehow that action would prove to be a useful signal to other potentially delinquent credit customers. As with all components of working capital, it ultimately boils down to expected benefits versus expected costs.

CHANGING CREDIT POLICIES

In an earlier section, we discussed the costs to the firm of selling on credit. Since most firms do not really have a choice of selling on credit or only for cash, the more important decision for credit managers and their staff is when to change the credit policy of the firm over time. To do that, a return-on-investment framework is appropriate for comparing credit alternatives. The reason is that a return-on-investment framework properly focuses on the investment which a firm makes in accounts receivable. It also allows the credit manager to systematically consider potential sales and profits, alternative credit terms including cash discounts, and bad debt expenses. Exhibit 5-6 shows how a proposed change in credit terms would be evaluated.

Suppose that a firm's existing credit terms (net 30) are expected to result in sales of 400,000 units. Each unit has a production cost of $9, sells for $10, and results in a profit (before bad debts) of $1. Expected profits (after bad debts) are $380,000, the collection period is 32 days, and the firm's average investment in accounts receivable (90 percent of value shown on the balance sheet) will be $315,800.

In an effort to increase sales, the marketing manager of the firm has proposed that credit terms be extended (net 40). It is expected that this will increase sales by 10 percent to 440,000 units. Bad debts will increase from 0.5 percent on existing terms to 1.0 percent for the extended terms. Expected profit will be $396,000, or an increase of $16,000. The other result of the proposal will be an increase in collection period to 46 days, a decrease in receivables turnover (365 days divided by the collection period), and an increase of $185,400 in the firm's investment in accounts receivable. As shown at the bottom of Exhibit 5-6, the expected return on investment for the proposal is 8.6 percent. If the firm's cost of capital was 10 percent, the proposal should *not* be accepted.

EXHIBIT 5-6

RETURN ON INVESTMENT CALCULATION FOR CHANGING THE FIRM'S CREDIT TERMS

	Existing terms	Proposed terms
Expected volume	400,000 units	440,000 units
Expected sales revenue	$4,000,000	$4,400,000
Expected profit (before bad debts)	$400,000	$440,000
Expected bad debt expense	$20,000 (.5%)	$44,000 (1.0%)
Expected profit (after bad debts)	$380,000	$396,000
Incremental profit	—	$16,000
Expected collection period	32 days	46 days
Accounts receivable turnover	11.4 times	7.9 times
Average accounts receivable	$350,900	$556,900
Average receivables investment	$315,800	$501,200
Incremental investment	—	$185,400

$$\text{Return on investment} = \frac{\text{incremental profit}}{\text{incremental investment}} = \frac{\$16,000}{\$185,400} = 8.6\%$$

Earlier in this chapter when credit terms were discussed, we showed how production cost and credit cost would be subtracted from the effective price of a product in order to obtain the profit per unit. Applying the same procedure to aggregate sales in the example here results in the following comparison:

	Existing terms	Proposed terms
Expected sales revenue	$4,000,000	$4,400,000
− Product cost	3,600,000	3,960,000
− Bad debt expense	20,000	44,000
− Credit cost	31,600	49,900
Expected profit	$ 348,400	$ 346,100

Expected profit is greater under the existing credit terms, and thus the same answer of *not* accepting the marketing proposal is obtained. Although the two procedures are equivalent, the return-on-investment framework is perhaps more useful since it allows one to see the investment implications more explicitly. The return-on-investment framework is also helpful in comparing proposed changes in two or more working capital components.

SOME IMPORTANT LINKAGES

We have considered some of the factors involved in managing accounts receivable. It remains to identify certain linkages that should not be ignored in evaluating alternative credit terms and policies. A first linkage is between credit terms and policy and the firm's total marketing effort. The potential profits to a firm depend upon the sales volume that is achieved. Marketing managers may at times seem to focus more on sales growth and market share than on the profits that remain after due consideration of all credit costs. Credit and financial managers should always force each proposed change in credit terms and policies to a bottom-line evaluation of their impact on firm profitability. The return-on-investment framework is helpful in doing that.

Another linkage is between credit policy and the inventory level of the firm. In Exhibit 5-6, we evaluated a proposed change in credit policy that was expected to increase sales by 10 percent. For most firms, an increase in sales volume of that amount would necessitate an upward adjustment in inventory level. If an increase in inventory level is necessitated, then the return-on-investment calculation should include the incremental investment in inventory along with the incremental investment in accounts receivable. Not to include both is to *overstate* the return on investment for the proposed change in credit policy. What this means is that the credit manager must be aware of the firm's inventory levels, and how inventory investments are related to investments in accounts receivable.

Another linkage is between credit policy and the production capacity of the firm. Suppose in the example of Exhibit 5-6 that the $9 cost per unit consisted of $2 fixed cost and $7 variable cost. If the firm were operating under capacity, management should be willing to grant more credit than if the firm were operating at capacity. The reason is that the expected profit per unit from additional sales is greater. Specifically, the expected profit for the proposed change in credit terms would be $3 per unit. If everything else in the example were the same, the return on investment for the proposal would be

$$\text{Return on investment} = \frac{\$96,000}{\$144,256} = 66.5\%$$

The value easily exceeds the firm's 10 percent cost of capital, and hence the proposed extension in credit terms would add to firm profitability.* The

*The details of how the numerator and denominator are calculated is left to a problem at the end of the chapter.

implication of the linkage between credit policy and capacity is that the credit manager must also be familiar with the production operation of the business. Management almost always should be willing to grant more credit when the firm is operating below capacity.

A related linkage is between credit policy and the cost structure of the firm. In particular, the firm's willingness to change credit terms should also depend on how variable costs of production are related to the fixed costs of the business. To show this, we repeat the example of a firm operating below capacity. But now the firm has a cost structure in which the $9.00 production cost includes $2.50 fixed cost and $6.50 variable cost. For the proposal of extended credit terms that is expected to lead to a 10 percent increase in sales volume, the return on investment would be

$$\text{Return on investment} = \frac{\$116,000}{\$133,900} = 86.6\%$$

The effect of a higher ratio of fixed costs to variable costs—or *operating leverage* as it is sometimes called—is to increase the return on investment for credit policy changes of firms operating under capacity. The implication is that a firm with a *higher* degree of operating leverage should be *more* willing to grant more credit than a firm having a lower degree of operating leverage. This helps to explain why telephone utility companies with higher

EXHIBIT 5-7

RETURN ON INVESTMENT CALCULATION FOR MORE EFFICIENT FIRM

	Existing terms	*Proposed terms*
Expected sales revenue	$4,000,000	$4,400,000
Expected profit (before bad debts)	600,000	660,000
Expected bad debts expense	20,000	44,000
Expected profit (after bad debts)	580,000	616,000
Incremental profit	—	36,000
Average accounts receivable	350,900	556,900
Average receivables investment	298,300	473,400
Incremental investment	—	175,100

$$\text{Return on investment} = \frac{\text{incremental profit}}{\text{incremental investment}} = \frac{\$36,000}{\$175,100} = 20.6\%$$

operating leverage often tend to grant credit more readily than food-processing or financial-service firms that typically have lower operating leverage.

The final linkage is between credit policy and efficiency of the firm's operations. What would happen to the evaluation of credit policy changes for a firm that was able to convert $10 of sales revenue (per unit) into $1.50 profit (instead of only $1 as before)? To answer that, it is necessary to repeat the entire calculation in Exhibit 5-7. We see that expected profit is higher and average receivable investment is lower as a result of a more efficient operation. Return on investment for the proposal of extended credit terms more than doubles from what it was in the regional example.

All of this serves to emphasize a key point of this *Guide:* that the credit manager and other financial managers cannot be unfamiliar with other aspects of their firm. Inventory levels, production capacity, operating leverage, and efficiency are examples of linkages that impact an evaluation of changes in credit terms and credit policies. In making decisions, financial managers must have a broad perspective that extends beyond the working capital component for which they are responsible.

SUMMARY

Many firms sell their products and services on a credit basis, thus creating accounts receivable on the balance sheet. The state-of-the-art for managing accounts receivable includes procedures for setting credit terms, analyzing credit applications, monitoring customer payment behavior, and applying pressure to delinquent customers. To evaluate proposed changes in the credit terms and policies of the business, a return-on-investment framework was discussed and illustrated. Important linkages to inventory levels, production capacity, operating leverage, and firm efficiency add to the complexity of managing accounts receivable.

Problem 5-1

Early in the chapter, probabilities were assigned to three outcomes (thirty-day payment, sixty-day payment, and bad debt) in order to calculate expected profit to Crescent Corporation. If the probability of thirty-day payment remains at 70 percent, what probability of bad debt would cause expected profit to drop to zero?

SOLUTION: The profit (loss) values remain the same with only two of the three probabilities changing. Let B represent the probability of a bad debt. The probability of 30-day payment is 70% and the probability of 60-day payment is $100\% - 70\% - B = 30\% - B$. Expected profit is given by

$$(.70)(\$26.86) + (.30 - B)(\$28.52) + (B)(-\$94.49)$$

Setting this equal to zero and solving for B

$$18.80 + 8.56 - 28.52B - 94.49B = 0$$
$$123.01B = 27.36$$
$$B = \frac{27.36}{123.01} = 22.2\%$$

This means that the chances of bad debts would have to increase to 22.2% in order for the expected outcome not to be a profit to Crescent.

Problem 5-2

Work through the details of calculating incremental profit and incremental investment as suggested in the footnote at the bottom of page 134. This is the case where a firm, operating under capacity, is considering a change in credit terms from net 30 to net 40 days.

SOLUTION: Calculation of profitability and receivables investment under the existing credit terms is shown in Exhibit 5-6. The appropriate calculation for incremental profitability would be

Sales revenue	$4,400,000
− Production cost	
(400,000 units) ($9)	3,600,000
(40,000 units) ($7)	280,000
− Bad debt expenses	44,000
Expected profit (extended terms)	$ 476,000
− Expected profit (existing terms)	380,000
Incremental profit	$ 96,000

The appropriate calculation for receivables investment would be

$$\text{Units in receivables (extended terms)} = \frac{440,000}{7.9} = 55,696$$

$$-\text{Units in receivables (existing terms)} = \frac{440,000}{11.4} = 35,088$$

Additional units in receivables	20,608
× Investment per unit	$7
Incremental investment	$144,256

Problem 5-3

In a similar fashion, work through the details of calculating incremental profit and incremental investment for the case of a firm that has a higher operating leverage—namely $2.50 fixed cost and $6.50 variable cost.

Problem 5-4

Using the relative weights and decision guidelines of the credit-scoring illustration discussed in the chapter, decide whether or not to grant credit to the following applicants:

Variable	Applicant 1	Applicant 2	Applicant 3
Age	20	50	70
Marital status	no	yes	yes
Occupation (code)	1	3	2
Time on last job	1 year	20 years	retired
Annual income	$6,000	$28,000	$14,000
Residence (code)	4	5	2
Home ownership	0 years	18 years	32 years
Telephone	yes	yes	yes

Problem 5-5

For a small wholesale firm that sells almost exclusively on credit, the following schedule of forecasted sales is prepared:

Month	Sales	Month	Sales	Month	Sales
January	$28,000	May	$48,000	September	$38,000
February	31,000	June	57,000	October	31,000
March	35,000	July	51,000	November	25,000
April	42,000	August	45,000	December	29,000

Management also forecasts that on average 20 percent of credit sales will be collected in the same month, 60 percent in the first month after the sale, 15 percent in the second month, and the remaining 5 percent in the third month. No bad debts are expected. Calculate the average collection period at the end of each quarter during the year. Also prepare an aging schedule at the end of each quarter.

Problem 5-6

An outline of sequential credit analysis was presented in Exhibit 5-3. Suppose that company files (Stage 1) indicate that a particular applicant has a "good history" of prompt payments. Based on prior experience, 98 percent of customers with a "good history" continue to pay promptly, while 2 percent become delinquent or do not pay. Other relevant facts include: (1) production cost is 90 percent of the sales price; (2) collection costs for delinquent accounts average $200; (3) bad debts are written off after six months; (4) the firm's cost of capital is 10 percent. Develop a decision rule which would be helpful in making a credit decision.

SOLUTION: Let X represent the dollar value of the credit requested. If the applicant continues to pay promptly, the benefit to the firm is

$$X(1 - 90\%) = .10\ X$$

If the applicant does *not* continue to pay promptly, then the cost to the firm is

Production cost	$.90X$
Collection cost	$200
Credit cost $(1/2\ \text{year})(10\%)(.90X) =$	$.045X$
Total cost	$\underline{\underline{\$200 + .945X}}$

These outcomes are then combined with the respective probabilities in order to obtain a single expression for expected profit

Outcome	*Profit to firm*	*Probability*	*Weighted profit*
Pays promptly	$.10\ X$	.98	$.098\ X$
Doesn't pay	$-(\$200 + .945\ X)$	.02	$-(\$4 + .0189\ X)$
Expected profit			$.0791\ X - \$4$

which is seen to depend on the size of the credit request. If expected profit is set equal to zero and solved, we obtain X = $50.57. For credit requests *smaller* than $50.57, credit should *not* be granted; for requests *greater* than

$50.57, credit should be granted. The reason is that for small credit requests, the potential profit on the sale is not large enough to justify the collection costs and bad debt expense that occur if the customer does not pay promptly.

SUGGESTED READINGS

Beckman, T. N. and R. S. Foster: CREDIT AND COLLECTIONS: MANAGEMENT AND THEORY, 8th ed. (New York: McGraw-Hill Book Company, 1969).

Cole, R. H.: CONSUMER AND COMMERCIAL CREDIT MANAGEMENT, 4th ed. (Homewood, Ill.: Richard D. Irwin, Inc., 1972).

Davey, P. J.: MANAGING TRADE RECEIVABLES (New York: The Conference Board, Inc., 1972).

Higgins, R. C.: FINANCIAL MANAGEMENT: THEORY AND APPLICATIONS (Chicago: Science Research Associates, Inc., 1977), Chapter 22.

Hutson, T. G. and J. Butterworth: MANAGEMENT OF TRADE CREDIT, 2d ed. (Essex, Great Britain: Gower Press Limited, 1974).

Lewellen, W. G. and R. W. Johnson: "Better Way to Monitor Accounts Receivable" HARVARD BUSINESS REVIEW, May–June 1972, pp. 101–109.

Mehta, D. R.: WORKING CAPITAL MANAGEMENT (Englewood Cliffs, N.J.: Prentice-Hall, Inc., 1974), Chapters 1–3.

Stone, B. K.: "The Payments-Pattern Approach to the Forecasting and Control of Accounts Receivable" FINANCIAL MANAGEMENT, Fall 1976, pp. 61–78.

6

MANAGING INVENTORY

We turn now to inventory. Among the current assets and fixed assets recorded on the balance sheet of the firm, inventory represents, on average, one of the largest investments made by an organization. The importance of inventory is more striking because the averages reflect some firms, such as in the services sector of the economy, which have almost no inventory recorded on their balance sheets. But for the vast majority of firms, inventory is a critical current asset that must be carefully planned and controlled. The management of inventory is complex because so many different types of materials and parts are needed for the products that are manufactured and distributed.

RATIONALE FOR INVENTORY

If we lived in a world that had no delays, inventory would not be necessary. Upon receipt of an order from a customer, a firm would instantaneously acquire the necessary materials and parts, and the product would be manufactured instantaneously. There would be no need for materials, parts, or in-process inventory. There would also be no need for finished-goods inventory since delivery to the customer would be instantaneous. The primary rationale for inventory, therefore, is to allow for inevitable delays in acquiring necessary resources, manufacturing products, and delivering them to customers. These delays are part of the operating cycle of the firm which was described with a piping system analogy in Exhibit 3-1. The extent of the delays differs considerably among firms, and this is why there is such a wide variation in inventory levels among business firms.

A related rationale for inventory is that managers have different feelings about how closely those time delays ought to be managed. Some managers prefer to be more cautious and maintain higher levels of inventory, while other managers are more aggressive and maintain lower levels of inventory.

We saw in Exhibit 1-10 that the degree of caution employed in managing inventory and other working capital components can have a direct effect on both the profitability and liquidity of the firm.

RESPONSIBILITY FOR INVENTORY

Unlike cash, marketable securities, and accounts receivable, for which there usually is a singular responsibility within the firm, inventory typically is a shared responsibility. The purchasing manager is responsible for the materials and parts which the firm acquires for use in the manufacturing process. The production manager is responsible for processing materials and parts, together with necessary labor and overhead, toward the planned output of the firm. The marketing manager is responsible for seeing that the orders generated by the sales force are met. The financial manager is responsible for assessing the investment which is made in various kinds of inventory, and how inventory is related to other investments made by the firm. These are key managers within the business firm, and so decisions about inventory are a company-wide responsibility.

There may be certain perspectives or biases toward inventory which these managers have because of their responsibilities. The purchasing manager may lean toward larger orders in order to reduce purchase prices. The production manager may lean toward larger stocks of materials and parts, as well as larger work-in-process inventory, so as to enhance a smooth manufacturing process. The marketing manager may lean toward larger inventories of finished goods so as to avoid unfilled orders and delayed or lost sales. Only the financial manager may lean toward smaller inventories because of the costs to the firm of larger investments in materials, parts, work in process, and finished goods.

Somehow these different perspectives and biases must be resolved in an overall inventory policy for the firm. Responsibility for inventory may be given to a committee which includes the different functional perspectives that have been mentioned. If responsibility for inventory is given to a single manager, it typically would be to the treasurer, comptroller, or vice president of finance. The reason is that financial managers are able to identify and estimate the different costs associated with varying inventory levels. And since those costs may be tied to the different functional perspectives, the financial manager is able to balance the different views toward inventory levels that naturally arise within the organization.

For large corporations, the extent to which inventory responsibility is centralized or decentralized is apt to parallel how overall management is centralized or decentralized. A firm with several divisions may give major responsibility for inventory to their divisional managers, but with broad inventory policy coming down from the corporate level. The extent of decentralization of inventory responsibility is likely to increase if the divisions manufacture and distribute dissimilar product lines. For smaller firms, inventory responsibility is likely to reside with a high-ranking financial officer. Arthur Hanson of Crescent Corporation is assigned responsibility for inventory, as well as for other working capital components.

DIFFERENT TYPES OF INVENTORY

Inventory is an asset which can be seen and counted. As such, inventory differs from the current assets which we have talked about thus far in the *Guide*. It is also complex because there are different types of inventory, as well as different sizes, shapes, and substances. There are three major types of inventory. First, there are materials such as lumber, steel, rubber, plastic, chemicals, paint, and other finishing substances. Materials inventory also includes supplies, parts, fasteners, and a myriad of small items necessary to manufacture a complex product. Even a relatively small firm, such as Crescent Corporation, may literally have hundreds of different items of parts and materials inventory.

The second major type of inventory is *work in process*. It consists of items that are partially assembled or partially processed, but not yet completed. The extent of work-in-process inventory for a given firm depends on the complexity of the finished item and the length of time necessary for its production.

The third major type of inventory consists of finished goods that are completed and ready to be sold to customers. Finished-goods inventory also consists of products that are purchased for resale by wholesaling and retailing firms.

The relative breakdown of inventory into parts and materials, work in process, and finished goods is quite different among firms. The breakdown depends upon the nature of the business and the way in which the inventory is necessary to facilitate the delays that occur prior to sale to customers. A particular item may be a finished-good type of inventory for one firm, but a material or part for another firm. For example, a chemical firm manufactures a particular substance that is used by a pharmaceutical firm in producing a proprietary drug item. An electronic control produced by one firm is used as a purchased part by the manufacturer of heavy moving equipment. Only for wholesaling or retailing firms are the same items both purchased and sold.

Another way of categorizing inventory is by the value of the firm's investment. At a point in time, each business has a list of items in inventory with a dollar value associated with each item. The total of all the dollar values would be the amount shown as "inventory" on the balance sheet of the organization. The value assigned to each item, and hence the total inventory valuation, depends upon the accounting method used by the firm. Three accounting methods for inventory valuation are FIFO, LIFO, and average cost. *First-in-first-out* (FIFO) means that the cost of goods sold out of inventory during a period reflects the cost of items purchased or produced earlier in time, while items remaining in inventory reflect more recent costs.

Last-in-first-out (LIFO) does just the opposite: the cost of goods sold out of inventory reflects the cost of items purchased or produced recently, while items remaining in inventory are valued on the basis of earlier costs. *Average cost* is a procedure of basing both cost of goods sold out of inventory and items remaining in inventory on an average-cost basis. The FIFO and LIFO methods tend to give more extreme results, while the average-cost method gives results between the extremes. Only if the costs of purchasing and production remain constant over time will all three accounting methods give identical results for cost of goods sold and inventory valuation.

Exhibit 6-1 presents a comparison of FIFO and LIFO inventory accounting methods.* The comparison is facilitated by an example of a simplified business that had but four financial transactions during the year. A balance sheet is prepared after each transaction in order to show its impact on the financial status of the business. In transaction 1, an entrepreneur invests $5,000 cash to start a small business that buys specialized parts for resale. Fifty common shares are issued. Transaction 2 is the purchase for cash of 100 parts at $20 each, or a cash outlay of $2,000. At that point, the balance sheet includes cash of $3,000 plus inventory of $2,000—both financed by the entrepreneur's savings. Transaction 3 is the purchase, three months later, of 50 additional parts at $40 each, or another $2,000 cash outlay. Now there are 150 parts in inventory with a total investment of $4,000.

Transaction 4a is the sale of 50 parts (at $60 per part) using the FIFO method of inventory accounting. Cost of parts sold is $1,000 (since the earlier parts are sold), taxable income is $2,000, federal taxes of $800 (40%) are paid in cash, and $1,200 of after-tax earnings are retained in the business. Earnings per share for the year would be $2.40, the firm would have cash of $3,200, and the ending inventory valuation would total $3,000. In contrast, transaction 4b is the sale of 50 parts under LIFO. Here the cost of parts sold is $2,000 (since the later parts are sold), taxes are $400, and retained earnings are $600. Earnings per share for the year would be $1.20, the firm would have cash of $3,600, and ending inventory would be $2,000.

Comparison of FIFO with LIFO is highlighted by looking at four aspects of the business for the year:

Accounting method	Assets	Earnings	Cash	Inventory
FIFO	$6,200	$2.40	$3,200	$3,000
LIFO	$5,600	$1.20	$3,600	$2,000

Under FIFO, the business is larger (in terms of assets), and has twice the earnings for the year. The business also has an inventory valuation under

*Comparison of FIFO and LIFO with average cost is left to a problem at the end of the chapter.

EXHIBIT 6-1

BALANCE SHEET COMPARISON OF FIFO VERSUS LIFO INVENTORY ACCOUNTING

Transaction	*Assets*		*Equity*	
1. Invest $5,000 in small auto parts business.	Cash	$5,000	Stock (50 shares)	$5,000
	Total	$5,000	Total	$5,000
2. Purchase for cash 100 parts at $20 per part.	Cash	$3,000	Stock (50 shares)	$5,000
	Inventory		Total	$5,000
	(100)(20)	2,000		
	Total	$5,000		
3. Purchase for cash 50 parts at $40 per part.	Cash	$1,000	Stock (50 shares)	$5,000
	Inventory		Total	$5,000
	(100)(20)	2,000		
	(50)(40)	2,000		
	Total	$5,000		
4a. Sell for cash 50 parts at $60 per part. Use FIFO.	Cash	$3,200	Stock (50 shares)	$5,000
	Inventory		Retained earnings	1,200
	(50)(20)	1,000	Total	$6,200
	(50)(40)	2,000		
	Total	$6,200		
4b. Sell for cash 50 parts at $60 per part. Use LIFO.	Cash	$3,600	Stock (50 shares)	$5,000
	Inventory		Retained earnings	600
	(100)(20)	2,000	Total	$5,600
	Total	$5,600		

FIFO that more accurately depicts recent prices of parts. Under LIFO, the business has more cash.

If you were the entrepreneur in the example, which accounting method would you prefer? Many investors seem preoccupied with earnings per share as a single measure of firm success. They would prefer FIFO. Other investors, realizing that earnings per share often is the result of various accounting methods (including the way in which inventory is valued), might intuitively opt for LIFO since it leads to a larger cash balance. The theory of finance has shown convincingly that cash flow ought to be more relevant than earnings as a measure of how the owners of a business have fared during a given time period. In addition to theory agreeing with intuition, practice also seems to agree—we have seen countless firms switch from FIFO to LIFO during the last few years when prices have increased steadily. For during a period of rising prices, LIFO reduces federal taxes, and more cash remains in the business.

Regardless of the accounting method used by the firm, it is possible for management to rank inventory items in order of decreasing value per item. If such a ranking or distribution was plotted for a business, it might look like the pattern in Exhibit 6-2. The horizontal scale depicts percentage of items in inventory for the business and ranges from 0 to 100 percent. The vertical scale shows the percentage of total investment in inventory, and also ranges

EXHIBIT 6-2

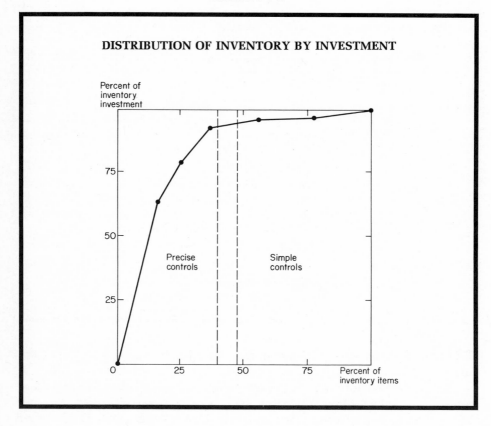

DISTRIBUTION OF INVENTORY BY INVESTMENT

from 0 to 100 percent. The inventory distribution curve reveals a typical pattern: a small percentage of the items in inventory constitutes a large proportion of the total investment made by the firm. We also see that the inventory items are divided roughly into two broad categories for which inventory control should be applied differently. For the first part of the distribution, more precise controls are appropriate for inventory because of the large investment in those high-valued inventory items. For the second part of the distribution, simpler controls are appropriate because investment per inventory item is smaller. The two vertical dashed lines in Exhibit 6-2 indicate that there is not a clear-cut demarcation between higher-valued and lower-valued inventory items. Before discussing technique of managing different types of inventory, it is useful to take an overall look at the problem of inventory management.

OVERVIEW OF AN INVENTORY SYSTEM

A schematic diagram of an inventory system is shown as Exhibit 2-3. Each different type of inventory held by a firm may be viewed as an inventory system consisting of three components. Regardless of the size, shape, value, or importance of the particular item, the three component parts of an inventory system are almost always present. First, there are customers. They include consumers who buy products from retailing and wholesaling firms. Or, they include firms that purchase materials, parts, and subassemblies for use in their production process. Customers can also refer to the next step in the manufacturing process, whereby the output of one stage of production is input to the next stage. In other words, the customer of the purchasing department is the manufacturing department. Thus, "customers" is situational depending upon the nature of inventory and how inventory is used. The polygons in Exhibit 6-3 indicate that an inventory system may involve several customers for each type of inventory.

The second component of an inventory system is inventory storage or inventory stocking points. It might be a warehouse, a distribution center, a storage bin, some empty space within a factory, or any other physical location where inventory is stored for a period of time. The rectangles in Exhibit 6-3 indicate that an inventory system may have several stocking points for each type of inventory. The third component of an inventory system consists of the sources of inventory to a business. It could be a supplier from which a firm purchases parts or materials. The source could be a manufacturing process within your own firm. The circles in Exhibit 6-3 indicate that a firm may have several sources of inventory.

Because there are many customers, stocking points, and sources for each type of inventory, one sees why inventory systems can be quite complex. Two steps or relationships serve to connect the three components of an inventory system. As seen in Exhibit 6-3, step 1 has to do with the pattern of customer demand for inventory that must be satisfied from the stocking

EXHIBIT 6-3

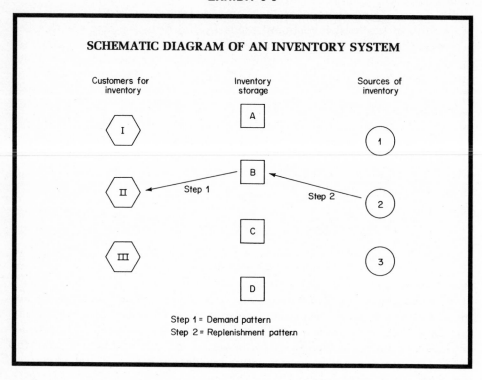

SCHEMATIC DIAGRAM OF AN INVENTORY SYSTEM

| Customers for inventory | Inventory storage | Sources of inventory |

Step 1 = Demand pattern
Step 2 = Replenishment pattern

points. Step 2 has to do with the pattern of replenishment from sources to the stocking points.

One way to understand different approaches to inventory management is to begin with the simplest inventory system: one source, one stocking point, and one customer. The usual procedure is to make estimates about step 1, and then decide how to best manage step 2. That is, management estimates the demand for a given inventory item, and then it determines the best strategy for replenishing the inventory stocking points from which that demand is to be satisfied. Since demand determines revenue to the firm or value in the next phase of production, the goal of an inventory system should be to minimize the costs associated with having inventory available at the storage point. In so doing, firm profitability is maximized.

Although more than one source, one stocking point, and one customer add to the complexity of an inventory system, the idea of trying to minimize the total of all costs associated with inventory does not change. Accordingly, we can set forth an appropriate goal for financial managers responsible for inventory as follows:

> The *goal of inventory management* is to replenish stocking points in such a way as to minimize the total of all associated costs, and thereby enhance the profitability of the organization.

As we shall see in the next section, the relevant costs to a business resemble the pattern depicted in Exhibit 2-4.

INVENTORY COSTS

There are five different costs to the firm that involve inventory. The first category of costs is the value of the inventory itself. For materials, supplies, and purchased parts, it would be the purchase price of each unit acquired. For work in process, it would be the cumulative cost of material, direct labor, and overhead of a particular item on its way toward completion. For finished-goods inventory, the first category would be the total production cost of a completed unit ready for sale to customers.

The second category of costs has to do with acquiring inventory. It includes the expenses of the firm in acquiring or processing inventory, apart from the value of the inventory itself. For materials and purchased parts, it would include purchasing costs such as the salaries and benefits of the purchasing department (managers, buyers, and secretaries), telephone calls and other paperwork necessary to place orders, the inspection function when those parts and materials arrive at the firm, and so forth. For finished-goods inventory, it would consist of the maintenance and retooling costs necessary to turn on the production process, either in a job-shop operation or in an intermittent production process. The second category often is referred to as setup costs. The costs of acquiring may be viewed as a fixed cost per purchase or production run, in the sense that once costs are incurred, the firm may either purchase or produce as many units as it wishes without incurring additional costs of this type.

The third category of costs has to do with holding or storing inventory. It is the cost component that usually is associated with inventory. Included in this category would be the costs of maintaining and managing warehouses or other storage facilities. It would include the costs of safety systems for guarding inventory. It would include estimated costs of inventory shrinkage that might occur from spoilage, theft, or obsolescence. And, it would also include the value (i.e., opportunity cost) of company funds tied up in inventory. In contrast to acquisition costs, holding costs may be viewed as variable costs in the sense that more units held in inventory result in greater holding costs. Estimates of holding costs ranging from 20 to 30 percent of the value of inventory are not uncommon.

The fourth category of costs has to do with shortage. In many ways, this is the most difficult category to estimate, even though it is a very real cost to most firms. What, for example, is the cost to Crescent Corporation if the firm is unable to meet an order for a number of its cleaning units? The cost might be simply a delay in filling the order for a few days. Or, the cost might be a lost profit on a sale that is not consummated. Worse yet, it might entail a lost customer. If word spreads about the inability of Crescent Corporation to fill orders, the cost of shortage conceivably could be even larger. For supplies, materials, and parts inventory, as well as work in process, shortage cost is different, though no less important. A shortage of necessary inventory means that the production operation of the firm is delayed or shut down until the necessary supplies, materials, or parts are acquired. If an entire manufacturing facility must be shut down because of a lack of inventory, the cost to the firm could be considerable.

The fifth category of costs associated with inventory applies as well to all components of working capital. It is the cost of deciding what to do. For inventory, it is the cost of deciding how best to manage an inventory system as depicted in Exhibit 6-3. Put another way, it is the system costs associated with inventory management. For example, management may need to develop a better information system, or an improved computational capability, for a particular inventory system. The distribution curve in Exhibit 6-2 suggests, however, that system costs should not be the same for all items held in inventory.

COST-BALANCING APPROACHES

The next step is to see how the five categories of costs are interrelated in an inventory system. An example will be helpful. Suppose, hypothetically, that Crescent Corporation is concerned about the inventory level of a plastic moulded part used in one of its electrical cleaning appliances. The plastic part is purchased from suppliers. At the present time, there are 9,722 parts in inventory. Management is interested in determining whether that is an appropriate level or not. The purchase cost for the part is $9, and thus there is a current investment of $87,498 in inventory. It is estimated that Crescent will need 240,000 parts during the next year. Demand for parts from the manufacturing operation is expected to be relatively constant during the year at the rate of 20,000 parts per month. Although the manufacturing schedule is expected to be constant throughout the year, management has decided to try and maintain a 1,000-unit safety stock of parts at all times. Based upon data obtained from the accounting department, management estimates that an acquisition cost of $200 is incurred each time the Crescent purchasing department processes an order to suppliers for additional parts. Management also estimates that the holding cost for each part held in inventory for a year is as follows:

Storage, safety, and shrinkage $0.60
Opportunity cost (10%) ($9)   0.90
Holding cost per unit per year $1.50

The opportunity cost component of holding cost reflects Crescent's 10 percent cost of capital.

In Exhibit 6-4, two alternative strategies for replenishing the inventory of plastic parts are indicated. The decision variable for management is the size of each purchase. Purchase size determines the average inventory on hand

EXHIBIT 6-4

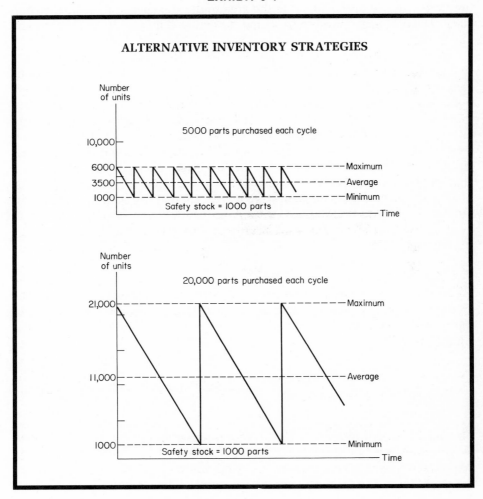

ALTERNATIVE INVENTORY STRATEGIES

throughout the year. If management decided on an order size of 5,000 parts, inventory would range between 1,000 and 6,000 parts, with an average of 3,500 parts. A larger purchase order of 20,000 parts would result in an average inventory of 11,000 parts, and a range of 1,000 (minimum) to 21,000 (maximum). The straight-line patterns of inventory levels in Exhibit 6-4 are based on assumptions of constant demand and instantaneous replenishment.

Exhibit 6-5 is a cost comparison for these and six other strategies ranging from the purchase of 1,000 parts (240 times per year) to 240,000 parts (only once per year). Average inventory increases from 1,500 to 121,000 parts at the extreme cases. Holding costs increase with purchase size at the rate of $1.50 per part. Acquisition costs decrease with purchase size at the rate of $200 per purchase. In terms of the inventory strategies in Exhibit 6-4, holding costs are proportional to the area under the curve, while acquisition costs depend on the number of inventory cycles (i.e., purchases) during the year.

Shortage costs are assumed not to exist in the example, and computational costs are not considered. Total costs thus are the sum of holding costs, acquisition costs, and the cost of the parts. As purchase quantity is increased, the total costs associated with inventory first decrease and then increase. The purchase quantity with the lowest total cost among the eight alternatives is 10,000 parts, for which average inventory is 6,000 parts, and total costs are $2,173,800. Many readers may have observed that the same solution would have been obtained by just considering holding costs and acquisition costs. The reason is the $2,160,000 annual purchase cost of the plastic parts is the same for each strategy of replenishing inventory. If dollar-holding costs and acquisition costs were plotted for the eight values of purchase quantity (or average inventory), the graph would resemble the pattern in Exhibit 2-4 which, in general terms, compared "costs of too little" with "costs of too much."

The 10,000-part solution in Exhibit 6-5 is that purchase quantity which provides the best balance of holding costs and acquisition costs—among the eight alternative strategies which were investigated. The *optimal* solution to the problem of how to replenish inventory stocking points is given by the square-root formula

$$\text{Optimal purchase quantity} = \sqrt{\frac{(2)(\text{annual demand})(\text{acquisition cost})}{\text{holding cost}}}$$

This formula, also referred to as the *economic order quantity (EOQ) model,* is the analytical solution to minimizing the total of holding costs and acquisition costs. The formula is based on an assumption of constant demand that is known with certainty, as well as an assumption of instantaneous replenishment of inventory each time a purchase is made.

EXHIBIT 6-5

COST COMPARISON OF ALTERNATIVE STRATEGIES

Purchase quantity	1,000	5,000	10,000	15,000	20,000	40,000	120,000	240,000
Number of purchases	240	48	24	16	12	6	2	1
Average inventory	1,500	3,500	6,000	8,500	11,000	21,000	61,000	121,000
Cost of parts	$2,160,000	$2,160,000	$2,160,000	$2,160,000	$2,160,000	$2,160,000	$2,160,000	$2,160,000
Holding costs	2,250	5,250	9,000	12,750	16,500	31,500	91,500	181,500
Acquisition costs	48,000	9,600	4,800	3,200	2,400	1,200	400	200
Total costs	$2,210,250	$2,174,850	$2,173,800	$2,175,950	$2,178,900	$2,192,700	$2,251,900	$2,341,700

For the example of replenishing plastic parts for Crescent Corporation, the optimal purchase quantity would be

$$\sqrt{\frac{(2)(240,000 \text{ units})(\$200 \text{ per order})}{\$1.50 \text{ per unit per year}}} = 8,000 \text{ parts}$$

For the optimal solution, there would be thirty purchases per year. Inventory level would range from a low of 1,000 parts (safety stock) to a high of 9,000 parts each time an order of parts is received. Average inventory would be 5,000 parts, and there would be a cost breakdown as follows:

Cost of parts (240,000)($9)	$2,160,000
Holding costs (5,000)($1.50)	7,500
Acquisition costs (30)($200)	6,000
Total cost	$2,173,500

The formula provides a solution (8,000 parts) that is $300 less expensive than the 10,000-part solution in Exhibit 6-5.

There are both advantages and disadvantages to using the formula. One advantage is that it is easy to use. Another advantage is that the formula helps to understand better the sensitivity of the inventory decision to the parameters of the problem. The optimal solution to replenishing inventory increases with the square root of demand, increases with the square root of holding cost, and decreases with the square root of acquisition cost.* Moreover, optimal purchase quantity does *not* depend on the size of the firm's safety stock. If Crescent management increased the safety stock for plastic parts by 4,000 units (from 1,000 to 5,000 units), the optimal purchase quantity would remain at 8,000 parts. Management should not be indifferent to the safety-stock level, however, since total inventory cost would increase by $1.50 for each part added to the safety stock, or the annual increase of $6,000.

A disadvantage of the cost-balancing formula is that its relative simplicity may cause some users not to be aware of the underlying assumptions, or of how and why the formula leads to the best balance of inventory costs. For most extensions, as we will see in successive sections, a set of numerical calculations (such as in Exhibit 6-5) is more useful than simply plugging the square-root formula. Regardless of how useful the EOQ formula is for a given problem, a cost-balancing approach helps the financial manager to understand how different inventory costs are interrelated. In particular, a cost-balancing approach is helpful in avoiding extreme solutions for which the total cost is excessive.

*Examples of sensitivity are provided in the problems at the end of the chapter.

In the previous chapter, proposed changes in credit policy were evaluated in terms of incremental return on investment. Before proceeding, it is well to demonstrate that cost-balancing models for inventory are consistent with evaluating changes in credit policy. Suppose that prior to the cost comparison in Exhibit 6-5, Crescent Corporation had been ordering plastic parts in quantities of 5,000 units. To change from purchase orders of 5,000 parts to purchase orders of 10,000 parts would require an incremental investment as follows:

Average inventory before change	
(1/2)(1,000 + 11,000)	6,000 parts
− Average inventory after change	
(1/2)(1,000 + 6,000)	3,500 parts
Increase in average inventory	2,500 parts
× Purchase cost per part	$9
Incremental investment	$22,500

Incremental profit for the change would result from a net reduction in total inventory costs

Decrease in acquisition costs	
(48 − 24 purchases)($200)	$4,800
− Increase in holding costs	
(2,500 parts)($0.60)	1,500
Incremental profit	$3,300

Return on investment for the change in inventory policy would be

$$\text{Return on investment} = \frac{\$ \ 3,300}{\$22,500} = 14.7\%$$

Since this result is well above Crescent's 10 percent cost of capital, the change in purchase quantity from 5,000 to 10,000 parts would add to the profitability of Crescent Corporation.

Although the example in this section has involved the purchasing of parts to be used in manufacturing, the same concept of balancing costs can be applied to the determination of production quantities, particularly when the production process is not a continuous assembly line. The important difference is that the costs of acquisition become the retooling and maintenance that are needed to turn on the production process for a given type of inventory. A cost-balancing approach also can be useful in discussing several extensions of the inventory problem. It is not within the scope of this book to pursue those extensions in great detail, though the state of the art does exist.[1] Instead, we shall review the extensions from the perspective of the financial manager who is concerned about inventory as one component of the firm's working capital.

SEASONAL DEMAND

One extension has to do with seasonality of demand. It is not realistic to expect many situations wherein the demand for a material, part, or product is uniform throughout the year. And yet, this is a key assumption on which the square-root formula depends. What happens instead when there is a seasonal pattern to demand, such as the summer high for sailing boats, or the December peak for toys? Although the cost-balancing approach of the prior section is not directly applicable, it does provide a point of departure. A manager might calculate the appropriate acquisition quantity for a given item of inventory assuming constant demand, and then make appropriate adjustments in inventory replenishment for the highs and lows during the year. That is, purchase (or production) quantities would be reduced as demand slackens during one season of the year, and increased as demand picks up during another season. The square-root formula tells us that the ideal purchase or production quantity should be in proportion to the square root of demand.

An alternative procedure which the manager might use is to divide the year into seasons within which demand is relatively constant. A cost-balancing approach could then be used to determine an appropriate inventory policy for each season. In some instances, the benefits of any attempt to use a more sophisticated analysis of seasonal demand would not be sufficient to cover the cost of the analysis. This is where the fifth cost component, the system costs of deciding what to do, becomes very important.

INVENTORY REPLENISHMENT

Another extension has to do with replenishment of inventory. The timeline diagram of demand in Exhibit 6-4 assumes an instantaneous replenishment of inventory at the beginning of each cycle. This assumption is almost never experienced in practice. It takes time to order, to produce, and to deliver.

[1]For comprehensive coverage, see E. S. Buffa and W. H. Taubert, *Production-Inventory Systems: Planning and Control* (Homewood, Ill.: Richard D. Irwin, Inc., revised edition, 1972), and G. Hadley and T. M. Whitin, *Analysis of Inventory Systems* (Englewood Cliffs, N.J.: Prentice-Hall, Inc., 1963). See also the three articles by J. F. Magee included in the suggested readings at the end of this chapter.

One way around this difficulty is to place orders for materials and parts, or inventory purchased for resale, prior to the point at which inventory falls to the safety-stock level. In the previous example, assume that management has decided to order 10,000 parts every two weeks. If the total time from purchase to receipt of parts is estimated to be one week, then the midpoint of each two-week cycle becomes the appropriate reorder point. That corresponds to an inventory level of 6,000 parts as shown in panel A of Exhibit 6-6.

For finished-goods inventory that is produced by the firm, a different pattern is necessary since inventory accumulation is gradual rather than instantaneous. One variation occurs when the rate of production is just equal to the rate of demand, and inventory level remains at the safety-stock level over time. That variation describes the inventory level of an item that is

EXHIBIT 6-6

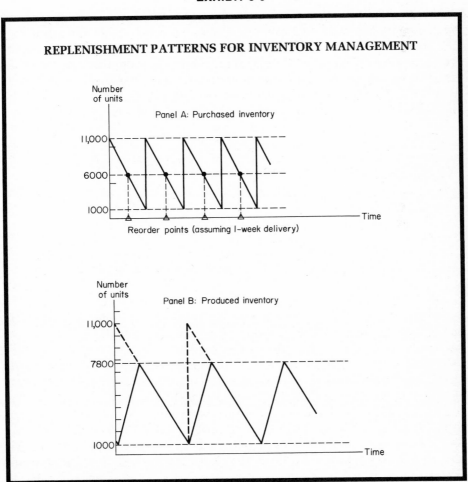

REPLENISHMENT PATTERNS FOR INVENTORY MANAGEMENT

Panel A: Purchased inventory

Reorder points (assuming 1-week delivery)

Panel B: Produced inventory

produced continually on an assembly line. For intermittent production—such as for different models or product sizes—the rate of production must exceed the rate of demand in order for there to be a buildup of inventory. Suppose that Crescent manufactures, rather than purchases, the plastic moulded parts in 10,000 unit production runs. Panel B of Exhibit 6-6 shows inventory accumulation when the rate of production is three times greater than the rate of demand. Net accumulation of parts during the replenishment phase of each cycle is twice the rate of depletion during the rest of the cycle. According to the graph, maximum inventory level during each cycle is 7,800 parts. Average inventory level for each cycle and thus throughout the year can be shown to be 4,900 parts, as opposed to 6,000 parts when replenishment is instantaneous. This means that holding costs are lower when instantaneous delivery of parts or product cannot be assumed.

PURCHASE DISCOUNTS

The possibility of purchase discounts requires another extension. It does not involve another pattern of inventory usage, but rather a varying parameter that must be reflected in the cost calculations. The square-root formula cannot be used when purchase discounts are available to the buyer because the cost per unit is not a constant. Nevertheless, a tabular cost comparison is still applicable. Suppose that the Crescent Corporation is able to buy the plastic moulded parts from suppliers according to the following schedule:

Quantity	Price	% discount
1–5999	$9.00	—
6,000–11,999	8.90	1.1
12,000–17,999	8.80	2.2
18,000–23,999	8.70	3.3
24,000–more	8.50	5.6

By buying larger quantities, the allowed discount is larger. This is why buyers and purchasing managers naturally may lean toward larger purchase quantities.

The effect of purchase discounts on the total costs associated with inventory is shown in Exhibit 6-7. The same eight inventory strategies as before are considered. Number of purchases, average inventory, and acquisition costs are exactly the same as in Exhibit 6-5 where a $9.00 cost per part is incurred for all purchase quantities. Holding costs are somewhat lower per unit for purchase quantities of 10,000 units or more. The biggest change, however, is seen in the costs of the parts themselves. For the extreme

EXHIBIT 6-7

COST COMPARISON REFLECTING PURCHASE DISCOUNTS

Purchase quantity	1,000	5,000	10,000	15,000	20,000	40,000	120,000	240,000
Applicable price	$9.00	$9.00	$8.90	$8.80	$8.70	$8.50	$8.50	$8.50
Number of purchases	240	48	24	16	12	6	2	1
Average inventory	1,500	3,500	6,000	8,500	11,000	21,000	61,000	121,000
Cost of parts	$2,160,000	$2,160,000	$2,136,000	$2,112,000	$2,088,000	$2,040,000	$2,040,000	$2,040,000
Holding cost per unit	$1.50	$1.50	$1.49	$1.48	$1.47	$1.45	$1.45	$1.45
Holding costs	2,250	5,250	8,940	12,580	16,170	30,450	88,450	175,450
Acquisition costs	48,000	9,600	4,800	3,200	2,400	1,200	400	200
Total costs	$2,210,250	$2,174,850	$2,149,740	$2,127,780	$2,106,570	$2,071,650	$2,128,850	$2,215,650

purchase quantity of 240,000 units ($8.50 price), the cost is $2,040,000 instead of $2,400,000—a savings of $360,000.

The most economical purchase quantity among the alternatives in Exhibit 6-7 is 40,000 parts. The total cost of that strategy is $2,071,650 and thus well below the $2,215,650 total cost if 240,000 parts are purchased only once per year. The reason is that the final quantity discount ($8.50 per part) begins at 24,000 units. A financial manager responsible for inventory ought to do a total cost calculation for the purchase quantity at each break point in the schedule, since the reduced cost per unit often tends to dominate both holding costs and acquisition costs, except for extreme strategies. In this instance, a 24,000-part purchase quantity leads to the following:

Cost of parts (240,000)($8.50)	$2,040,000
Holding costs (13,000)($1.45)	18,850
Acquisition costs (10)($200)	2,000
Total cost	$2,060,850

This is the optimal solution for the case of purchase discounts.

INFLATION EFFECTS

Inflation has become a way of life. If the prices of materials, parts, supplies, and production continue to increase over time, financial managers must consider the financial implications. In an earlier section, we saw how LIFO and FIFO accounting methods affect cost of goods sold, federal taxes, earnings, cash, and inventory valuation during a period of rising prices. It is tempting for a purchasing manager to stockpile materials and parts at the beginning of the year with some confidence that prices of those materials and parts will be higher by the end of the year. Still, holding costs also will be higher for such a strategy, and thus it is necessary to consider all relevant costs before deciding on a particular strategy of replenishing inventory.

Exhibit 6-8 provides a cost comparison of alternative inventory strategies during a period in which prices are increasing at the rate of 1 percent per month. Continuing with the same example, the monthly prices of plastic moulded parts to Crescent Corporation would be

January	$9.00	May	$9.37	September	$ 9.75
February	9.09	June	9.46	October	9.84
March	9.18	July	9.55	November	9.94
April	9.27	August	9.65	December	10.04

EXHIBIT 6-8

COST COMPARISON REFLECTING INFLATION

Purchase quantity	1,000	5,000	10,000	15,000	20,000	40,000	120,000	240,000
Applicable price	$9.51	$9.51	$9.51	$9.51	$9.51	$9.47	$9.28	$9.00
Number of purchases	240	'48	24	16	12	6	2	1
Average inventory	1,500	3,500	6,000	8,500	11,000	21,000	61,000	121,000
Cost of parts	$2,282,400	$2,282,400	$2,282,400	$2,282,400	$2,282,400	$2,272,800	$2,227,200	$2,160,000
Holding costs	2,329	5,434	9,315	13,196	17,078	32,603	94,703	187,853
Acquisition costs	50,736	10,147	5,074	3,382	2,537	1,265	412	200
Total costs	$2,335,465	$2,297,981	$2,296,789	$2,298,978	$2,302,015	$2,306,668	$2,322,315	$2,348,053

If all 240,000 parts are purchased in January, the price would be $9.00 per unit for a total of $2,160,000. If two purchases are made during the year (January and July), the average price would be ($9.00 + 9.55) ÷ 2 = $9.28 per part, with a total acquisition cost of $2,227,200. For all strategies involving purchase quantities of 20,000 parts or less, the average price for all twelve months would be $9.51 for a total acquisition cost of $2,282,400.

Holding costs are incurred continually throughout the year. The average cost per unit per year is $1.553 and is multiplied by average inventory to obtain the holding cost associated with each inventory strategy. Acquisition costs during a period of inflation depend on when purchases are made. The average acquisition cost per order increases with the number of orders made during the year. As purchase quantity increases, total costs associated with each strategy first decrease and then increase in much the same way as before. The total cost relationship has the same basic shape and the lowest total cost occurs for a purchase quantity of 10,000 parts, just as in Exhibit 6-5. The reason for this result is that inflation causes all cost components to increase, and the net effect is that the optimal solution does not change with inflation. That result was not obvious before the cost calculation in Exhibit 6-8 was prepared. The implication is that the financial manager responsible for inventory decisions should calculate the total inventory costs for various replenishment strategies under the set of assumptions, including inflation, that best describes the manager's expectations of the future.

UNCERTAINTY AND SHORTAGE

Another important extension of the cost-balancing approach has to do with shortage. Many managers contend that they do not tolerate shortage. Or, at least they assert that shortage is never deliberately planned. Other managers state that the unavailability of certain key materials and parts has become a critical problem in recent years—so much so that when those materials or parts do become available, they purchase as much as they can. Such a strategy, according to those managers, is doubly attractive if the prices of materials and parts are subject to rapid inflation.

The cost-balancing approach discussed this far in the chapter (Exhibits 6-4 through 6-8) has not reflected shortage for two reasons. First, the demand for plastic parts by Crescent Corporation was assumed with certainty to be constant during the year at the rate of 20,000 units per month. Second, Crescent management established a safety stock of 1,000 parts. Actually, these two reasons are contradictory. For if demand is known with certainty, there is no need for a safety stock. Put differently, a safety stock is really a hedge by management against not knowing for certain either the amount or timing of demand.

One approach to shortage is to deliberately build it into the cost-balancing framework such as in Exhibit 6-9. In other words, shortage is planned. During each cycle, there is a period when inventory level goes negative, thus indicating a time when the firm cannot fill orders. This is the case of

EXHIBIT 6-9

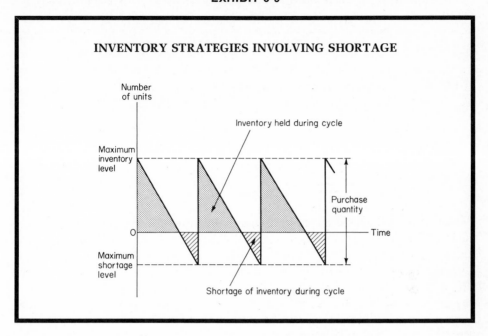

INVENTORY STRATEGIES INVOLVING SHORTAGE

shortage under conditions of certainty. If a shortage cost per unit per year is estimated, then it becomes a fourth cost component to be included in the analysis. For each strategy for replenishing inventory, total cost includes the value of parts purchased, purchasing costs, holding costs, and shortage costs. Just as dollar-holding costs are proportional to the triangular area of positive inventory at the beginning of each cycle, dollar-shortage costs are proportional to the area of negative inventory at the end of each cycle. The analogous square-root formula for determining the optimal purchase quantity with planned shortage is as follows:

$$\begin{array}{c}\text{Optimal purchase} \\ \text{quantity} \\ \text{with shortage}\end{array} = \left(\begin{array}{c}\text{optimal purchase} \\ \text{quantity} \\ \text{without storage}\end{array}\right) \sqrt{\frac{\text{(holding cost + shortage cost)}}{\text{shortage cost}}}$$

Notice that the adjustment factor involves holding cost and shortage cost, both measured in dollars per part per year.

In the example, suppose that the production manager of Crescent Corporation estimates that shortage costs—in terms of a delayed manufacturing process—are $16 per unit per year. Recalling that the optimal purchase quantity without shortage was 8,000 parts, we plug the formula and obtain

$$(8{,}000 \text{ parts}) \sqrt{\frac{\$1.50 + 16.00}{\$16.00}} = (8{,}000)(1.046) = 8{,}368 \text{ parts}$$

as the optimal purchase quantity. The maximum inventory level during each cycle is

$$(8,000 \text{ parts}) \sqrt{\frac{\$16.00}{\$1.50 + 16.00}} = (8,000)(.956) = 7,648 \text{ parts}$$

which means that the extent of shortage is

Optimal purchase quantity	8,368 parts
− Maximum inventory level	−7,648 parts
Maximum shortage level	720 parts

during each inventory cycle.

Our earlier comments about using a formula for decision-making are again applicable. It is easy to use, and it affords an insight into shortage: the higher shortage cost is relative to holding cost, the closer the adjustment factor is to unity; optimal purchase quantity changes very little, and very little shortage is anticipated. Conversely, a smaller shortage cost leads to a larger adjustment factor, a larger purchase quantity, and a larger anticipated shortage. A disadvantage of the formula is that the underlying assumptions must be met. An additional assumption in extending the cost-balancing approach to shortage is that back orders are immediately filled each time another quantity of parts is received.

An alternative approach to handling the problem of uncertainty in inventory decision-making is with the use of probability estimates. To illustrate, suppose that after a careful cost comparison, Crescent management has decided to purchase 10,000 plastic moulded parts every two weeks. Based on conversations with the production manager, the demand for plastic parts in the manufacturing process during each two-week cycle is specified with a probability distribution. Expected demand is calculated.

Demand	Probability	Weighted demand
9,000 parts	.05	450 parts
9,500	.15	1,425
10,000	.60	6,000
10,500	.15	1,575
11,000	.05	550
Expected demand		10,000 parts

The result is 10,000 parts, the same value used in the earlier examples, but under conditions of certainty.

EXHIBIT 6-10

COST COMPARISON OF SAFETY-STOCK LEVELS

Safety stock	Shortage	Probability, %	Expected shortage	Shortage cost	Holding cost*	Total cost
0	0	80 ⎫				
	500	15 ⎬	125 parts	$2,000	$ 0	$2,000
	1,000	5 ⎭				
500	0	95 ⎫	25	400	750	1,150†
	500	5 ⎭				
1,000	0	100	0	0	1,500	1,500
1,500	0	100	0	0	2,250	2,250

*Just of the safety stock.
†Optimal solution.

Management is concerned as to whether or not a 1,000-part safety stock is adequate in view of the uncertainty of demand. A cost analysis of alternative safety-stock levels is presented in Exhibit 6-10. Estimates of holding cost and shortage cost are $1.50 and $16.00 per unit per year, respectively. Safety stocks of 0, 500, 1,000, and 1,500 parts are examined. Demand probabilities are combined with each safety-stock level to arrive at an expected shortage. For a zero safety stock, the probability of meeting demand (i.e., zero shortage) with a 10,000-part purchase quantity is 80 percent (the sum of the first three probabilities in the demand distribution), the probability of a 500-part shortage is 15 percent, and the probability of a 1,000-part shortage is 5 percent. Expected shortage is found to be 125 parts. Expected shortage is 25 parts for a safety stock of 500, and 0 for safety stocks of 1,000 units or more. When shortage costs are added to the holding costs, a total cost is obtained for each safety-stock level. In Exhibit 6-10 it is seen that the optimal safety stock of 500 parts is less expensive than either a zero safety stock or the 1,000-part safety stock which results in no expected shortage. The results of this cost analysis are quite sensitive both to demand probabilities and estimates of shortage cost.

STRATEGY IMPLEMENTATION

We now have reviewed several aspects of inventory management within the context of a cost-balancing approach. In each instance, we have seen that the financial manager must be careful to assess the impact of an inventory decision on all relevant costs. The focal point has been the choice of an optimal strategy of inventory replenishment in response to the demand for each inventory item. One limitation has been that only a single item of inventory was considered in each instance. It remains to consider inventory management within the context of a firm that holds scores, and even hundreds, of different items in inventory.

If a firm has only a few items of inventory, then presumably a cost-balancing model could be applied to each. But if many items of inventory are held, it may not be practical to do so. An alternative is to classify inventory into basic categories—according to size, type, or storage requirements—and to concentrate more detailed cost analyses on those categories where difficulty is experienced. A firm, for example, might focus on inventory items that are utilized in a troublesome production process. Management could analyze the inventory problems of a warehouse where excessive shortages have been reported. Or, management might focus on the purchasing practices of a particular division experiencing financial difficulty.

Another approach is to undertake detailed cost comparisons for those items that require a relatively large investment, or for which the costs of acquisition, holding, and/or shortage are large. This would include the first part of a firm's inventory distribution as depicted in Exhibit 6-2. For low-valued inventory items, the firm can develop simple guidelines for replenishment based on visual inspection of current inventory levels and an awareness of historical demand patterns. In trying to decide on which inventory items more precise controls are needed, the system costs must be considered. In smaller firms, this might be the rental cost of an inventory-control system. In larger firms, system costs might also include the salaries of systems analysts who help to develop inventory controls. For very large firms, system costs might involve extensive developmental costs. Economic theory suggests that inventory controls ought to be applied to additional inventory items as long as expected benefits to the firm exceed the additional costs of developing and maintaining the system costs. Admittedly, this is difficult to ascertain in advance.

Many inventory-control systems consist of an information or record-keeping function, coupled with a control function that alerts management to situations needing special attention. The output of an inventory-control system often is a computer printout prepared weekly, or even daily. The printout includes a current count of the number of each item held in inventory. The printout also includes upper and lower control limits against which the current counts can be compared by management.

Exhibit 6-11 portrays graphically how an inventory-control system would be used. At point A, management is alerted to an inventory level that has risen above the upper control limit, and for which holding costs are becoming excessive. At point B, management is alerted to an inventory level that

EXHIBIT 6-11

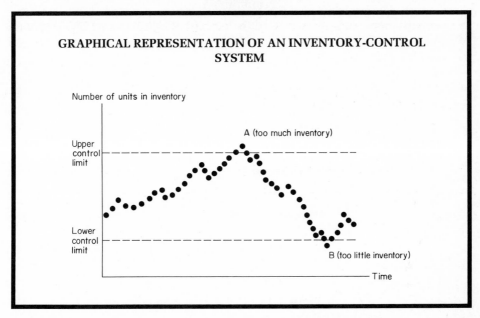

GRAPHICAL REPRESENTATION OF AN INVENTORY-CONTROL
SYSTEM

has fallen below the lower control limit, and for which the chances of
shortage are becoming significant. Two observations about an inventory-
control system should be made. First, the usefulness of the system depends
heavily on the accuracy of the inventory counts that are presented. The
complexity of inventory inflows and outflows over time necessitates a periodic physical count to ensure that management has correct data on which to
make decisions. Second, the upper and lower control limits must not be set
arbitrarily, but rather in response to the various costs associated with a
particular item of inventory. This brings us full circle since much of this
chapter has focused on cost comparisons of alternative strategies for replenishing inventory.

SUMMARY

Inventory results from inevitable delays in the manufacturing of products
and distribution to customers. The different types of inventory held by many
firms collectively represent one of its largest investments. Inventory storage
should be replenished in response to demand for each inventory item and a
careful analysis of all relevant costs associated with inventory. A cost-
balancing approach was applied to a simple inventory problem, and then
extended to include consideration of seasonal demand, purchase discounts,
inflation, shortage, and uncertainty.

Problem 6-1

In the chapter an example was used to compare the FIFO and LIFO methods of inventory valuation. Show how the average-cost method gives results between that of FIFO and LIFO.

SOLUTION: After purchasing 100 parts at a price of $20 and then 50 parts at a price of $40, the average cost per part would be

$$\frac{\$4,000 \text{ investment}}{150 \text{ parts}} = \$26.67 \text{ per part}$$

The income statement would become

Revenue (50)($60)	$3,000
− Cost of parts (50)($26.67)	1,333
Taxable income	$1,667
− Federal taxes (40%)	667
Retained earnings	$1,000

and the ending balance sheet would be

Assets		Equity	
Cash	$3,333	Stock (50 shares)	$5,000
Inventory		Retained earnings	1,000
(100)($26.67)	2,667	Total	$6,000
Total	$6,000		

To show how the average-costing method compares with FIFO and LIFO, we compare earnings per share and cash as follows:

Accounting method	Earnings	Cash
FIFO	$2.40	$3,200
Average costing	2.00	3,333
LIFO	1.20	3,600

Problem 6-2

Use a return-on-investment framework to evaluate change of Crescent's purchase quantity of plastic parts from 10,000 to 8,000 parts.

SOLUTION: Following the procedure used in the chapter, the average inventory would decrease from 6,000 to 5,000 parts. The incremental loss would be

Decrease in holding costs	
(1,000 parts)($0.60)	$ 600
− Increase in acquisition costs	
(30 − 24 purchases)($200)	1,200
Incremental loss	$ 600

But there would also be a reduction in inventory investment of ($1,000 parts) ($9) = $9,000. This would lead to

$$\text{Return on investment} = \frac{-\$600}{-\$9,000} = 6.7\%$$

For changes that decrease investment, the return on investment should be *lower* than the firm's cost of capital in order for the change to enhance firm profitability. Since cost of capital for Crescent is 10%, the 8,000-part purchase quantity would be a profitable change.

Problem 6-3

The example of Crescent Corporation buying plastic moulded parts included the following parameters: annual demand of 240,000 parts, $9 purchase price per part, safety stock of 1,000 parts, acquisition costs of $200 per purchase, and holding costs of $1.50 per unit per year. Use the square-root formula to test, individually and collectively, the following parameter changes: annual demand 360,000 parts, safety stock of 4,000 parts, acquisition costs of $300 per purchase, and holding costs of $5 per unit per year.

Problem 6-4

Redo the cost comparison in Exhibit 6-8 for an inflation rate of 2 percent per month.

Problem 6-5

Following the approach in Exhibit 6-9, what would be the optimal purchase quantity of plastic parts, if shortage cost was estimated to be only $2 per unit per year? What is the implication of the result?

Problem 6-6

Following the approach in Exhibit 6-10, what is the optimal safety stock if shortage cost is only $2 per unit per year? What is the implication of the result?

Problem 6-7

The daily newspaper of a large midwestern city is trying to decide how often to bill their 1 million subscribers. The subscription rate is $4 per month. The costs of each billing are $50,000. If management estimates the newspaper's cost of capital to be 10 percent, how often should subscribers be billed?

SOLUTION: This problem has to do with accounts receivable, but it is amenable to the cost-balancing approach discussed in this chapter. It is a good example of constant demand throughout the year. A tabular procedure is helpful.

Billings per year	1	2	3	4	6	12
No. months billed	12	6	4	3	2	1
Average receivables	$24,000,000	$12,000,000	$8,000,000	$6,000,000	$4,000,000	$2,000,000
Holding costs	2,400,000	1,200,000	800,000	600,000	400,000	200,000
Billing costs	50,000	100,000	150,000	200,000	300,000	600,000
Total costs	$ 2,450,000	$ 1,300,000	$ 950,000	$ 800,000	$ 700,000	$ 800,000

It shows that billing every two months would be the least expensive strategy among the six evaluated. The optimal answer can be obtained with an application of the square-root formula

Optimal billing quantity

$$= \sqrt{\frac{(2)(12,000,000 \text{ monthly subscriptions})(\$50,000)}{(\$4 \text{ per subscription})(.10)}} = 1,732,000$$

In other words, the optimal billing would be 1¾ months (or about every seven weeks). For that strategy, the cost breakdown would be

Holding costs ($3,500,000 average receivables)(.10)	$350,000
Billing costs (12 ÷ 1¾)($50,000)	343,000
Total costs	$693,000

which is $7,000 lower than the two-month billing solution from the tabular procedure.

SUGGESTED READINGS

Beranek, W.: WORKING CAPITAL MANAGEMENT (Belmont, Calif.: Wadsworth Publishing Company, Inc., 1966), Chapters 5–6.

Buffa, E. S. and W. H. Taubert: PRODUCTION-INVENTORY SYSTEMS: PLANNING AND CONTROL (Homewood, Ill.: Richard D. Irwin, Inc., revised edition, 1972).

Hadley, G. and T. M. Whitin: ANALYSIS OF INVENTORY SYSTEMS (Englewood Cliffs, N.J.: Prentice-Hall, Inc., 1963).

INVENTORY MANAGEMENT IN INDUSTRY (New York: National Industrial Conference Board, Inc., 1958).

Levin, R. I. and C. A. Kirkpatrick: QUANTITATIVE APPROACHES TO MANAGEMENT, 2d ed. (New York: McGraw-Hill Book Company, 1971), Chapters 6–7.

Magee, J. F.: "Guides to Inventory Policy: Functions and Lot Sizes," HARVARD BUSINESS REVIEW, January–February 1956, pp. 49–60.

————: "Guides to Inventory Policy: Problems of Uncertainty," HARVARD BUSINESS REVIEW, March–April 1956, pp. 103–116.

————: "Guides to Inventory Policy: Anticipating Future Needs," HARVARD BUSINESS REVIEW, May–June 1956, pp. 57–70.

Mehta, D. R.: WORKING CAPITAL MANAGEMENT (Englewood Cliffs, N.J.: Prentice-Hall, Inc., 1974), Chapters 4–5.

Smith, K. V., (ed.): READINGS ON THE MANAGEMENT OF WORKING CAPITAL (St. Paul, Minn.: West Publishing Company, 1974), Section IV.

Wilson, F. C.: SHORT-TERM FINANCIAL MANAGEMENT (Homewood, Ill.: Dow Jones-Irwin, 1975), Chapter 7.

7

MANAGING PAYABLES AND ACCRUALS

This and the following chapter deal with sources of working capital financing. There are several sources of short-term financing for a firm including trade credit, various accruals, and short-term borrowing. In this chapter, we consider the management of trade credit, or accounts payable as it appears on the firm's balance sheet. We also consider the management of other accruals.

RATIONALE FOR PAYABLES AND ACCRUALS

Many firms could never get started in business were it not for their suppliers. Manufacturing firms would not be able to obtain adequate financing from alternative sources in order to pay cash for the raw materials and parts needed in the production process. Wholesaling and retailing firms would not be able to pay cash for the products and merchandise which they purchase for resale. Large established firms could conceivably finance materials and parts through other financial sources, but they tend not to do so. Indeed, accounts payable (or just "payables" as we will frequently refer to trade credit in this chapter) was seen in the first chapter (Exhibit 1-9) to represent a large portion of short-term financing for nonfinancial corporations. Short-term financing is also made available through "other accruals." This includes wages and salaries payable to employees and managers, and taxes payable to federal and local governments. Accruals represent another large portion of short-term financing for nonfinancial corporations.

A common characteristic of payables and accruals is that they are spontaneous (i.e., self-adjusting) sources of financing. As sales expand, the firm necessarily purchases more materials and parts, hence payables increase. More labor and management are needed and hence wages and salaries payable increase. If the firm is successful in its endeavors, profits are enhanced and taxes payable increase as well. Conversely, when sales decrease, so do purchases, payables, accruals, and taxes. In other words, upward and downward movements in firm sales are accompanied by upward and downward adjustments in the financing made available from these short-term spontaneous sources.

Since most firms buy as well as sell on credit, payables on the financing side of the balance sheet are paralleled—though not necessarily equaled— by receivables on the investment side of the balance sheet. The term *net credit* is sometimes used to mean accounts receivable minus accounts payable. Defined in this way, net credit is a positive value when the firm is a net supplier of credit, and it is a negative value when the firm is a net user of credit. Exhibit 7-1 presents the net-credit position of a sample of nine industrial corporations in 1976. The sample was chosen to be representative, both in size and type of business. We see that the larger firms tended to be net suppliers of credit, while the smaller firms tended to be net users of credit.

The aggregate working capital of nonfinancial corporations at the end of 1975 was as follows:

Cash and equivalents	$ 87.5 billion	Accounts payable	$288.0 billion
Accounts receivable	298.2	Other accruals	169.5
Inventory	285.0		

We see that accounts payable was comparable in size both to accounts receivable and to inventory. The aggregate net-credit position of nonfinancial firms at the end of 1975 was $10.2 billion. An interesting observation is that aggregate accounts payable actually exceeded aggregate inventory. Since inventory included work in process and finished goods, this means that firms were receiving financing from trade credit in excess of the materials and parts which they purchased from suppliers. One possible explanation for this seemingly impossible observation is the trend toward LIFO inventory valuation by firms as discussed in Chapter 6. Another possible explanation is that firms were processing materials and parts into products and selling those products before paying suppliers.

Trade credit involves the acquisition of materials, parts, and supplies needed by the firm, and a delay between the date of their acquisition and the date of payment to the supplier. Financing from employees and managers also results from a delay between the date value (in services) is received by the firm, and when payment for those services is made. Important aspects in managing payables are the timing of purchases, the terms of purchases, the cost to the firm of financing obtained from suppliers, and decisions about when and how suppliers should be paid. Managing accruals involves a

EXHIBIT 7-1

NET CREDIT POSITION OF SELECTED U.S. FIRMS, 1976

Corporation	Statement date	Accounts receivable	Accounts payable	Net credit
Firestone Tire & Rubber	Oct. 31, 1976	$682,600,000	$274,800,000	$407,800,000
Caterpillar Tractor	Dec. 31, 1976	597,100,000	481,600,000	115,500,000
Gillette	Dec. 31, 1976	294,400,000	100,100,000	194,300,000
Heublein	June 30, 1976	221,900,000	60,300,000	161,600,000
Campbell Soup	Aug. 1, 1976	103,000,000	110,800,000	(7,800,000)
Memorex Corporation	Dec. 31, 1976	56,100,000	43,900,000	12,200,000
Melville Corporation	Dec. 31, 1976	17,900,000	109,200,000	(91,300,000)
Host International	Dec. 31, 1976	6,811,000	14,251,000	(7,440,000)
American Precision Instrument	Dec. 31, 1976	2,397,000	2,999,000	(602,000)

Source: Moody's Industrial Manual, 1977.

recognition that various accruals are a form of short-term financing, and how the timing of payments to employees, governments, and others affects the cost of that financing. Following the procedure in previous chapters, it is well to set forth an appropriate managerial goal as follows:

> The *goal of payables and accruals management* is to provide as much spontaneous financing as possible at zero cost to the organization.

RESPONSIBILITY FOR PAYABLES AND ACCRUALS

Managerial responsibility for accounts payable begins with the purchasing manager who places orders for needed materials and parts, and ends with the treasurer or other financial manager who effects their payment. This split responsibility is somewhat different from accounts receivable management. Usually the credit manager is equally involved both in granting credit and in all collection activities. In some firms, the credit manager participates in the credit aspects of the firm's purchasing, but in many others, the job description of the credit manager does not mention purchasing or payables. Responsibility for other accruals typically resides with a high-level financial manager. In the case of Crescent Corporation, Arthur Hanson perceives accounts payable and other accruals as important components of working capital for which he has ultimate responsibility.

For firms involved in manufacturing, a purchasing function is essential to acquire the materials and parts necessary to ensure a timely and efficient production process. For firms involved in wholesaling or retailing, the purchasing function provides the products that will be resold to other customers. Purchasing is thus a key function in the operating of many firms—of all sizes and all types of business. For a small manufacturing business, purchasing may involve one or two office employees who include buying among other responsibilities. For a small retailing store, the buying may be done by the owner-manager. But for a larger organization, purchasing activity may necessitate an entire department that includes many clerical personnel, buyers, and managers. For business organizations that have divisions and facilities located across the country or around the world, purchasing becomes a significant part of the total activity. It is usually handled at a decentralized level, though there may be a centralized control for the whole company.

PURCHASING ON CREDIT

Suppliers would of course prefer to sell their materials, parts, and products on a cash basis. But as mentioned in Chapter 5, we have evolved into a credit type of economy, in which competition perpetuates credit transactions between companies, and between companies and customers. Our interest here is purchasing on credit.

Purchasing is not an isolated activity, but rather a part of the total process whereby a business organization goes about preparing products and services for sale to its customers.[1] The following action steps ultimately involve purchasing:

1. Preparing a sales budget
2. Preparing a production budget
3. Determining what and when to purchase
4. Determining which suppliers to use
5. Determining what credit terms to accept
6. Receiving purchases and ensuring quality
7. Determining when and how to pay invoices

The first three of these steps are part of the total planning activity as discussed in Chapter 2, while the seventh step has to do with disbursing cash, as discussed in Chapter 3. The other three steps are really at the heart of the purchasing activity within the business firm. They sometimes are part of the firm's material management program. Textbooks on purchasing and procurement also include chapters on the legal aspects of purchasing, quality assurance, value analysis, negotiation strategies, and evaluation of the entire purchasing activity.

There are significant cost implications to firms of not having materials and parts when needed, or of receiving materials and parts of unacceptable quality. We will not pursue those cost implications here. From the perspective of working capital management, and certainly of financial management in general, we are concerned about the nature and cost implications of the credit terms offered by suppliers, as well as the cost implications of the firms' response to those terms.

TYPES AND TERMS OF TRADE CREDIT

Most firms utilize trade credit, but the institutional procedures are not identical. In this section, we briefly review some of the different types and terms of trade credit that have a bearing on the amount of financing available from payables. Subsequent sections consider the cost implications of trade credit.

[1]For extensive discussion, see W. B. England, *Procurement: Principles and Cases*, 4th ed. (Homewood, Ill.: Richard D. Irwin, Inc., 1962).

One of the most frequent types of trade credit is referred to as *open-account financing*. It is the simplest procedure, whereby the firm purchases materials or parts and pays for them at a later date. Exact timing of the payment—and hence of the conclusion of the transaction—depends upon how and when the supplier presents an invoice to the firm, and how the firm responds to that request for payment. The procedure continues over time from transaction to transaction. For consumer credit, a somewhat similar procedure occurs when an individual obtains food, lodging, transportation, or other services on credit by using a travel card (American Express, Diner's Club, etc.). The individual pays for those services when paying the monthly bill. The main difference between open-account financing for commercial credit and the use of travel cards in consumer credit is the nature of the billing. In commercial credit, the invoicing is tied to a particular transaction, while in consumer credit, invoicing is done a regular basis (usually monthly) and reflects all uses of the travel card by the individual during the period.

Revolving credit, which again pertains to consumer credit, is the procedure that accompanies the use of plastic charge cards issued by banks, gasoline companies, and department stores. The difference here is that the individual consumer is given a choice as to how much of the monthly invoice may be paid. The choice ranges from a specified minimum up to the full amount that is owed. The monthly accounting for revolving credit is illustrated in the following:

Previous revolving balance	$186.84
− Payment received	87.02
Remaining balance	99.82
+ New purchases	64.38
+ Finance charge	1.55
New revolving balance	$165.75

The finance charge is based on the average daily balance in the account and thus reflects payments made by the consumer during the month. In recent years, the finance charge for many firms selling on credit has been 1.5 percent monthly, or 18 percent on an annual basis.

Certain bank credit-card plans (Bank of America, Master Charge, etc.) also allow an individual to borrow cash as well as to charge for services and commodities. An advance of cash typically entails an additional charge (often 1 percent to 2 percent) that is added to the unpaid balance along with the amount of the advance itself. The joint effect of a front-end charge for borrowed funds and the monthly financial charge on the unpaid balance makes this type of credit very expensive.

Even though revolving credit involves individuals rather than business firms, it was included here because it emphasizes the payment options that are given to the consumer. The analagous procedure in trade credit is the cash discount which the supplier may offer to the buying firm. As we saw in Chapter 3, a cash discount is an economic inducement to encourage the buyer to pay faster.

A *consignment* is an arrangement whereby a supplier forwards merchandise to a retailer without actually selling it to the retailer. If the retailer is able to sell the merchandise, then the supplier is paid. If not, the merchandise is returned to the supplier. Since title does not pass to the retailer when merchandise is placed on consignment, there is no effect on the retailer's balance sheet, either to inventory or to accounts payable. Nevertheless, consignment may be viewed as free trade credit, since merchandise is provided to the retailer without obligation or cost.

Another type of institutional procedure is referred to as *seasonal dating*. This is when a firm places an order for certain seasonal goods, but with the shipping and billing procedures determined by the nature of that particular industry. For example, a toy manufacturer may arrange to sell merchandise to retail outlets rather evenly throughout the year, but with a clear recognition that the majority of the retailers' toy sales will be during the Christmas holidays. The billings for those toys may be arranged so that the retailers can pay for the toys following the time that they sell most of them to their customers. In contrast, manufacturers of garden tools or outboard motors may allow shipments to retail outlets not to be paid until the summer months when those products are sold to the public.

Specific credit terms already have been mentioned in Chapters 3 and 5. To reiterate, "net 30" means that the seller expects the invoiced amount to be paid by the thirtieth day following the sale. The terms "2/10, net 30" means that, in addition, the buyer is entitled to a 2 percent cash discount off the invoiced amount if payment is made by the tenth day following the sale. The terms "2/10, net 30, EOM" is the same except that the payment period does not begin until the end of the month in which the sale and billing occur.

The next two sections explore the financial implications of credit transactions. Several dates associated with a transaction should be noted: (1) the day an order for parts or materials is placed, (2) the day those parts or materials are received by the buying firm, (3) the day the invoice is received from the supplier, (4) the day the payment is mailed, and (5) the day the cash account of the buyer is reduced by the amount of the payment. The reader may recall that these dates were identified in the schematic diagram of float in Exhibit 3-6. Our interest here is in the bottom half of that diagram, specifically, the positive float that arises from delayed payments. For purposes of discussion, we will assume that legal title to the parts or materials passes to the buyer when the shipment is received. We will also assume that the postmarked date of the payment constitutes the day of legal payment.

COST OF OPEN-ACCOUNT TRADE CREDIT

From the standpoint of working capital management, the two important variables associated with accounts payable are the amount of the financing made available to the firm, and the cost of that financing. We will examine those variables for different credit terms. For purposes of illustration, let us suppose that Crescent Corporation has placed an order for $1,000 worth of small bearings to be used in the production of one of the firm's cleaning appliances. And suppose further that Crescent's cost of capital is estimated to be 10 percent.

Exhibit 7-2 is a timeline diagram of the relevant events when Crescent buys the bearings under the open-account terms of "net 30." To simplify discussion, we assume that the invoice for the purchase was included with the shipment of bearings. Exhibit 7-2 includes four possible responses by Crescent to the credit terms. Positive float is equal to delayed payment time *plus* mail and clearing time. Delayed payment time is a conscious choice by management, while mail and clearing time depends on the U.S. Postal Service and the location and procedures of the supplier's commercial banks. In order to focus on management decisions about payment time, we assume that mail and clearing time averages six days.

Alternative 1 is a payment before the due date, say in twenty days. Crescent has $1,000 worth of value at no cost (0 percent) to the firm for twenty days (without mail and processing float) or twenty-six days (with that additional float). The percentage cost is zero because there is no penalty to Crescent in waiting twenty days to mail payment to the supplier. The dollar value to Crescent of the trade-credit financing associated with alternative 1 is

$$\$1,000 \times 10\% \times \frac{20 \text{ days delayed payment}}{365 \text{ days in year}} = \$5.48$$

without consideration of mail and clearing float, and it is

$$\$1,000 \times 10\% \times \frac{26 \text{ days positive float}}{365 \text{ days in year}} = \$7.12$$

if total positive float is considered.* From those calculations, it is clear Crescent receives a distinct benefit from the availability of trade credit, and further that the benefit is enhanced by virtue of the slow postal system. Calculations for alternative 2 (delayed payment of thirty days) are similar, and the results clearly show that the dollar benefit of trade credit increases as the firm delays payment.

Some readers, recalling the adage that "there is no such thing as a free

---

*It would seem clear that the second calculation, which includes mail and clearing time, is a more accurate measure of the action taken by management. Both calculations are included here in order to emphasize the value of the additional component of positive float.

EXHIBIT 7-2

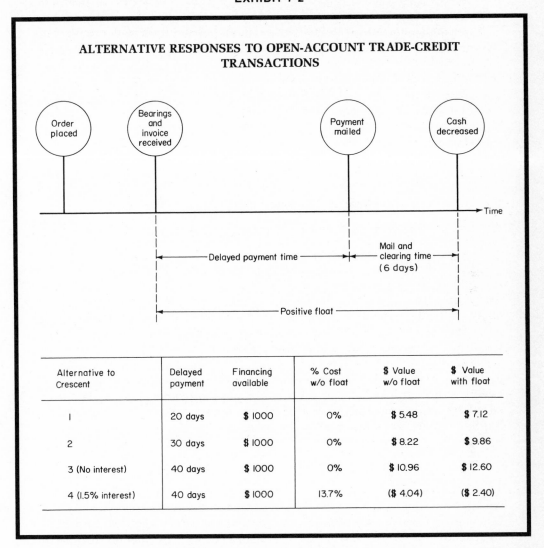

ALTERNATIVE RESPONSES TO OPEN-ACCOUNT TRADE-CREDIT TRANSACTIONS

Alternative to Crescent	Delayed payment	Financing available	% Cost w/o float	$ Value w/o float	$ Value with float
1	20 days	$ 1000	0%	$ 5.48	$ 7.12
2	30 days	$ 1000	0%	$ 8.22	$ 9.86
3 (No interest)	40 days	$ 1000	0%	$ 10.96	$ 12.60
4 (1.5% interest)	40 days	$ 1000	13.7%	($ 4.04)	($ 2.40)

lunch,'' may argue that trade-credit financing cannot really be free, since suppliers certainly must realize the possibility of delayed payment when they set prices on materials and parts. That is true, but still the calculations here are all based on the supplier's established price of $1,000 for the bearings, regardless of how the price was set. If the price of the bearings was raised to $1,100 by the supplier, the percentage cost of the first two alternatives in Exhibit 7-2 would still be zero. The dollar value of the financing would be higher because $1,100 would replace $1,000 in the calculation as the value of the bearings received by Crescent. At the same time, the total profitability to Crescent would be lower if the price of an input (such as bearings) into cost of goods sold were to increase.

Some managers deliberately delay payment beyond the due date specified in the credit terms of suppliers. Suppose the delayed payment is forty days. The financial consequences of this are seen in Exhibit 7-2 to depend on how the supplier responds. If the supplier does nothing (alternative 3), the percentage cost of the trade-credit financing remains zero, while the dollar benefit to Crescent increases, just as before. But if the supplier adds a finance charge (say 1.5 percent or $15) at the end of forty days (alternative 4), the consequences are markedly different. The percentage cost of the trade-credit financing (without mail and clearing float) becomes

$$\frac{\$15 \text{ penalty charge}}{\$1,000 \text{ value}} \times \frac{365 \text{ days in year}}{40 \text{ days delayed payment}} = 13.7\%$$

The dollar value of this alternative turns out to be a loss of $4.04 as follows:

$$\$1,000 \left(10\% \times \frac{40 \text{ days delayed payment}}{365 \text{ days in year}} - 1.5\% \text{ penalty} \right) = \$4.04$$

The implication of these calculations is that management must be careful about delayed payments beyond the due date specified in credit terms, since a financial charge can effectively change a dollar benefit into a dollar cost to the firm. Whether or not a financial charge is levied by the supplier is situational. It ultimately depends on the relative financial strengths of buyer and seller in the credit transaction, as well as the degree of competitiveness among suppliers. Arthur Hanson must be aware of the likely behavior of suppliers before reaching a final decision among alternatives such as in Exhibit 7-2. A safe alternative is simply to pay on the due date.

COST OF TRADE CREDIT INVOLVING DISCOUNTS

To see the significant impact of cash discounts on trade-credit transactions, we alter the illustration so that the credit terms on the purchase of $1,000 of bearings by Crescent Corporation are "2/10, net 30." The general impact of such credit terms has already been considered, but the specific results of alternatives open to the buying firm have not. Exhibit 7-3 presents again the timeline of relevant events, and the economic consequences of five alternative responses by Crescent Corporation are summarized. Mail and clearing time again is assumed to be six days.

Although the timeline of events is not changed, the option of a cash discount substantially changes the consequences. The offer of a cash discount by the supplier effectively reduces the price of the materials or parts being purchased. The true price of a product or service is its cash price. Therefore, the amount of reduction in price associated with a cash discount

EXHIBIT 7-3

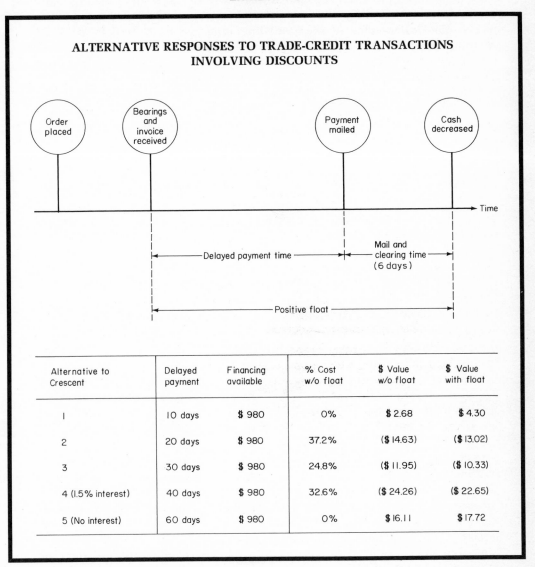

ALTERNATIVE RESPONSES TO TRADE-CREDIT TRANSACTIONS
INVOLVING DISCOUNTS

Alternative to Crescent	Delayed payment	Financing available	% Cost w/o float	$ Value w/o float	$ Value with float
1	10 days	$ 980	0%	$ 2.68	$ 4.30
2	20 days	$ 980	37.2%	($ 14.63)	($ 13.02)
3	30 days	$ 980	24.8%	($ 11.95)	($ 10.33)
4 (1.5% interest)	40 days	$ 980	32.6%	($ 24.26)	($ 22.65)
5 (No interest)	60 days	$ 980	0%	$ 16.11	$ 17.72

becomes an effective penalty to the buyer—similar to an interest charge—if the discount is not taken.

In the illustration, a 2 percent discount on a $1,000 invoice amounts to $20, and so the true price of the bearings is $980. The true price is the amount of the financing for each of the five alternatives shown in Exhibit 7-3. If Crescent delays payment for ten days (alternative 1) and thus qualifies for the discount, there is a zero percentage cost for the $980 financing made available to Crescent by the supplier. Using a calculation procedure as before, the dollar value of the $980 financing can be shown to be $2.68 (without float) or $4.30 (with float).

Payment of the full $1,000 (discount foregone) in twenty days (alternative 2) is seen to be expensive, both in the percentage cost

$$\frac{\$20 \text{ foregone discount}}{\$980 \text{ financing}} \times \frac{365 \text{ days in year}}{20 \text{ days delayed payment}} = 37.2\%$$

and in the dollar loss to Crescent

$$\$980 \times 10\% \times \frac{20 \text{ days delayed payment}}{365 \text{ days in year}} - \$20 \text{ foregone} = \$14.63$$

The dollar loss decreases to ($13.02) if total positive float of twenty-six days is used in the latter calculation. Waiting until the thirty-day due date for payment (alternative 3) reduces the percentage and dollar costs somewhat, but they still are relatively high. Delaying payment for forty days, coupled with a 1.5 percent interest charge for late payment levied by the supplier (alternative 4), results in a 32.6 percent cost to Crescent and a loss of ($22.65) if total positive float is considered. The clear implications of the first four alternatives in Exhibit 7-3 are twofold: (1) Crescent management should take the cash discount if at all possible, and (2) if that is not possible, payment should be made on the due date specified in the credit terms.

Before proceeding, it may be useful to compare the calculations of Exhibit 7-3 with the standard coverage of cash discounts (i.e., 2/10, net 30) in many finance textbooks. Dollar values of financing available from accounts payable are never mentioned. Invariably, the percentage cost of *not* taking the cash discount is shown to be 37.2 percent. That result is really the *difference* between paying $980 (with the discount) on the tenth day or paying $1,000 (without the discount) on the thirtieth day. The 37.2 percent result is then contrasted with the firm's cost of capital, to show that the firm should take the cash discount offered by the supplier. The 37.2 percent result is also the maximum rate which Crescent should be willing to pay to a banker or other lender in order to borrow the money necessary to take the cash discount offered by the supplier. However, the 37.2 percent result is *not* the financing cost to Crescent for the bearings. The financing cost is 24.8 percent as shown for alternative 3 in Exhibit 7-3.

DISBURSEMENT ANALYSIS

In Chapter 3, it was suggested that careful choice of disbursement locations can be used to extend positive float. That possibility was not reflected in the above cost calculations for trade credit, since a mail and clearing time of six days was assumed. In addition to choosing among alternative responses to credit terms offered by suppliers, management must also decide which bank accounts to use in paying suppliers. A simple example will be used to illustrate how management might conduct a disbursement analysis.[2]

Suppose that a firm headquartered in Boston makes average monthly payments to suppliers in three cities.

City	Monthly payment
Boston	$110,000
New York	190,000
Seattle	80,000

The firm has bank accounts in each of the three cities that could be used for disbursements. Each supplier also has a depository account in the same bank in its city. Management estimates the following check clearing times between its disbursement accounts and the suppliers' depository accounts:

Buyer's disbursement accounts	Suppliers' depository accounts		
	Boston	New York	Seattle
Boston	0 days	1.9 days	5.9 days
New York	1.1	0	5.1
Seattle	4.2	5.0	0

The firm's cost of capital is 12 percent. The cost of using each bank account for disbursement purposes is estimated to be $150 per month. The problem is to decide which accounts to use for disbursement.

Analysis of positive float is shown in Exhibit 7-4. First, a system of disbursing from a single city is considered. The values in the table are found by multiplying the monthly payments by the estimated check clearing times. For example, if the firm disbursed only from Boston, the positive float generated in paying suppliers in New York would be

$$(\$190,000 \text{ payment})(1.9 \text{ days}) = \$361,000$$

For each city, the total positive float is calculated, and Seattle is seen to be the best choice. Similar calculations are made for two- and three-bank

[2]The illustration is based on discussions and an example from L. J. Gitman, D. K. Forrester, and J. R. Forrester, Jr., "Maximizing Cash Disbursement Float," *Financial Management*, Summer 1976, pp. 15–24.

EXHIBIT 7-4

ILLUSTRATION OF DISBURSEMENT ANALYSIS (IN DOLLARS)

Buyer's disbursement accounts	Suppliers' depository accounts			Total positive float
	Boston	*New York*	*Seattle*	
One-bank system				
Boston	0	361,000	472,000	833,000
New York	121,000	0	408,000	529,000
Seattle	462,000	950,000	0	1,412,000*
Two-bank system				
Boston and New York	121,000	361,000	472,000	954,000
Boston and Seattle	462,000	950,000	472,000	1,884,000*
New York and Seattle	462,000	950,000	408,000	1,820,000
Three-bank system				
Boston, New York, and Seattle	462,000	950,000	472,000	1,884,000*

*Maximum positive float for that system.

disbursement systems. In each case, an assumption is made that disbursements to a particular supplier are made from the city with the longest check-clearing time.

In Exhibit 7-5, the value to the firm of the positive float is calculated. For a one-bank system (i.e., Seattle), the monthly value of the disbursement float would be

$$\frac{\$1,412,000 \text{ positive float}}{365 \text{ days in year}} \times 12\% = \$464$$

Division by 365 days is necessary because the values of total positive float are in units of dollar-days. When the monthly cost of each system is subtracted from the monthly benefit, a net benefit for that system is obtained. As seen in Exhibit 7-5, the optimal solution is a disbursement system from two cities: Boston and Seattle. Specifically, suppliers in Boston and New York

EXHIBIT 7-5

FINAL SOLUTION FOR DISBURSEMENT ANALYSIS (IN DOLLARS)

System	Positive float	Value of float*	System cost	Net benefit
One-bank				
Seattle	1,412,000	464	150	314
Two-bank				
Boston and Seattle	1,884,000	619	300	319†
Three-bank				
Boston, New York, and Seattle	1,884,000	619	450	169

*Value of float = (positive float)(12%) ÷ (365 days in year).
†Optimal solution.

would be paid with checks drawn on the Seattle bank, while Seattle suppliers would be paid with checks from the Boston bank account.

Many readers will notice the similarity between the illustration of disbursement analysis presented here and the lockbox analysis presented in Chapter 3. The main difference is that management should use lockbox analysis to *minimize* the net benefit of negative float, and use disbursement analysis to *maximize* the net benefit of positive float. A determination of how best to disburse payments to suppliers is one more aspect in the management of cash flow and accounts payable.

SUPPLIER RELATIONSHIPS

We have focused at some length on the cost implications of trade credit because that is a key aspect in the management of payables. There are other aspects that should also be considered. While the percentage and dollar costs to the firm of a credit transaction are important in the firm's overall financial management, so too is the longer-range relationship between a firm and its many suppliers. As such, the shorter-range economics should not be given undue weight in decisions regarding payment alternatives.

Consider Crescent's decision alternatives in Exhibit 7-3. Alternative 5, to wait sixty days and *still* take the cash discount, is clearly optimal in terms of either percentage or dollar cost. The percentage cost is zero, and the dollar benefit of $17.72 (with total float) greatly exceeds the benefits of the first four alternatives. Such a decision (which many firms make routinely), implemented over time, may eventually force a supplier out of business. If so, the costs to Crescent of finding another suitable supplier might be considerable. Moreover, if the supplier is large relative to a small buyer like Crescent, many managers would not jeopardize their source of supply by trying alternative 5. Many managers also would not choose alternative 5 because of the ethical issue. Perhaps the best guideline is simply to take advantage of cash discounts when available, but not extend payment beyond the due date.

For many firms, payments made to suppliers exceed payments to employees, bankers, governments, creditors, and owners. Moreover, the quality of the materials, parts, and products purchased from suppliers is an important determinant in the quality of products, either manufactured or purchased for resale. In manufacturing, the availability of materials and parts has a critical bearing on the continuity and efficiency of the manufacturing process. In wholesaling and retailing, availability of products directly affects the products that can be offered for resale. The implicit costs of both quality and availability must be carefully considered alongside of the explicit financial costs of trade-credit financing. All of this serves to underscore the importance of a broad view of accounts payable, just as with any other component of working capital.

MANAGING OTHER ACCRUALS

Other accruals, such as salaries and taxes payable, are similar to trade credit in that they are a spontaneous source of financing to the firm. They differ from trade credit in that they are much less a decision variable. In other words, management is relatively constrained in terms of what can be done to influence accruals as a source of financing.

Some managers may not realize that they, together with their fellow employees, are a source of financing to their firm. Indeed, all employees of an organization help to finance their firm since they are not paid for their services on a day-by-day basis. Instead, they are paid at the end of the week, every two weeks, or perhaps at the end of the month. A salary of $1,000 earned by an employee or manager but not yet paid is not much different from $1,000 borrowed from the firm's commercial bank. Managers also may not realize that they are providing financing to their firm without charge. While the bank charges interest on borrowed money, employees do not do so. All of us essentially provide free financing to our employers.

For firms in a seasonal business, wages and salaries payable represent a spontaneous and flexible source of financing. During the busier part of the year when more employees are used in the production process, the amount of financing available from wages and salaries payable increases. Conversely, employees' financing decreases during the slower part of the business cycle or during the slack seasons of the year. In this sense, wages and salaries payable resemble trade credit from suppliers.

From a management perspective, there really is not much that can be done about this particular source of financing. Some leeway exists in that a firm may choose to pay its employees less frequently. For example, it might choose to pay monthly rather than semimonthly. Because there are laws in many states that dictate how frequently employees must be paid, there is an upper limit to the amount of additional financing that can be obtained by an overt management decision to pay employees (including themselves) less frequently.

In Chapter 3, it was mentioned that some firms have chosen to pay their employees by draft rather than by a negotiable check. This is an alternative way that payment can be delayed even further. In such an instance, employees receive their checks just as quickly, but the amount of financing will remain (on the balance sheet) for a longer period until the bank draft works its way back to the firm's bank and the cash account is decreased. To the extent that a firm can increase its wages and salaries payable, it represents additional, zero-cost financing to the firm.

The taxes that are owed to various governments constitute another accrual that becomes part of the firm's short-term financing. Property taxes and federal income taxes do not become due at the moment they are incurred, but rather their payment is delayed until a later date. Taxes payable are also a free source of financing in that there is no additional payment made to the government. However, if the firm is required to accumulate funds in a special checking account in anticipation of a future tax payment, it can be argued there is an opportunity cost to the firm since those funds otherwise cannot be used. Since the timing of tax payments is specified by government bodies, including the Internal Revenue Service, there is little that a firm can do about this free source of short-term financing. An exception would occur if a firm deliberately decided to delay tax payments beyond the due date, even though a known penalty would result. There have been reported cases in foreign countries where firms have deliberately avoided paying taxes to their governments, recognizing that the penalties for late tax payments were less than the interest rates charged by banks and other lenders on comparable amounts of financing.

A final point is that other accruals should be monitored and managed, even though management decision-making is limited. Payments to employees and governments represent a significant part of the firm's total cash flow, and the extent of positive float associated with other accruals is highly predictable. Relationships with employees and ultimately with governments are really no less important than supplier relationships, particularly if management takes a longer-range viewpoint.

SUMMARY

Accounts payable is one of the larger and certainly one of the most important sources of financing to the firm. Payables result from the firm's purchasing activity and are influenced by a variety of different credit terms and institutional practices. The financial implications of trade credit depend both on the credit terms offered by suppliers and on how management decides to respond to those terms. Accruals are another important source of spontaneous financing to the firm. The cost of accruals are free. Financial managers must ensure continuing relationships with suppliers, as well as with employees and governments.

Problem 7-1

Show calculations for the dollar value of financing under alternative 1 in Exhibit 7-3.

SOLUTION: Considering only the time of delayed payment, we obtain

$$\$980 \times 10\% \times \frac{10 \text{ days delayed payment}}{365 \text{ days in year}} = \$2.68$$

If total positive float of 10 + 6 = 16 days is reflected, we have

$$\$980 \times 10\% \times \frac{16 \text{ days positive float}}{365 \text{ days in year}} = \$4.30$$

These are the dollar values reported in Exhibit 7-3.

Problem 7-2

A manufacturing firm has a $6 million total payroll twice a month. If the firm's cost of capital is estimated to be 12.5 percent, what is the benefit to the firm of paying employees only once per month.

SOLUTION: If the size of the firm's work force remains fixed over time, then wages and salaries are accrued at a constant rate. For a $6 million semi-monthly payroll, the average amount of financing provided by employees is half of the payroll, or $3 million. If the payroll becomes $12 million on a monthly basis, then the average financing during the month would become $6 million. Since this is also the average financing during the year, the benefit to the firm would be

$$(\$6 \text{ million} - \$3 \text{ million})(.125) = \$375,000$$

There would also be a significant impact on the firm's cash budget at the time such a change was implemented.

Problem 7-3

Calculate the dollar costs of alternatives 4 and 5 in Exhibit 7-3.

Problem 7-4

Crescent Corporation is considering changing credit terms to its customers from 2/10, net 30 to 3/10, net 30. In order to anticipate how customers may respond, management decides to see how Crescent would react if its suppliers made a similar change. Repeat the calculations of Exhibit 7-3 using 3/10, net 30.

SUGGESTED READINGS

Davey, P. J.: MANAGING TRADE RECEIVABLES (New York: The Conference Board, Inc., 1972).

England, W. B.: PROCUREMENT: PRINCIPLES AND CASES, 4th ed. (Homewood, Ill.: Richard D. Irwin, Inc., 1962).

Gitman, L. J., D. K. Forrester, and J. R. Forrester, Jr.: "Maximizing Cash Disbursement Float," FINANCIAL MANAGEMENT, Summer 1976, pp. 15–24.

Heinritz, S. F. and P. V. Farrell: PURCHASING: PRINCIPLES AND APPLICATIONS, 5th ed. (Englewood Cliffs, N.J.: Prentice-Hall, Inc., 1971).

Johnson, R. W.: FINANCIAL MANAGEMENT, 4th ed. (Boston: Allyn and Bacon, Inc., 1971), Chapter 12.

Ramamoorthy, V. E.: WORKING CAPITAL MANAGEMENT (Madras, India: Institute for Financial Management and Research, 1976), Chapter 9.

Sinnickson, L.: "Obtaining Trade Credit," in J. F. Weston and M. B. Goudzwaard (eds.), TREASURER'S HANDBOOK (Homewood, Ill.: Dow Jones-Irwin, 1977), Chapter 25.

Sweetser, A. G.: FINANCING GOODS (Albert G. Sweetser, 1957), Chapter 5.

8

MANAGING SHORT-TERM BORROWING

We come now to short-term borrowing, which is a second major component of working capital financing. Although it is a smaller percentage of total financing than accounts payable, short-term borrowing is extremely important because its characteristics are different and tend to complement payables and accruals. Short-term borrowing includes financing made available by individuals, other firms, and financial institutions. Of particular importance is short-term borrowing from commercial banks.

RATIONALE FOR BORROWING

In the previous chapter, we examined the rationale for payables and accruals. Short-term borrowing is another source of short-term financing to the firm that differs from payables and accruals in certain respects. First, the firm actually is acquiring dollars rather than materials and products from suppliers or time and services from employees. Second, short-term borrowing represents a deliberately planned and hence nonspontaneous source of financing. This is in contrast to accounts payable and various accruals which tend to rise and fall with the sales volume of the firm. Third, the typical transaction is much larger for short-term borrowing than for payables and accruals. Fourth, the cost to the firm of short-term borrowing is *not* zero, as is the case for properly managed payables and accruals.

Exhibit 8-1 depicts graphically how borrowing is used over time to help balance the longer-term uses and sources of funds within the organization with the shorter-term needs and sources. Panel A depicts how the fixed assets and current assets might vary over a two-year period. Panel B shows the gradual increase of long-term financing as a result of retained earnings, and a slightly different seasonal pattern for the short-term financing available from payables and accruals. Sources and uses are brought together in panel C. For brief periods during the two years, total sources exceed total

EXHIBIT 8-1

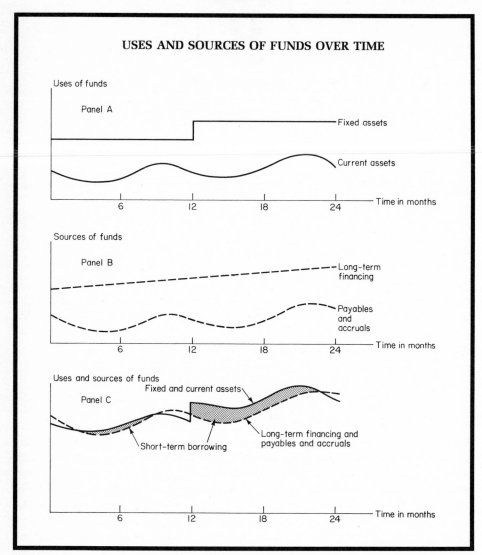

USES AND SOURCES OF FUNDS OVER TIME

Uses of funds

Panel A

Fixed assets

Current assets

6   12   18   24   Time in months

Sources of funds

Panel B

Long-term financing

Payables and accruals

6   12   18   24   Time in months

Uses and sources of funds

Fixed and current assets

Panel C

Short-term borrowing

Long-term financing and payables and accruals

6   12   18   24   Time in months

uses, and there is an excess of funds that can be invested in marketable securities. But for the middle portion of the first year and much of the second year, uses exceed sources, and short-term borrowing is necessitated. The need for short-term borrowing could also be identified with a diagram that traced permanent and temporary sources and uses of funds over time. The reader may recall from Chapter 1 that permanent levels of working capital are those amounts of various current assets and current liabilities that persist from year to year and are not influenced by short-range business fluctuations.

The pattern of uses and sources of funds in Exhibit 8-1 serves to emphasize that the need for short-term borrowing is unique from month to month and year to year. The need for short-term borrowing also differs from firm to firm, since growth rates, earnings capacity, dividend policies, and availability of trade credit differ for industries and for firms within industries. Such differences are why short-term borrowing is the result or outcome of cash budgeting, rather than an input to the planning for firm liquidity. We saw in Chapter 2 that careful cash budgeting is the appropriate tool for planning the borrowing requirements of an organization.

The irregular pattern in Exhibit 8-1 suggests two alternative ways that a firm might try to balance its sources and uses of funds. The first alternative is to arrange for some lender—most likely a commercial bank—to provide the needed borrowing from month to month. Such an arrangement is often referred to as a *line of credit*. The second alternative is to borrow for a longer period, say a year, an amount equal to the maximum need during the year, and thereby have an excess of funds during certain months.

Short-term borrowing usually takes the form of an account balance in a commercial bank or other financial institution. However, all of the cash in the account may not be available for immediate use by the firm. The reason is that the lender, as payment for the funds provided, may place constraints on the use of the account balance. An arrangement such as this is referred to as a *compensating balance*. Credit lines, compensating balances, and other features of short-term borrowing will be discussed further in this chapter.

RESPONSIBILITY FOR BORROWING

Regardless of the lender or of the specific terms, short-term borrowing results in cash available to the firm. This is in contrast to payables and accruals where financing takes the form of materials, parts, or products available to the firm. In addition, short-term borrowing usually involves far fewer transactions, but each transaction might involve much larger dollar amounts. A firm thus might do business with scores or even hundreds of suppliers, while interacting with only a few short-term lenders.

As a result of that characteristic, the responsibility for short-term borrowing is at a higher, more centralized level in the organization. The treasurer or financial vice president would usually be responsible for negotiating short-term loans to the firm. For Crescent Corporation, Arthur Hanson is the primary contact with commercial banks and other sources of financing. High-level responsibility is appropriate because the necessary borrowing for a firm is the culmination of a planning process that brings together all aspects of the business. For example, the cash budgeting exercise for Crescent (in Chapter 2) reflected plans for sales, production, purchasing, capital expenditures, and dividend payments. High-level responsibility is also appropriate because the firm's various bank accounts (see especially Exhibit 3-9) comprise the network for cash flow within the organization. For a decentralized firm, the responsibility for short-term borrowing would normally be delegated to local management.

Regardless of what manager is assigned responsibility for short-term borrowing—either for the total firm or for a component of the business—an appropriate goal can be specified:

> The *goal of short-term borrowing management* is to provide necessary nonspontaneous funds at the lowest possible cost to the organization.

In the sections which follow, we explore types and costs of short-term borrowing.

TYPES OF BORROWING

Though all short-term borrowing results in needed cash to the firm, there are many different types of borrowing arrangements from different sources. Our categorization and brief description of types of borrowing is based on the *source* of the short-term financing.

A first type of short-term borrowing is that obtained from individuals. That type of financing would be shown on the balance sheet as notes payable. It would most likely occur for smaller firms for which short-term borrowing might not be available from other sources. For a new firm just getting started, borrowing from family and friends may well be the only source of nonspontaneous financing available. Often it may represent additional money put into the business by owner-managers. Collateral typically is not part of the loan agreement. While the terms of the borrowing may call for repayment within a year, often this is a flexible requirement since the future of the business is so uncertain during the early weeks and months of a new venture.

A second type of short-term borrowing is in the form of commercial paper, which is promissory notes sold by large firms to other business firms and financial institutions. Commercial paper was one of six types of marketable securities discussed in Chapter 4. The promissory notes are unsecured, they are usually issued in denominations of $1 million, and their maturities range from 3 to 270 days, although typically the maturities are less than 30 days. Commercial paper is sold to business firms and financial institutions directly, or issued indirectly through securities dealers. Yields on commercial paper are generally about 0.5 percent lower than the rate paid on loans from commercial banks to their best corporate clients. The advantages of commercial paper include its lower interest rate, flexibility in managing cash flow, and the prestige associated with a firm that is able to obtain such short-term financing. A disadvantage of commercial paper is that it is not available to smaller firms or to larger firms experiencing financial difficulty.

Loans from commercial banks are a third type of short-term borrowing. Commercial loans are by far the largest source described here and, in the aggregate, are second in size only to trade credit as a source of short-term financing. Loans to business firms are the major product offered by commercial banks. Loans are of all sizes and include a variety of different features and terms according to the relative needs and financial status of the borrower. Other services provided by commercial banks include lockbox collection systems, information systems for firms with multiple divisions and bank accounts, general business counseling, and sometimes even referral business. The last two of these serve to emphasize the importance of the overall relationship between a business firm and its commercial banks.

A fourth type of short-term borrowing is from commercial finance corporations that specialize in loans tied to specific collateral such as inventory or accounts receivable. Commercial finance companies also provide financing to a firm during short periods each year when commercial banks require that the customer firm pay off its short-term loan so as to distinguish it from longer-term financing. Commercial finance companies also tend to make loans to riskier firms, though at higher interest rates. Because of their specialization and willingness to lend to riskier firms, commercial finance companies tend to complement rather than to compete directly with commercial banks. They are much less important than commercial banks in the total picture of short-term financing provided to business firms.

Certain terms involved in short-term borrowing should be defined. A *simple interest loan* consists of a principal amount borrowed for a designated length of time, repaid at the designated maturity, along with the designated interest payment. A *discounted loan* differs in that the interest payment is paid in advance, thereby reducing the amount of funds made available to the borrower. A *working capital loan* is a short-term loan, usually with a maturity of a year or less, that is made to a firm for the expressed purpose of investing in accounts receivable and/or inventory. A *term loan* involves periodic equal payments to a bank (including both interest and principal repayment) over a longer period, say three to five years. A *compensating balance* is the average account balance which a banker requests that the firm maintain over the life of the loan. A typical compensating balance might be 15 percent to 25 percent of the amount borrowed. The implication of a compensating balance is that the borrowing firm is not able to utilize the full amount of the funds legally borrowed and on which interest is paid. A *line of credit* is an agreement whereby a commercial bank agrees to lend to the borrower on request up to a specified amount. The borrower pays interest on the funds actually borrowed, and often a small commitment fee (perhaps 0.5 percent to 1.0 percent) on the amount of the line not borrowed as well. Alternatively, a 10 + 10 percent charge for a line of credit would mean that the bank asks for 10 percent (in balances) of the line of credit, plus 10 percent more on the amount actually borrowed. If the total line is borrowed, the compensating balance would be 20 percent.[1]

COLLATERAL FOR BORROWING

Another aspect of short-term borrowing is the possible presence of collateral as part of the lending agreement. Although loans from all sources reflect the credit worthiness of the borrower, claims on the assets of the borrower are often specified as additional collateral for a loan. Fixtures and equipment are possible collateral for term loans or other long-term borrowing, while inventory and accounts receivable constitute the usual collateral for short-term borrowing. We will begin with short-term borrowing having inventory as collateral.

Inventory is a useful form of collateral because it is physical and can be seen and counted. The lender decides what particular items of inventory held by the firm are worth (based on cost or market value), and then agrees to advance some prescribed percentage of that value as a loan to the firm.* The nature of particular inventory and its relative stage in the production process affects its estimated value as collateral. Raw materials and finished goods have a higher collateral value than work-in-process inventory, because they are liquidated more readily. The lender does not expect to have to liquidate the inventory in order to recover the loan principal. Rather, the pledging of inventory is viewed as an extra precaution in connection with a loan that is expected to be repaid by the borrower.

Physical possession of the inventory is also specified as part of the collateral arrangement. In some cases, the borrower retains the pledged inventory, and pays the lender when that inventory is sold or used. This is the procedure typically used for consumer durables, such as appliances and automobiles, where the presence of a serial number on each inventory item is an easy way to keep track of the collateral. It is not as easy to keep track of parts, materials, and nondurable goods, and the pledged inventory may be entrusted to a third party for safeguarding. If pledged inventory is kept off the premises of the borrowing firm, it is held in a *public warehouse* by a company that provides warehousing services as part of collateral arrangements. If, instead, the inventory is kept on the premises of the borrower, but under the control of a bonded warehouse operator, the arrangement is referred to as a *field warehouse*.

Accounts receivable is a different type of collateral for short-term borrow-

---

[1]For more detailed discussion of compensating balances, see H. G. Hamel and F. J. Walsh, Jr., *Commercial Banking Arrangements* (New York: The Conference Board, Inc., 1968).

*Examples of percentage guidelines used in collateralized loans are presented in a subsequent section.

ing because it is a nonphysical claim on a future payment by the borrower's customer. The simplest procedure is for the receivables to be pledged as collateral for the loan. As with inventory, the lender accepts certain of the receivables as collateral, and then agrees to advance some prescribed percentage of the value of the receivables as a loan to the firm.

Factoring is also frequently mentioned in connection with receivables financing. Taken literally, *factoring* is when a firm sells its accounts receivable to another firm. A *factor* is a person or firm that is willing to purchase the accounts receivable of another firm. Some commercial finance companies are willing to factor receivables. Many commercial banks also offer factoring as a subsidiary service. Usually, receivables are "factored" at a discount from the face amount owed. The amount of the discount is thus the price which a firm pays to pass on the risk of collecting the receivables to the factor. *Factoring with recourse* means that the firm which sold the products or merchandise eventually would have to make good on an uncollected account, and thus the factor or commercial finance company is simply advancing cash to the firm. In contrast, *factoring without recourse* means that the buyer of the receivables accepts the full risk of the invoices being paid. The balance sheet changes for factoring are an increase in cash and a decrease in accounts receivable. *Maturity factoring* is when accounts receivable are sold to a third party, but payment to the firm is delayed for a period approximately equal to when the receivables should be paid. There is no financing involved in maturity factoring. The more frequent practice in factoring is when a cash advance is made to the firm by the factor, thus providing funds at the time of need. In that instance, financing is made available to the firm, but it is not secured financing since the collateral has in fact been sold.

Factoring of accounts receivable by a firm needing cash is frequently viewed as a signal of financial weakness. In some instances, this is true when a firm in financial difficulty may be forced to sell its receivables at a substantial discount (almost like a pawn shop transaction) in order to pay its employees or suppliers. But in other instances, factoring is institutionalized as the way to obtain short-term financing, and it is not necessarily a signal of financial weakness. For example, prosperous manufacturing firms in the textile industry have factored their receivables as a routine matter for decades.

COST OF BORROWING

The cost of short-term borrowing is an important aspect to be considered. The cost structure for short-term borrowing is quite different from that of payables and accruals, where we have seen that the cost of spontaneous financing can be zero. The cost of short-term borrowing is never zero. But the cost is seldom as high as the cost for trade credit when cash discounts are not taken by the firm. The cost of short-term borrowing to the firm is also more complicated when the lender is a commercial bank, because of other services that may be provided by the bank. We review now a series of different lending arrangements, for the purpose of determining in each instance the true interest cost. The *true interest cost* is defined as the percentage cost to the firm of the funds actually available for use. In order to make comparisons between the different types of financing, it is convenient to express the true interest cost as an annual percentage rate. Four different lending arrangements are shown schematically in Exhibit 8-2. The example concerns Crescent Corporation borrowing funds for the first six months of the year. Arthur Hanson estimates that $30,000 is needed.

The first lending arrangement is a "simple interest," one-period loan. Because of Crescent's earnings potential and financial strength, its commercial bank agrees to provide a short-term loan of $30,000 at an annual stated interest rate of 8.5 percent. Panel A of Exhibit 8-2 is a timeline diagram of the cash flows that occur. When the loan is created, $30,000 is added to Crescent's checking account. Six months later, the principal is paid back to the bank, together with a single interest payment as follows:

Principal repaid	$30,000
Interest ($30,000) (8.5%) (1/2 year)	1,275
Total payment	$31,275

Working backward, the true interest cost for the lending arrangement is

$$\frac{\$1,275 \text{ interest}}{\$30,000 \text{ principal}} \times \frac{12 \text{ months in year}}{6\text{-month loan}} = 8.5\%$$

The true interest cost is just equal to the stated rate in this arrangement.

A second lending arrangement is a "discounted," one-period loan. The only change is that Crescent's commercial bank stipulates that the interest must be paid in advance. As seen in panel B of Exhibit 8-2, only $28,725 is added to Crescent's checking account. The $30,000 principal is paid back to the bank at the end of six months. The true interest cost to Crescent for this arrangement is as follows:

$$\frac{\$1,275 \text{ interest}}{\$28,725 \text{ available cash}} \times \frac{12 \text{ months in year}}{6\text{-month loan}} = 8.9\%$$

Discounting the loan thus has the effect of increasing Crescent's true interest cost to 8.9 percent from the 8.5 percent stated rate.

A third lending arrangement is when the commercial bank requests that Crescent maintain a compensating balance in its checking account, on average, during the six-month life of the loan. Suppose that for Crescent's $30,000 loan, the bank requests a compensating balance of 20 percent, or $6,000. Panel C of Exhibit 8-2 shows that the relevant cash flows are $24,000

EXHIBIT 8-2

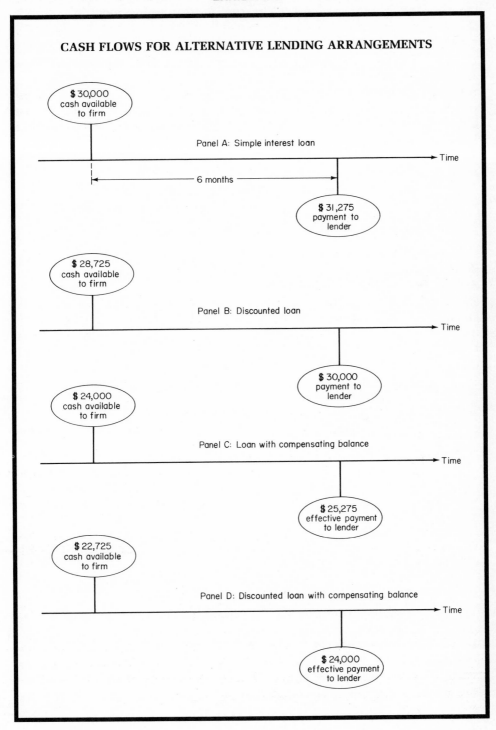

CASH FLOWS FOR ALTERNATIVE LENDING ARRANGEMENTS

$30,000 cash available to firm

Panel A: Simple interest loan

Time

6 months

$31,275 payment to lender

$28,725 cash available to firm

Panel B: Discounted loan

Time

$30,000 payment to lender

$24,000 cash available to firm

Panel C: Loan with compensating balance

Time

$25,275 effective payment to lender

$22,725 cash available to firm

Panel D: Discounted loan with compensating balance

Time

$24,000 effective payment to lender

to Crescent when the loan is set up, and $25,275 back to the bank after six months. The true interest cost to Crescent for this arrangement is

$$\frac{\$1,275 \text{ interest}}{\$24,000 \text{ available cash}} \times \frac{12 \text{ months in year}}{6\text{-month loan}} = 10.6\%$$

Since compensating balances are typically in the 15 percent to 25 percent range, it is clear that they have a significant impact on the true interest cost of short-term borrowing. If the loan is discounted and a compensating balance is required, the true interest cost of borrowing is even higher. Panel D of Exhibit 8-2 shows the relevant cash flows. The appropriate calculation is given by

$$\frac{\$1,275 \text{ interest}}{\$22,725 \text{ available cash}} \times \frac{12 \text{ months in year}}{6\text{-month loan}} = 11.2\%$$

The cost of borrowing is also increased because a line of credit is not fully used. Suppose that Crescent Corporation's commercial bank agrees to an $80,000 line of credit, but the firm only needs to borrow $30,000 during the six-month period. In addition to the 8.5 percent interest paid on the funds actually borrowed, Crescent is charged a commitment fee of 1 percent on the unused portion of the line of credit. The unused portion of the line amounts to $50,000 in the following illustration. The total payment to the bank would be

Principal repaid	$30,000
Interest ($30,000) (8.5%) (1/2 year)	1,275
Commitment fee ($50,000) (1.0%) (1/2 year)	250
Total payment	$31,525

Again assuming a 20 percent compensating balance, the true interest cost to Crescent would be

$$\frac{\$1,525 \text{ interest and fee}}{\$24,000 \text{ available cash}} \times \frac{12 \text{ months in year}}{6\text{-month loan}} = 12.7\%$$

If Crescent's bank charged for the line of credit with required balances instead of a dollar fee, the true interest cost could be even higher. Suppose the bank required balances on the 10 + 10 percent basis previously mentioned. The total compensating balance would be

> (10%) ($80,000 line of credit) $ 8,000
> (10%) ($30,000 borrowed)   3,000
>
> Total compensating balance $11,000

This would mean that only $19,000 of the $30,000 borrowed by Crescent would be available for use. As a result, the true interest cost would be

$$\frac{\$1,275 \text{ interest}}{\$19,000 \text{ available cash}} \times \frac{12 \text{ months in year}}{6\text{-month loan}} = 13.4\%$$

These calculations demonstrate that the costs to a firm of short-term borrowing increase as a result of discounting, compensating balances, and commitment fees. There will also be differences in the costs of short-term borrowing based on the degree of risk as perceived by the lender. A higher rate of interest is usually charged on loans to firms which are judged to be greater business and/or financial risks. *Business risk* is the uncertainty inherent in the operations of a business firm. Technology, competition, and government regulation are factors that add to business risk. *Financial risk* is the additional uncertainty faced by the owners of the business as debt financing is added to the firm's capital structure.

In practice, interest rates on short-term borrowing tend to be tied to the *prime rate*, which is the interest rate charged by the lending commercial banks to their best corporate customers. The prime rate tends to vary over time as a result of the demand and supply for funds in the economy. As seen in the following summary, the prime rate increased until about the middle of 1974, and has gradually decreased since.*

	1973	1974	1975	1976	1977
Mid-year	7.75%	11.75%	7.07%	7.20%	6.75%
Year-end	9.75	10.50	7.26	6.35	7.75

In recent years we have read much about the high cost of funds borrowed by individuals and by business firms. The true interest costs for alternative loans to Crescent Corporation, which ranged from 8.5 percent to 13.4 percent, are representative of recent borrowing costs. Yet, when we realize that interest payments and commitment fees paid to lenders are legitimate

*The values shown here are measured at six-month intervals and thus differ from the annual values of the prime rate which appeared in Exhibit 4-4.

deductions for tax purposes, the after-tax costs are considerably lower. If Crescent's marginal federal tax rate is 45 percent, then the true interest cost of a particular lending arrangement would have to be multiplied by 100 percent − 45 percent = 55 percent in order to obtain the after-tax cost of the borrowing. The range of costs for the alternative loans to Crescent would become 4.7 percent to 7.4 percent on an after-tax basis.

To summarize, the costs of short-term borrowing to a firm begin with the existing prime rate. A risk premium is added in order to establish the stated rate on loans that are requested by a given firm. The true interest cost calculation then adjusts the stated rate for additional factors in the loan agreement, such as a compensating balance and/or a line of credit. Finally, an after-tax calculation leads to the direct, out-of-pocket cost to the firm. For the case of an $80,000 line (on a 10 + 10 percent basis), the cost of short-term borrowing to Crescent Corporation can be broken down as follows:

Prime rate	7.5%
+ Risk premium	1.0
Stated rate	8.5%
+ Compensating balance	2.1
+ Line of credit commitment fee	2.8
Before-tax true interest cost	13.4%
− Federal government subsidy (45%)	6.0
After-tax true interest cost	7.4%

In addition to all these factors, there may be indirect costs for short-term borrowing, such as the cost of the inconvenience caused by having inventory or accounts receivable tied up as collateral, or the costs of other constraints that are written into the lending agreement by the lender. If the bank requires that Crescent's loan be paid off (i.e., "cleaned up") for a few weeks each year, Arthur Hanson must carefully plan the cash flows of the business to ensure continuity of operations. Finally, our brief discussion of after-tax costs to the firm does not really reflect the complexity of the problem, since the government's recognition of deductible charges occurs later. For example, an interest payment in the summer of year one has no impact of the cash flows of the firm until the spring of year two. This point serves to emphasize once again the importance of careful cash budgeting.

A final point has to do with the relative costs of secured and unsecured borrowing. At first blush, it would seem that loans secured by inventory or accounts receivables ought to carry a lower stated interest rate. For a given business firm, the presence of collateral may improve the borrowing terms. But looking across all loans made by commercial banks and other lenders, the cost structure is just the opposite—namely, secured loans cost more than unsecured loans. The reason is that the presence of collateral does not offset the higher risk of the borrowing firm that necessitated the collateral. Bankers often assert that loans to riskier firms carry high interest rates; the idea is to induce management of those firms to improve their financial status so that the next loan may possibly be on an unsecured basis at a lower interest rate. Because of the impact of interest charges on firm profitability, a business firm should always strive to borrow on an unsecured basis at a lower interest rate.

APPRAISING BORROWING POTENTIAL

Managing short-term borrowing includes a determination of how much borrowing is needed (both long-term and short-term), when the borrowing is needed, what type of loan is most suitable, which lenders to approach, which terms are appropriate, and what is the true interest cost to the firm. In preparing to negotiate a loan from a given lender, management should consider just how much borrowing the firm might be able to obtain. In other words, it is useful to appraise the borrowing potential of a firm. Borrowing potential depends on the financial situation of the borrower as reflected in both its current balance sheet and recent income statement. Borrowing potential also depends on the purposes for which the loan is being obtained, certain guidelines that are used by lenders in setting loan limits, and the overall availability of financing within the economy. We will illustrate how the borrowing potential of Crescent Corporation might be determined, both on a secured and an unsecured basis. For convenience, Crescent's year-end 1977 balance sheet is presented again as Exhibit 8-3.

Suppose, first, that the future operations of Crescent are judged to be so risky that lenders are likely to require collateral in connection with any borrowing. For secured loans, the lender is particularly interested in the type and value of collateral available for the loan. For raw-material inventory that has alternative uses by other firms in various industries, the lender might advance 50 percent to 70 percent of the value shown on the balance sheet. The percentage advance on work-in-process inventory is less than this (perhaps 20 percent to 30 percent at most), because it seldom can be used directly by another firm. Finished-goods inventory usually brings the highest percentage advance (60 percent to 90 percent), because it can be sold immediately. Accounts receivable are more liquid than inventory and thus often bring a higher collateral value. A typical procedure would be a lender approving 85 percent to 95 percent of the firm's accounts receivable, and then offering to advance to the borrower as much as 80 percent to 90 percent of the face amount of those approved receivables.

The actual percentage advance from the lender depends on the nature of the business, its potential collateral, and the relationship between lender and borrower. The percentages are likely to be higher to a borrower who is

EXHIBIT 8-3

CRESCENT CORPORATION
BALANCE SHEET FOR YEAR-END 1977

Assets		Liabilities and Equity	
Cash	$ 98,836	Accounts payable	$ 126,400
Accounts receivable	504,000	Notes payable	200,000
Installment notes receivable	201,600	Other Accruals	288,000
Inventory		Total current liabilities	$ 614,400
Raw materials	347,600		
		Total equity	1,598,218
Finished goods	182,960		
Prepaid expenses	46,022	Total liabilities and equity	$2,212,618
Total current assets	$1,381,018		
Net fixed assets	831,600		
Total assets	$2,212,618		

well-known and has had prior loans with that lender. For inventory, borrowing potential is likely to be higher if the inventory is to be held in a field or public warehouse whereby the borrowing arrangement is known to the public and to other creditors of the borrowing firm. For receivables financing, the borrowing potential reflects the firm's credit customers (how many and how much) as well as the credit worthiness of those customers.

To illustrate how guidelines such as these might be used in practice, let us suppose that the *middle* of the percentage ranges suggested here is proposed to Crescent by the lender. The borrowing potential secured by inventory is as follows:

Raw material (60%) ($173,800) $104,280
Finished goods (75%) ($91,480)   68,610
Borrowing potential for inventory $172,890

For receivables financing, the borrowing potential is calculated as follows:

Accounts receivable $ 504,000
× Approved by lender   90%
                                   $453,600
× Advanced by lender   85%
Borrowing potential for receivables $ 385,560

The total borrowing potential for secured financing to Crescent would thus be appraised as

Borrowing potential for inventory $172,890
Borrowing potential for receivables   385,560
Total secured borrowing potential $558,450

Suppose, instead, that Crescent's operations have continued to be profitable and that lenders will be willing to make loans on an unsecured basis. The guidelines used by lenders for unsecured financing depend on the overall financial strength of the borrower because there is no priority position among creditors. Attention usually focuses on the overall working capital position of the firm. One simple guideline used by lenders is to advance 40 percent to 60 percent of the net working capital of the firm. Again using the middle of that percentage range, we obtain

Current assets $1,381,018
− Current liabilities   614,400
Working capital $ 766,618
× Advanced by lender   50%
Unsecured borrowing potential $ 383,309

as the borrowing potential for Crescent Corporation on an unsecured basis.

An alternative guideline that might be used by a lender is to advance funds up to the point that the firm's current ratio, or perhaps some other selected ratio, falls to a prescribed level. Suppose for Crescent that a minimum level of 1.8 for the current ratio was prescribed by a lender. Since the creation of a short-term loan of size L increases both cash (current assets) and notes payable (current liabilities) by the amount L, the result for Crescent would be

$$\text{Current ratio} = \frac{\$1,381,018 + L}{614,400 + L}$$

If this current ratio expression is set equal to 1.8 and solved for L, we obtain $L = \$343,873$ as the unsecured borrowing potential under this guideline. The lender might also use a combination of guidelines, such as a prescribed percentage of net working capital, *provided* the current ratio does not fall below a prescribed level. For example, an unsecured loan of $383,309 (from the preceding paragraph) would cause Crescent's current ratio to fall to a value of

$$\frac{\$1,381,018 + 383,309}{\$614,400 + 383,309} = 1.77$$

which is below the 1.8 target, and thus the combination guideline would *not* be satisfied.

LENDER RELATIONSHIPS

The illustration of how financial managers might appraise the borrowing potential of their firm was done without mentioning the interest rate that might be charged by the lender or any other requirements, other than collateral, that might be specified in the loan agreement. The point is that short-term borrowing includes a number of different considerations that must be brought together in the final negotiations for a loan. In addition, there will be further communication between borrower and lender throughout the life of any loan. All of this is part of the lender relationship which the responsible financial manager must maintain. In this final section, we consider additional aspects of the lender relationship. Since loans from commercial banks represent by far the largest part of short-term financing to a firm, we will focus on banker relationships.

We begin by reviewing the contents of the loan proposal, an important document used by the borrower in trying to obtain financing. Although the format is not the same in each instance, the following items would normally be included in a proposal for short-term borrowing:

1. Concise statement of the purpose of the requested loan
2. Description of the borrowing firm, its products and markets

3. Description of the organizational structure, including biographical information on the key officers and managers

4. Recent financial statements, audited if possible

5. Projected income statement for the next year, or at least the lifetime of the requested loan

6. Projected cash-flow statement for the next year, or at least the lifetime of the requested loan

7. Specification of alternative sources from which the bank can expect to be repaid

8. Description of additional financial commitments or pending loan proposals

9. Specification of the nature and procedures for any collateral if the requested loan is to be secured

10. Business references

For the prospective lender, the first four of these items provide perspective on the requested loan. Items 5 and 6 are part of financial planning by the firm. Item 7 is particularly important to the banker because it indicates how and when the loan is expected to be repaid. This cannot be complete unless all future financing plans (item 8) are included in the projections. Item 9 normally would be included only if it was clear, before the fact, that collateral will be required by the lender. Item 10 is particularly apropos when it is the first time a loan is sought.

If the banker decides that the proposal has merit, then the details of a possible loan are developed. For a small firm just getting started in business, this may amount to the banker specifying the terms and the borrower deciding whether to accept or not. For larger businesses, and especially when the firm has already borrowed from that bank, developing the terms of the loan may involve negotiations between borrower and lender. In either case, a loan that is finally agreed upon by both sides will include in the loan agreement the terms of the loan, a repayment schedule, and a plan whereby designated financial managers of the borrowing firm will interact on some regular basis with designated loan officers of the commercial bank. During the lifetime of the loan, the lender will want to remain informed as to how the plans of the borrower are materializing, any deviations from the repayment schedule, and the emergence of future plans that may impact subsequent financial arrangements between the firm and the bank or other lenders.

Apart from the actual funds made available in a loan, the commercial bank may provide other services to the borrowing firm. The loan may be part of a larger line of credit established for the borrower. The checking account set up for the loan may also be used for deposits and check withdrawals on a regular basis. Alternatively, other accounts may be set up for cash collections and cash disbursements, possibly on a zero-balance basis (as described in Chapter 3). The bank may also help the firm in considering the relative merits of a lockbox collection system, and in operating such a system if it is deemed appropriate. The commercial bank trust department may be engaged as manager of the firm's pension and profit-sharing plans. There may also be other services such as safe deposit boxes, data processing, real estate, leasing, and international transactions.

Commercial banking is a profit-oriented business, and bankers do not provide all of those services for free. Thus far only the interest payment on a particular loan and the commitment fee on an unused credit line have been mentioned, but these are for short-term financing that is actually provided. The additional services provided by a commercial bank are paid for with a cash fee, or through compensating balances. Exhibit 8-4 shows how a commercial bank might report monthly on the activities of a customer for whom bank services are being paid in balances. The monthly dollar value of bank services is shown to be $91.48. Cash inflows and cash outflows are reflected. The necessary balance (using 6 percent annually, or 0.5 percent monthly) as the allowed rate would be calculated as follows:

$$\frac{\$91,480 \text{ monthly activity charges}}{.5\% \text{ monthly allowed rate}} = \$18,296$$

As seen in Exhibit 8-4, the firm had an average available balance of $27,941 during the month, and thus there was an average $9,645 extra balance available. A report such as Exhibit 8-4 helps the financial manager to plan the cash flows so that funds maintained in checking accounts are used effectively. While cash payment for services rendered by a bank might seem more straightforward, many commercial banks prefer to be paid through account balances, since deposits on hand are a measure of bank size and activity.

It also has been argued that the use of compensating balances tends to obscure the real costs of the financing and ancillary services provided by a bank. It is doubtful that firms ever "underpay" for financing and services from banks, and other lenders for that matter. Instead, it is plausible that often business firms "overpay." It is incumbent on the responsible financial manager of the borrowing firm to ensure that payments to the firm's bankers—either in cash or in balances—are appropriate for the mix of financing and services actually received. Toward ensuring fair payment, the manager ought to insist on a periodic account analysis from the bank (such as in Exhibit 8-4), just as the bank insists on certain reports from the borrower in connection with a loan.

To reiterate, the lender relationship is a key part of working capital management. It helps to ensure that the firm obtains necessary short-term financing at appropriate interest rates and with other credit terms. The

EXHIBIT 8-4

HYPOTHETICAL BALANCE AND ACTIVITY REPORT

Balance Report

Average daily account balance during month	$28,837
−Average negative float	896
Average available balance	$27,941

Activity Report

	In units	Price	Amount	
Account maintenance	1	$5.000	$ 5.000	
Checks deposited	228	0.035	7.980	
Checks paid	187	0.200	37.400	
Depository transfers	11	0.100	1.100	
Marketable securities transactions	15	2.000	30.000	
Safe deposit box	1	10.000	10.000	
Total activity charges			$91,480	
−Balance required to support activity charges (6%)				18,296
Balance available for additional services				$ 9,645

---

lending relationship helps the firm to obtain useful services that extend beyond just short-term borrowing. Also, the lender relationship allows the responsible manager to make sure that compensation to lenders for financing and services is not excessive.

SUMMARY

Short-term borrowing is used to balance the working capital needs of the firm with the spontaneous financing provided through payables and accruals. Various types and terms of short-term borrowing have been discussed with special attention to the use of collateral and the true interest cost to the firm. The lender relationship also includes the acquisition of nonfinancial services by the firm and payment for those services, often with compensating balances.

Problem 8-1

Suppose that a firm borrows $100,000 for one year for investing in working capital during a period of rapid growth. The stated interest rate is 9 percent. What is the true interest rate (before taxes) if interest is paid to the lender (1) annually, (2) semiannually, and (3) quarterly?

SOLUTION: The annual interest is (9%) ($100,000) = $9,000.

1. If interest of $9,000 is paid at the end of the year, the true interest rate is

$$\left(\frac{\$9,000}{\$100,000} + 1\right)^1 - 1 = 9.0\%$$

2. If interest of (1/2) ($9,000) = $4,500 is paid at the end of each six-month period, the true interest rate is

$$\left(\frac{\$4,500}{\$100,000} + 1\right)^2 - 1 = 9.2\%$$

3. If interest of (1/4) ($9,000) = $2,250 is paid at the end of each quarter, the true interest rate is

$$\left(\frac{\$2,250}{\$100,000} + 1\right)^4 - 1 = 9.3\%$$

Hence, more frequent payment of interest increases the true interest cost paid by the firm.

Problem 8-2

A firm orders a quantity of a chemical substance worth $20,000 for use in manufacturing. The supplier offers to sell the substance under the terms "1/10, net 40." Management estimates that the firm will not have adequate cash to pay the ($20,000) (1-1%) = $19,800 discounted price by the tenth day of the month. A local bank offers to lend the firm $20,000 for one month at an interest rate of 10 percent paid in advance. Should management take the loan in order to take the cash discount offered by the supplier?

SOLUTION: This problem necessitates a comparison of the cost of two options to the firm. The cost of *not* taking the cash discount is

$$\frac{\$200 \text{ foregone discount}}{\$19,800 \text{ financing}} \times \frac{365 \text{ days in year}}{30 \text{ days delayed payment}} = 12.29\%$$

Interest on the 1-month bank loan is

$$10\% \times \$20,000 \times \frac{\text{1-month loan}}{\text{12 months in year}} = \$166.67$$

Since the loan is discounted, the available cash to the firm is

$$\$20,000.00 - 166.67 = \$19,833.33$$

The true interest cost of the loan is

$$\frac{\$166.67 \text{ interest}}{\$19,833.33 \text{ available cash}} \times \frac{\text{12 months in year}}{\text{1-month loan}} = 10.08\%$$

Since the cost of the loan is less than the cost of foregoing the cash discount offered by the supplier, management should take the loan.

Problem 8-3

A firm negotiates a one-year, $400,000 line of credit with its commercial bank. The stated rate is 8.8 percent, and the balance requirements are 10 + 10 percent as discussed in the chapter. Calculate the true interest cost if the actual amount borrowed is

1. $100,000

2. $200,000

3. $300,000

4. $400,000

Problem 8-4

For each of the four lending arrangements in Exhibit 8-3, calculate the true interest cost if the stated rate charged by the bank is increased from 8.5 percent to 9.0 percent. Also calculate the true after-tax interest cost for each lending arrangement, assuming that Crescent's marginal tax rate is 40 percent.

Problem 8-5

Redo the analysis of borrowing potential in the chapter, but use the lower end of the range for each guideline. How much less short-term borrowing is available in each instance?

Problem 8-6

Recall the retail bookstore example used in Chapter 2. Suppose that business proved to be so successful during the first eighteen months that you and your partner decide to expand your operations. To acquire extra financing, the local bank has agreed to provide a $10,000 working capital loan at an annual rate of 10.25 percent. What are the cash flows and true interest costs for the following arrangements?

1. Simple interest loan

2. Discounted loan

3. Loan with 20 percent compensating balance

4. Discounted loan with 20 percent compensating balance

SUGGESTED READINGS

Alexander, D. H.: BANKING FOR THE NON-BANKER (Seattle: D. H. A. & Associates, 1974).

Hamel, H. G. and F. J. Walsh, Jr.: COMMERCIAL BANKING ARRANGEMENTS (New York: The Conference Board, Inc., 1968).

Lordan, J. F.: THE BANKING SIDE OF CORPORATE CASH MANAGEMENT (Boston: Financial Publishing Company, 1973), Chapter VI.

"New Credit Package for the Small Borrower," BUSINESS WEEK, September 5, 1977, pp. 74–75.

Smith, K. V., (ed.): READINGS ON THE MANAGEMENT OF WORKING CAPITAL (St. Paul, Minn.: West Publishing Company, 1974), Section V.

Sweetser, A. G.: FINANCING GOODS (Albert G. Sweetser, 1957).

Weston, J. F. and M. B. Goudzwaard (eds.): TREASURER' HANDBOOK (Homewood, Ill.: Dow Jones-Irwin, 1976), Part VII.

9

CONTROLLING WORKING CAPITAL

The final chapter of the *Guide* deals with the controlling of working capital by financial managers. Control is not the final step in the management process, but rather a central part of the ongoing job of managing the financial and other resources of the organization. Our discussion will include the control of individual current assets, current liabilities, as well as important linkages between certain balance sheet accounts. The chapter also includes an illustration that ties together many of the topics discussed in the *Guide*.

RATIONALE FOR CONTROLLING

Controlling is a key function of management. While authors differ somewhat on a complete listing of management functions, planning, organizing, and controlling are always included. In simplest terms, planning has to do with setting forth what the business firm is going to do, while organizing has to do with marshaling the needed resources and executing the planned activities and programs of the business. To complete the circle, controlling has to do with monitoring activities and programs toward ensuring that the expressed goals of the organization are accomplished.

Management control can be defined further in terms of its scope. One possibility is to list the different products, divisions, business units, or profit centers that will be monitored and controlled. Another possibility is to list the different management functions (recall Exhibit 2-1) for which planning takes place and for which followup control is needed. It may also be useful to distinguish between control of efficiency (input as related to output) and control of effectiveness (output as related to firm goals).

Probing further, there is less agreement among writers as to the nature of control. A first thought is to view control in terms of results—what actually occurs as compared to what was planned. A second thought is to center not so much on results, but rather on the interpretation of those results, particularly if trends over time can be identified. A third thought about control is to emphasize the corrective actions that are necessary to get the firm back on a straight path toward accomplishment of its goals. Finally, a fourth thought about control is to focus on the managers who must measure results and determine proper actions to be taken. The viewpoint adopted here is that control reflects all four thoughts, and that managers must be aware of results, of implication of results, of the possible need for corrective actions, and of the human aspects of implementing corrective actions. Moreover, there must be a balance given to control alongside the other functions of management. Planning without followup control will prove frustrating, just as attempted control without adequate planning will most likely be futile. Other pitfalls include trying to control every last detail (including trivia) of a project, or of trying to control so tightly that undue resources are spent on minor corrective actions that really are unnecessary.

Our concern in this chapter is not with control in a broad sense, but with financial control, and in particular with the control of working capital. Because control is not an isolated management function, it is not surprising that aspects of control have already surfaced in the six chapters of the *Guide* dealing with particular current assets and current liabilities. In Exhibit 3-1, the piping analogy for managing cash included certain valves corresponding to possible management control of the firm's overall cash flow. The management of marketable securities in Chapter 4 included the review of a control limit model which triggers additions to or withdrawals from the securities portfolio. In Chapter 5, we compared alternative methods of monitoring accounts receivable and suggested that the use of certain ratios may be misleading. The nature of computerized inventory-control systems was reviewed in the final section of Chapter 6. Then in Chapters 7 and 8, we discussed the important relationships between a firm and its suppliers and lenders. To maintain those relationships, financial managers must monitor and control the relevant terms of those financial agreements, as well as the pattern of payments by the firm.

RESPONSIBILITY FOR CONTROLLING

Who is responsible for controlling the working capital of the firm? The answer is similar to that for the planning of working capital given in Chapter 2. Controlling ought to involve all managers who are in any way involved with the various components of working capital. Throughout the *Guide*, we have seen that this means the treasurer, the controller, the credit managers, various managers concerned with inventory, and perhaps higher management levels within the firm.

The final responsibility for controlling working capital typically resides with the highest financial manager. For example, Mr. Arthur Hanson, vice president of finance for Crescent Corporation, is ultimately responsible for the working capital of his firm. It is the job of the top financial manager, whatever the title, to design an overall system of controls that properly reflects all components of working capital, and which places working capital in perspective vis-á-vis overall financial controlling.

One control procedure is to monitor the level of each current asset and current liability over time. A more frequent and fruitful procedure is to monitor certain financial ratios that are calculated from the financial statements of the firm. Despite some disadvantages with financial ratios, their use permits financial managers to monitor both flows and levels of working capital. In the remainder of this chapter, we will consider individual ratios for controlling firm liquidity and firm profitability, and then certain combinations of ratios that may be helpful in controlling working capital. We will also consider control from a broader, systems viewpoint, with particular attention paid to complex trade-offs that must often be made by management.

LIQUIDITY RATIOS

The *current ratio* is almost always the first financial ratio to be mentioned, and it is probably the most frequently used of all the financial ratios. We begin with the current ratio because it is a convenient vehicle for discussing certain disadvantages in using ratios. Our procedure for the current ratio (and other ratios to follow) will be to define the ratio and then illustrate for the Crescent Corporation.* Calculations are based on data from Crescent's year-end 1977 financial statement which, for convenience, is reproduced here as Exhibits 9-1 and 9-2. The first ratio is

$$\text{Current ratio} = \frac{\text{current assets}}{\text{current liabilities}} = \frac{\$1,381,018}{\$614,400} = 2.25$$

Since this ratio shows the number of times that the firm's short-term obligations could be paid if its short-term assets were converted to cash, the current ratio is used as an overall measure of firm liquidity.

Immediately, one is faced with the question of what is a reasonable level for the current ratio. Is a value of 2.25 too low? Or is it too high? The answer, of course, is that financial managers who monitor overall working capital must have a perspective on how a firm's current ratio has varied over time, as well as how it compares with the current ratios of other firms in its industry. More on this appears in a subsequent section.

Another question is the extent to which management of a firm can influence financial ratios calculated from its financial statements. While the question is relevant in varying degrees to many ratios, it is especially relevant for the current ratio. To illustrate, suppose that just before the end of 1977, Crescent paid off $80,000 of its notes payable to a commercial bank.

---

*Some of the ratios have already been defined in the *Guide*. For completeness of the discussion here, all definitions will be reiterated.

EXHIBIT 9-1

CRESCENT CORPORATION
INCOME STATEMENT FOR THE YEAR 1977

Net sales	$8,110,900
Cost of goods sold	4,216,700
Gross profit	$3,894,200
Selling expenses	2,383,000
Administrative expenses	850,300
Earnings before interest and taxes	$ 660,900*
Interest	20,500
Earnings before taxes	$ 640,400
Federal taxes payable	288,000
Earnings after taxes	$ 352,400
Common stock dividends (on 40,000 shares)	80,000
Added to retained earnings	$ 272,400

*After deducting $60,000 of depreciation included in cost of goods sold, selling expenses, and administrative expenses.

The year-end balance sheet for 1977 (Exhibit 9-1) would show cash reduced to $18,836 and notes payable reduced to $120,000. The resulting current ratio would be

$$\frac{\$1,381,018 - 80,000}{\$614,400 - 80,000} = 2.43$$

instead of 2.25 as reported above. Crescent Corporation would show an improved liquidity position, even though nothing has really changed in terms of the firm's inherent financial strength. That is, paying off part of a current liability really has not altered Crescent's viability as an ongoing business. If a firm's current ratio is greater than unity, then any cash payment to reduce a current liability—be it to suppliers, employees, bankers, or government—will effectively increase the firm's current ratio. This phenomenon, sometimes referred to as "window dressing," is not illegal,

EXHIBIT 9-2

CRESCENT CORPORATION
BALANCE SHEET FOR YEAR-END 1977

Assets			Liabilities and Equity	
Cash		$ 98,836	Accounts payable	$ 126,400
Accounts receivable		504,000	Notes payable	200,000
Installment notes receivable		201,600	Federal taxes payable	288,000
			Total current liabilities	$ 614,400
Inventory				
Raw material		173,800	Common stock and surplus	$ 400,000
Finished goods		91,480		
Prepaid expenses		46,022	Retained earnings	932,938
Total current assets		$1,115,738	Total equity	$1,332,938
			Total liabilities and equity	$1,947,338
Land		$ 91,600		
Buildings	$800,000			
Acc. depreciation	360,000	440,000		
Machinery	$672,000			
Acc. depreciation	372,000	300,000		
Net fixed assets		$ 831,600		
Total assets		$1,947,338		

---

and can be used to improve a firm's short-term financial picture. Window dressing should be recognized by management to be a cosmetic rather than a substantive action.

The *quick ratio* (or the *acid-test ratio* as it is sometimes called) is similar to the current ratio except that inventory is subtracted from the current assets. The reason for excluding inventory is that it is the least liquid of the firm's current assets, and may not be very helpful in meeting immediate financial obligations. Specifically,

$$\text{Quick ratio} = \frac{\text{current assets} - \text{inventory}}{\text{current liabilities}}$$

$$= \frac{\$1,381,018 - 347,600 - 182,960}{\$614,400} = 1.38$$

The result is a value which suggests a lower level of firm liquidity.

Using the same logic, one might agree that only cash is immediately available to pay short-term financial obligations. Hence, one could define a *cash ratio* as follows:

$$\text{Cash ratio} = \frac{\text{cash \& equivalents}}{\text{current liabilities}} = \frac{\$98,836}{\$614,400} = 0.16$$

Furthermore, if the required compensating balance for a short-term bank loan (say 15 percent for Crescent) is subtracted from cash and equivalents, and notes payable from current liabilities, one could obtain the *available ratio*. In other words,

$$\text{Available ratio} = \frac{\text{cash \& equivalents} - \text{compensating balance}}{\text{current liabilities} - \text{notes payable}}$$

$$= \frac{\$98,836 - (15\%)(\$200,000)}{\$614,400 - 200,000} = 0.32$$

These latter two ratios, which are not as popular as the current ratio or the quick ratio, show, respectively, the extent to which all current liabilities and all current liabilities excepting short-term borrowing could be paid immediately (without attempting to liquidate receivables or inventory).

Turnover ratios are also used to monitor and control liquidity. Because turnover ratios involve sales as well as the various current assets, they measure flows as well as levels of working capital. Consider accounts receivable. *Receivables turnover* is given by

$$\text{Receivables turnover} = \frac{\text{annual sales}}{\text{year-end receivables}}$$

$$= \frac{\$8,110,900}{\$504,000 + 201,600} = 11.5 \text{ times}$$

For Crescent, this means that accounts receivable and installment notes receivable together are turning over just slightly more than once per month.*

Another version of a turnover ratio is to divide it into the number of days

---

*If the firm is growing rapidly, it is better to divide by the average value of receivables for the beginning and end of the period. For illustrations in this chapter, we will use just the year-end 1977 value.

in one year. The result is the number of *days sales outstanding* for the particular current asset. For accounts receivable, we have

$$\text{Days sales in receivables} = \frac{365 \text{ days}}{\text{receivables turnover}}$$

$$= \frac{365}{11.5 \text{ times}} = 32 \text{ days}$$

Days sales in receivables is often referred to as the *collection period* for a business firm. Since the collection period for Crescent Corporation is just over one month, we have the same interpretation for the two equivalent ratios.

Days sales outstanding can also be calculated for cash and for inventory. Because inventory is valued at cost, it is customary to utilize cost of goods sold, rather than sales, in calculating days sales in inventory. Cash turnover turns out to be 82.1 times for Crescent, while inventory turnover is 7.9 times for 1977. The corresponding values are four days sales in cash and forty-six days sales in inventory.

The liquidity position for Crescent Corporation can be summarized in the following tabulation of financial ratios:

Liquidity ratios for Crescent

Current ratio = 2.25
Quick ratio = 1.38
Cash ratio = 0.16
Available ratio = 0.32
Days sales in cash = 4 days
Days sales in receivables = 32 days
Days sales in inventory = 46 days

While there are other ratios that could be devised to measure liquidity, the seven ratios defined and illustrated here are adequate in most situations.

PROFITABILITY RATIOS

The profitability position of the firm can also be portrayed by a number of different ratios. The usual procedure is to compare after-tax earnings with particular benchmarks from either the income statement or the balance sheet. For the income statement, the *profit margin* relates after-tax earnings to sales as follows:

$$\text{Profit margin} = \frac{\text{earnings after taxes}}{\text{sales}} = \frac{\$352,400}{\$8,110,900} = 4.3\%$$

This ratio shows what portion of a dollar from customers remains after all constituencies—suppliers, employers, government, bankers, etc.—have been paid.

For the balance sheet, earnings can be related to total assets, or to total equity, depending on whether the focus is on the total resources used in the business or just those resources provided by the owners of the firm. Specifically, we obtain

$$\text{Return on assets} = \frac{\text{earnings after taxes}}{\text{total assets}} = \frac{\$352,400}{\$2,212,018} = 15.9\%$$

$$\text{Return on equity} = \frac{\text{earnings after taxes}}{\text{total equity}} = \frac{\$352,400}{\$1,598,218} = 22.0\%$$

respectively. The difference between these two values is that owners benefited from positive financial leverage. That is, Crescent Corporation benefited from the lower cost of funds provided by the creditors of the firm. The relationship between operating leverage and financial leverage is explored in a problem at the end of the chapter.

Probably the most popular measure of profitability is *earnings per share.* It relates the success of the firm to each share of common stock. For Crescent, there were 40,000 shares of common stock outstanding at the end of 1977. The calculation gives

$$\text{Earnings per share} = \frac{\text{earnings after taxes}}{\text{common shares outstanding}} = \frac{\$352,400}{40,000} = \$8.81$$

The other measures of profitability that are based on a share of ownership are cash flow per share and return per share. As seen in Exhibit 9-1, total depreciation charges for Crescent during 1977 were $60,000. That value is used in calculating cash flow per share as follows:

$$\text{Cash flow per share} = \frac{\text{earnings after taxes} + \text{depreciation}}{\text{common shares outstanding}}$$
$$= \frac{\$352,400 + 60,000}{40,000} = \$10.31$$

Because of the importance of cash flow to the firm, cash flow per share is frequently used by analysts as an indicator of firm success over time. As discussed and illustrated in Chapter 1, depreciation charges do not generate cash directly, but they are a source of cash to the firm since depreciation charges reduce taxable earnings and annual tax payments to the government. Assuming, further, that the market price of Crescent's common stock increased from $54.50 to $62.00 during 1977, and noting from Exhibit 9-1 that dividends of $2.00 per share were paid during 1977, return per share is given by

$$\text{Return per share} = \frac{\text{appreciation per share} + \text{dividends per share}}{\text{beginning price per share}}$$
$$= \frac{(\$62.00 - 54.50) + \$2.00}{\$54.50} = 17.4\%$$

Return per share is often used in discussing the relative attractiveness of the firm's common stock from an investment perspective. Inherent in per share return is the firm's price-earnings ratio defined as follows:

$$\text{Price-earnings ratio} = \frac{\text{price per share}}{\text{earnings per share}} = \frac{\$62.00}{\$8.81} = 7.0 \text{ times}$$

The price-earnings ratio is a measure of how all investors in the stock market for a given common stock collectively view the future prospects of a firm.

In the previous section, it was suggested that management can to some extent influence how certain of its liquidity ratios look at year-end. The same is true for profitability ratios. In particular, there are a series of accounting treatments and adjustments that influence the after-tax earnings of the firm. And earnings, we have seen, are the basis for all of the profitability ratios. Anyone analyzing the profitability of a given firm should be aware of how the accounting variations have been handled by the firm. Some of the accounting variations are the method of valuing inventory (see Chapter 6), the handling of investments in subsidiaries and other companies, the treatment of mergers and acquisitions, the reporting of foreign earnings, pension-fund accounting, depreciation methods, investment tax credits, and so on.[1]

The profitability position for our illustration firm, Crescent Corporation, can also be summarized in a tabulation of financial ratios

---

Profitability ratios for Crescent

Profit margin = 4.3%
Return on assets = 15.9%
Return on equity = 22.0%
Earnings per share = $8.81
Cash flow per share = $10.31
Return per share = 17.4%
Price-earnings ratio = 7.0 times

Again, there are other ratios that could be constructed, but for most situations, the seven ratios defined and illustrated here are sufficient to give a useful perspective on firm profitability.

[1]For detailed discussion and illustration of these and other accounting adjustments, see K. V. Smith and D. K. Eiteman, *Essentials of Investing* (Homewood, Ill.: Richard D. Irwin, Inc., 1974), Chapter 10.

COMPOSITE RATIOS

Ensuring adequate liquidity for the firm and enhancing firm profitability were identified in Chapter 1 of the *Guide* as two parts of the proper goal for managing working capital. Seven measures of liquidity and seven measures of profitability have been identified and illustrated here. In addition to monitoring these individual measures over time, and making appropriate comparisons with other firms in the same industry, it is well to consider composite measures of liquidity and profitability for better control of working capital.

For liquidity, the "days sales" ratios can be added in order to see how rapidly a dollar flows through the operating cycle of cash to inventory to receivables and back to cash. For Crescent, we have

Days sales in cash	4 days
Days sales in inventory	46 days
Days sales in receivables	32 days
Operating cycle	82 days

This result means that it takes eighty-two days for a dollar to complete the operating cycle. The shorter the length of the operating cycle, the more liquid the firm is judged to be. If the operating cycle gets longer over time, then management should attempt to pinpoint the reasons for the reduced liquidity. In contrast, procedures for reducing the length of the operating cycle are useful since liquidity is improved.

The operating cycle framework also allows financial managers to evaluate where they should devote additional resources to improving firm liquidity. In the case of Crescent, primary attention should be given to inventory and receivables since they are the longest components in the cycle. There probably is not a great deal that can be done to improve cash since it is such a small part of the operating cycle.

For profitability, the *Du Pont system* of financial control is the most well-known composite ratio. Actually, it is a detailed breakdown of return on assets, which was one of the ratios already defined. The first level breakdown is as follows:

$$\frac{\text{Earnings after taxes}}{\text{Total assets}} = \frac{\text{earnings after taxes}}{\text{sales}} \times \frac{\text{sales}}{\text{total assets}}$$

or

$$\text{Return on assets} = \text{profit margin} \times \text{total assets turnover}$$

For Crescent, a profit margin of 4.3 percent and total asset turnover of 3.7 times combine to give its 15.9 percent return on assets.

In subsequent levels of the Du Pont system, the income statement is used to breakdown earnings, while the balance sheet is used to breakdown the firm's total assets. Exhibit 9-3 is one version of the duPont system that

EXHIBIT 9-3

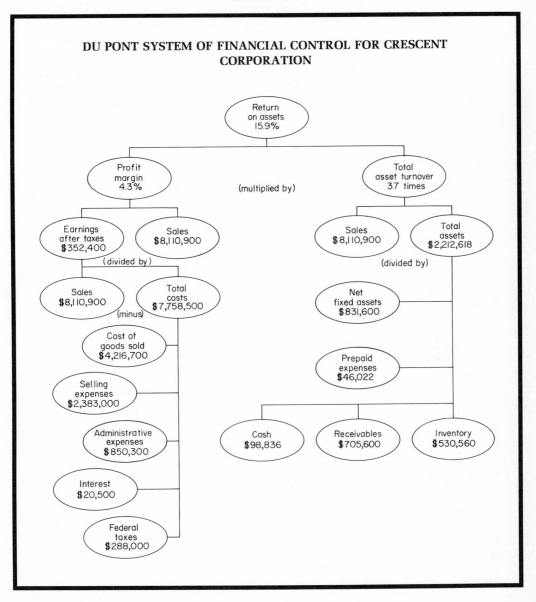

DU PONT SYSTEM OF FINANCIAL CONTROL FOR CRESCENT
CORPORATION

Return on assets 15.9%

Profit margin 4.3%   (multiplied by)   Total asset turnover 3.7 times

Earnings after taxes $352,400   Sales $8,110,900   Sales $8,110,900   Total assets $2,212,618

(divided by)   (divided by)

Sales $8,110,900   Total costs $7,758,500   Net fixed assets $831,600

(minus)

Cost of goods sold $4,216,700   Prepaid expenses $46,022

Selling expenses $2,383,000

Administrative expenses $850,300   Cash $98,836   Receivables $705,600   Inventory $530,560

Interest $20,500

Federal taxes $288,000

highlights the role of working capital.[2] Cash, receivables, and inventory are shown as components of total assets. Working capital management also impacts the firm's income statement, although that impact is not seen directly in Exhibit 9-3. Credit policy affects sales, purchasing policy and inventory policy affect cost of goods sold, while interest on short-term borrowing is part of the total costs of the organization.

Another composite ratio was devised in 1968 by Edward Altman as a means to predict corporate bankruptcy.[3] The composite ratio, called a Z-score, is a weighted average of five financial ratios. The relative weights are calculated using multiple discriminant analysis, in a manner analagous to that used to develop credit-scoring systems as described in Chapter 5. Professor Altman also determined the following guidelines for interpreting the Z-score: if the score is less than 2.0, the firm is in serious danger of

---

[2]Exhibit 9-3 follows a version of the Du Pont system suggested in J. F. Weston and E. F. Brigham, *Managerial Finance,* 5th ed. (Hinsdale, Ill.: The Dryden Press, Inc., 1975), Chapter 2. An alternative version is found in E. A. Helfert, *Techniques of Financial Analysis,* 4th ed. (Homewood, Ill.: Richard D. Irwin, Inc., 1976), Chapter 2.

[3]E. I. Altman, "Financial Ratios, Discriminant Analysis and the Prediction of Corporate Bankruptcy," *Journal of Finance,* September 1968, pp. 589–609.

EXHIBIT 9-4

ILLUSTRATION OF BANKRUPTCY TEST FOR CRESCENT CORPORATION

Ratio	Value	Weight	Weighted value
$\dfrac{\text{Working capital}}{\text{Total assets}}$	$\dfrac{\$1,381,018}{\$2,212,618} = .624$	1.2	.749
$\dfrac{\text{Retained earnings}}{\text{Total assets}}$	$\dfrac{\$1,198,218}{\$2,212,618} = .541$	1.4	.758
$\dfrac{\text{Earnings before interest and taxes}}{\text{Total assets}}$	$\dfrac{\$660,900}{\$2,212,618} = .299$	3.3	.987
$\dfrac{\text{Market value of equity}}{\text{Total debt}}$	$\dfrac{(40,000)\,(\$62)}{\$614,400} = 4.04$	0.6	2.42
$\dfrac{\text{Sales}}{\text{Total assets}}$	$\dfrac{\$8,110,900}{\$2,212,618} = 3.67$	1.0	3.67
		Total Z-score	8.58

bankruptcy; if the score is between 2.0 and 3.0, the future outcome is not clear; if the score is greater than 3.0, the firm is in no danger of financial difficulty.

Exhibit 9-4 is a calculation of the Z-score for Crescent Corporation as of the end of 1977. We see that the first ratio reflects the working capital position of the firm. The weighted average Z-score for Crescent is 8.58 and this is well above the 3.0 critical level. One reason is the low level of debt in Crescent's capital structure. Another reason is Crescent's high level of asset turnover. Advantages of the bankruptcy test include the fact that it is simple, and that management can observe changes over time in the five components of the composite ratio.

MONITORING FINANCIAL RATIOS

Calculating liquidity and profitability ratios, or combinations of financial ratios, is not enough. Indeed, managers can only make use of ratios in financial control if they are able to draw inferences from the level of particular ratios, or changes in ratios over time. One way for a manager to draw inferences about the liquidity and profitability of a firm is to compare selected ratios with that of other firms in the same industry. Fortunately, there are financial data available that facilitate such comparisons.

One useful source, and probably the best known, is an annual publication by Dun & Bradstreet, Inc., *Key Business Ratios*. It contains median and quartile values of fourteen ratios for 125 lines of business in the retailing, wholesaling, and manufacturing and construction sectors of the United States economy. The median is the value for which 50 percent of the values in the sample are greater. A quartile is the value for which 25 percent of the values in the sample are greater (or lower). Exhibit 9-5 traces the median values of the current ratio for selected sectors and industries over a recent decade. Clear trends are noted for some industries, but trends are less clear for other industries. The value of "two" often has been mentioned as a reasonable level for a firm's current ratio. The data in Exhibit 9-5 suggest that value is representative of many types of business in all sectors, but it is not a suitable benchmark for each and every industry. As a benchmark for control, it is desirable to have values that are appropriate for a specific industry.

Among the industries represented in Exhibit 9-5, "household appliances" in the manufacturing and construction sector is the single industry that is closest to Crescent Corporation. In order to focus on how financial ratios can be monitored over time, it is convenient to use the household appliances industry as a benchmark. Exhibit 9-6 shows how four of the ratios—two for measuring liquidity and two for profitability—have varied over the past decade. For each ratio, the three quartile values for firms in the household appliance industry are plotted. To reiterate, the first quartile for each industry is the value for which 25 percent of firms in the industry have a higher

EXHIBIT 9-5

MEDIAN VALUES OF CURRENT RATIO FOR SELECTED INDUSTRIES, 1965–1975

Sector and industry	1965	1967	1969	1971	1973	1975
Retailing						
Department stores	3.37	3.09	2.76	2.89	2.82	2.81
Gasoline stations	2.22	2.31	2.08	1.79	1.90	1.73
Grocery stores	1.97	1.86	1.69	1.73	1.76	1.63
Household appliance stores	2.21	2.09	2.20	1.95	1.87	2.00
Wholesaling						
Electrical appliances	2.23	1.99	1.86	1.91	1.76	1.86
Hardware	2.98	2.79	2.89	2.89	2.69	2.87
Meat products	2.43	1.95	1.80	1.89	1.93	1.74
Tires and tubes	1.85	1.92	1.93	1.80	1.69	1.78
Manufacturing and construction						
Drugs	2.94	2.69	2.24	2.90	2.75	2.46
General contractors	1.51	1.52	1.45	1.54	1.42	1.43
Household appliances	2.67	2.40	2.37	2.65	2.47	3.03
Office fixtures	1.98	2.23	2.08	2.27	2.17	2.94

Source: Dun & Bradstreet, Inc., *Key Business Ratios,* selected annual issues.

ratio, while the third quartile is the value for which 25 percent of firms have a lower ratio. The second quartile is the median value.

Superimposed on the quartile values for each ratio are the actual values for a hypothetical company. They do *not* represent the progress of Crescent Corporation, because data for our illustrative firm were not available prior to 1977, and Dun & Bradstreet has not yet published its industry ratios for 1977. For the hypothetical company, an examination of the four ratios over time reveals how it has fared in terms of ensuring liquidity and enhancing profitability. The current ratio appears to have been unnecessarily high until 1975 when it fell to just above the industry median. The collection period (i.e., days sales in receivables) was also too high during the late 1960s, but it was sharply reduced in the early 1970s. We are given no data on inventory, but it may also be too high, thus contributing to the above-average current ratio. In terms of profitability, the profit margin of the hypothetical company has consistently remained within the first and third quartiles, although it has been below the median in recent years. Return on equity has also been between the first and third quartiles, except that it has been above the

EXHIBIT 9-6

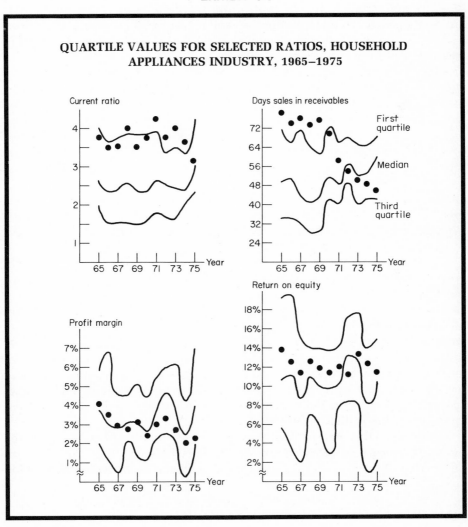

QUARTILE VALUES FOR SELECTED RATIOS, HOUSEHOLD
APPLIANCES INDUSTRY, 1965–1975

median value for all except one observation. So even though profit margin for the hypothetical company is below the industry median, the firm has managed all its assets in such a way that the return to owners has been above average. The important point is that for using quartile values for the industry, a manager can track the progress of the firm in terms of liquidity and profitability.

MULTIPLE TRADE-OFFS

This *Guide* has progressed on the assertion that liquidity and profitability are the two key goals in managing working capital. Preceding sections of this final chapter have identified a total of fourteen individual measures of liquidity and profitability. In controlling working capital, it is likely that financial managers tend to monitor several measures of progress for the firm. It is well, therefore, to take a closer look at the complexity of multiple measures within the context of control.

Suppose for the moment that two measures are being monitored by firm management: current ratio L (for liquidity) and return on equity P (for profitability). The top panel of Exhibit 9-7 is a two-dimensional plot of these measures. Let the position (P^*, L^*) represent the most recent values of liquidity and profitability. Both decisions by management and external developments in the industry and overall economy can cause the position of the firm to change—and that change must be into one of *four* regions. Greater profitability and greater liquidity describe the first region, which is clearly superior to the present position. Conversely, less profitability and less liquidity describe all points in the third region, which is clearly inferior to the present position. The other two regions involve trade-offs—either less profitability and more liquidity, or more profitability but less liquidity.

The bottom panel of Exhibit 9-7 is a three-dimensional plot wherein receivables turnover Q is added as a third measure.* Any movement from the current position (P^*, L^*, Q^*) is into one of *eight* regions: one is clearly superior, one is clearly inferior, and the other six regions all involve trade-offs among the three goals. For example, one of the six trade-off regions would be characterized by greater return on equity and greater receivables turnover, but lower current ratio. Another trade-off region would be characterized by greater receivables turnover and greater current ratio, but lower return on equity. Clearly the evaluation of six trade-off regions in three-goal space is more difficult than evaluation of two trade-off regions in two-goal space at the top of Exhibit 9-7.

It is possible to generalize the above to a larger number of goals. If N is the number of measures being monitored by management, then changes from one period to another in N-goal space is into one of 2^N regions, of which

---

*Receivables turnover is used instead of days sales in receivables (collection period) so that a higher value is considered "better" than a lower value.

EXHIBIT 9-7

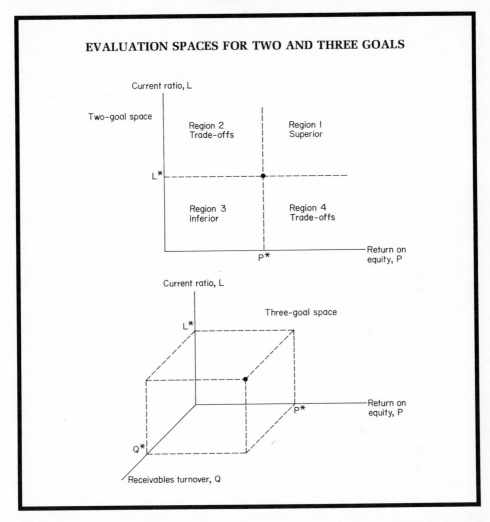

EVALUATION SPACES FOR TWO AND THREE GOALS

only one is clearly superior, and only one is clearly inferior. This means that the remaining $2^N - 2$ regions involve trade-offs among the various measures being monitored. For N = 4 measures, that would be 14 possible trade-offs, while for the N = 14 measures identified in this chapter, there would be 16,382 possible trade-offs! Clearly management control becomes complex as the number of measures of profitability, liquidity, and other goals of the firm is expanded.

To illustrate, we consider four measures for Crescent Corporation: current ratio and receivables turnover for liquidity, and profit margin and return on equity for profitability. The 1977 values for the four ratios have already been calculated. Using the projected financial statements for Crescent in Chapter 2 (Figures 1 through 19), the same four measures can be calculated for 1978. We obtain

Ratio	1977 actual	1978 projected
Current ratio	2.25	3.14
Receivables turnover	11.5 times	11.1 times
Profit margin	4.32%	6.44%
Return on equity	22.0%	27.7%

Thus three of the four ratios are expected to improve for Crescent during 1978.

But suppose that midway through 1978, management ascertains that its optimistic plans are likely not to materialize. In order to decide which actions should be taken, management settles on three possible plans.* The projected results of those three plans are as follows:

Ratio	1977 actual	Plan 1	Plan 2	Plan 3
Current	2.25	2.30	2.05	2.05
Receivables turnover	11.5 times	12.0 times	9.8 times	9.8 times
Profit margin	4.32%	4.12%	6.40%	4.20%
Return on equity	22.0%	20.7%	30.1%	33.0%

Since the 1978 projected ratios are not deemed feasible at the midyear evaluation, the 1977 values are used for the purpose of comparison. In this simplistic illustration, plan 1 focuses on tighter collection procedures for Crescent, plan 2 focuses on manufacturing efficiency, while plan 3 focuses on adding financial leverage via a long-term debt issue.

The projected results of the three plans reveal the trade-offs that must be made. For plan 1, the two liquidity ratios improve, but the profitability ratios worsen. The opposite occurs for plan 2, as the profitability ratios improve but the liquidity ratios worsen. For plan 3, the only improved ratio is return

*In practice, there would be many possible actions and combinations of actions that management could take. To simplify discussion here, we assume that there are only three possibilities.

on equity. These being the only possibilities, Arthur Hanson and other managers of Crescent must decide what package of changes is preferable overall. Which plan makes Crescent Corporation look better at the end of 1978? Which plan would owners prefer? Which plan is most consistent with the plans for 1979 and beyond? No mechanical procedure is likely to help in making that decision, and it ultimately boils down to managerial judgment. It should be noted, however, that working capital considerations are a central part of the complexity that accompanies multiple measures.

CORRECTIVE ACTIONS

Having seen the complexity of monitoring the progress of the firm over time, it remains to consider more specifically the corrective actions which should be taken when progress departs from plan. Many managers would probably assert that corrective action is the real heart of dynamic management and is likely to be the dimension that separates effective management from ineffective management. The sensitivity to needed corrective actions, the timing and amount of the actions, and the behavioral aspects of how the actions are taken are all part of management control.

With respect to controlling working capital, it is useful to identify "changes" that can be made by financial managers as corrective actions. Exhibit 9-8 is a list of seventeen possible changes. The list is representative rather than exhaustive of all possibilities. The reader may notice that the list of changes parallels the organization of this *Guide,* in particular Chapters 3 through 8. Some of the changes result from internal decisions by management (e.g., 3, 5, 6, and 9), while the effects of other changes depend, in large part, on the behavior of customers, suppliers, and lenders external to the organization (1, 7, 12, and 15). Certain changes in Exhibit 9-8 reflect management's willingness to assume risk (4 and 11). Other changes are an attempt to influence float (2, 3, and 14).

How should management decide to take a particular corrective action? A general guideline is that the decision to take corrective action should depend on the relative benefits and costs of somehow moving the firm back toward the plan, or more specifically toward the established goals of the organization. The notion of comparing the benefits of a corrective action against the costs of the change has been a consistent theme in this *Guide.* In Chapter 3, it was suggested that the financial manager responsible for cash ought to compare benefits with costs when considering the various decisions that impact firm float. Implicit in the discussion of strategies for managing marketable securities in Chapter 4 was the idea that only some firms are able to afford more sophisticated control systems. In Chapter 5, the potential costs of certain collection procedures were mentioned as being an important factor in deciding what to do about overdue account receivable. It

EXHIBIT 9-8

POSSIBLE CORRECTIVE ACTIONS FOR WORKING CAPITAL

1. Change discounts offered customers
2. Change collection network
3. Change disbursement network
4. Change size of operating cash balance
5. Change method of investing surplus cash

⎫ Managing cash and marketable securities

6. Change cutoff score for credit applications
7. Change frequency of followup payment notices

⎫ Managing receivables

8. Change inventory valuation methods
9. Change inventory order quantities
10. Change distribution network
11. Change inventory safety stocks

⎫ Managing inventory

12. Change suppliers used
13. Change response to supplier discounts
14. Change payroll procedures

⎫ Managing payables and accruals

15. Change lenders used
16. Change payment methods
17. Change collateral arrangements

⎫ Managing short-term borrowing

was suggested in Chapter 6 that the firm should implement simpler (and hence less expensive) controls for those numerous inventory items that comprise a relatively small part of the firm's total investment in inventory. In Chapter 7, it was argued that managerial response to credit terms offered by suppliers should consider the explicit costs to the firm, and also the implicit costs inherent in supplier relationships. And in Chapter 8, a similar argument involving costs and benefits was made concerning lender relationships.

CONTROL IN PERSPECTIVE

As management begins to evaluate the relative benefits and costs of various changes, such as in Exhibit 9-8, the subject of working capital management comes together as a whole. In other words, it is at the level of financial control—and specifically in trying to move the firm toward its expressed goals—that we can really see why financial managers must adopt a perspective that extends beyond just individual working capital components. Furthermore, a broader perspective emphasizes the importance of linkages between working capital accounts. For example, management should not change a firm's cash balance without due consideration of the impact on the various services obtained from commercial bankers. Management should not relax the firm's credit policy without duly considering additional inventory investment that might be needed. Changes in credit policy should also be based on the level of capacity at which the firm is producing, as well as the firm's degree of operating leverage. Management should recognize the relationship between the firm's inventory level and the short-term financing obtained from its suppliers. Management should be aware of the additional linkages that are created when the firm's short-term borrowing necessitates receivables and/or inventory being pledged as collateral.

Of course, not all of the changes in Exhibit 9-8 would be feasible, let alone desirable, for a given firm at a particular point in time. For each change that is feasible, financial managers should identify the expected benefits and costs toward an evaluation of whether it would help the firm move toward its expressed goals. Change 1, for example, is a change in the cash discounts which the firm offers to its credit customers. A cash discount is tantamount to a reduction in price. Suppose the discount is increased. To the extent that customers take advantage of a larger discount by paying their bills sooner, the firm's investment in accounts receivable is reduced. The expected dollar benefit of change 1 reflects the extent of the discount, faster payments that are required from credit customers, and the proportion of credit customers that are expected to take the discount. The expected dollar cost of change 1 is the reduced profit to the firm as a result of credit customers that avail themselves of a larger discount. Return on investment for change 1 is defined as reduced profit divided by reduced investment in receivables.

A return-on-investment (ROI) framework is also a systematic way to compare the benefits and costs of several corrective actions that may seem appropriate in controlling working capital. To illustrate, suppose that financial executives for a firm are considering four changes in working capital from the list in Exhibit 9-8 (2, 5, 6, and 9). Exhibit 9-9 includes for each change a brief description, quantitative estimates of both benefits and costs, and a calculation of the return on investment for that change. To simplify the illustration, corporate taxes are not included.

Before attempting to find the best decision, it is useful to pinpoint certain features of the changes summarized in Exhibit 9-9. Changes 6 and 9 are

EXHIBIT 9-9

ILLUSTRATION OF FOUR PROPOSED CHANGES IN WORKING CAPITAL

Change	Description	Estimated benefit	Estimated cost	Return on investment
2	Change collection network: Implement lockbox collection system in five metropolitan areas.	Reduced average collection time of one week. $50,000 lower investment in negative float.	Service fees to five banks for managing lockboxes. $7,000 annual fee.	$\dfrac{(\$7,000)}{(\$50,000)} = 14\%^*$
5	Change method of investing surplus cash: Hire manager for firm's portfolio of marketable securities.	Increased average yield on surplus cash balances. $(1.5\%)(\$2,400,000) =$ $36,000 annually.	Total compensation package of added manager. $30,000 annually.	$\dfrac{\$36,000 - 30,000}{\$30,000} = 20\%$
6	Change cutoff score for credit applications: Relax credit by decreasing credit cutoff score.	Increased profit from added sales, net of likely increased bad debts. $54,000 annually.	Added investment in accounts receivable and inventory. $300,000.	$\dfrac{\$54,000}{\$300,000} = 18\%$
9	Change inventory order quantities: Increase purchase quantities for parts used in manufacturing in response to supplier quantity discounts.	Increased profits (decreased total costs) associated with acquiring the parts. $13,000 annually.	Increased average inventory and hence investment in inventory. $100,000.	$\dfrac{\$13,000}{\$100,000} = 13\%$

*When both numerator and denominator are negative, a lower ratio is preferable to a higher ratio.

similar in that additional investments in current assets are expected to lead to increased annual profits and cash flows to the firm. In addition, change 6 reflects an important linkage wherein estimated cost includes additional investment in both accounts receivable and inventory. For change 2, a reduced investment in a current asset (i.e., cash) is made possible through a reduced expense and hence a reduced annual profit to the firm. For "reduced investments" of this sort, the associated return on investment must be *less* than the firm's cost of capital in order to be attractive to the firm.* For change 5, an added annual compensation expense leads to an added annual expected increase in additional revenue (i.e., portfolio yield) to the firm. Since the firm must make an advance commitment for the new position, it is appropriate to think of the $30,000 annual salary as an annual "investment," just as with the other three proposed changes in Exhibit 9-9.

Suppose that the firm's cost of capital is estimated to be 15 percent. If the four proposed changes in working capital are judged to be independent, and if no investment constraint is imposed by management, then changes 2, 5, and 6 would be acceptable according to the usual criterion of return on investment exceeding cost of capital for the firm. However, if management imposed a dollar investment constraint on changes which can be made to working capital, then the various projects must be considered in combination. Exhibit 9-10 is a complete enumeration of all combinations of the four proposed changes in the illustration. Without any changes in working capital, the firm is expected to earn 15 percent on its investment (i.e., total assets) of $1 million. The optimal choice of projects is indicated for each of several investment constraints. For investment (i.e., total asset) constraints of $1.05 million (5 percent growth in firm size) or $1.15 million (15 percent growth), changes 2 and 5 should be implemented. For a constraint of $1.25 million (25 percent growth), the combination of changes 2 and 6 is optimal. If there is no investment constraint imposed by management, then changes 2, 5, and 6 should all be implemented. The aggregate result of those three changes in working capital would be to increase the return on investment of the firm from 15.00 percent to 15.86 percent.

If the illustration were to consider additional changes, then a complete enumeration would reflect a larger number of alternatives. For ten possible changes, 1,024 combinations would have to be considered. For all seventeen changes, such as in Exhibit 9-8, a total of 131,072 combinations would have to be evaluated.† Fortunately, there are sophisticated linear programming techniques that can be used to find the optimal solution when the scope of the problem is that large.

---

*See Problem 9-3 for further elaboration of this point.

†This result is obtained by calculating the total number of combinations that are possible, with each project being either *in* or *out* of each combination. For the four alternatives in the illustration, there are a total of sixteen combinations as shown in Exhibit 9-10. If all seventeen changes had been considered, Exhibit 9-10 would have been quite lengthy!

EXHIBIT 9-10

OPTIMAL CHOICE OF WORKING CAPITAL PROJECTS FOR SELECTED CAPITAL CONSTRAINTS

Projects	Return*	Investment*	Return on investment	Investment constraint*			
				1,050	1,150	1,250	Unlimited
none	150	1,000	15.00%				
2	143	950	15.05				
5	156	1,030	15.15				
6	204	1,300	15.69	no†		no	
9	163	1,100	14.82	no			
2,5	149	980	15.20	optimal	optimal		
2,6	197	1,250	15.76	no	no	optimal	
2,9	156	1,050	14.86	no			
5,6	210	1,330	15.79	no	no	no	
5,9	169	1,130	14.96	no			
6,9	217	1,400	15.50	no	no	no	
2,5,6	203	1,280	15.86	no	no	no	optimal
2,5,9	162	1,080	15.00	no			
2,6,9	210	1,350	15.56	no	no	no	
5,6,9	223	1,430	15.59	no	no	no	
2,5,6,9	216	1,380	15.65	no	no	no	

*In thousands of dollars.
†no = project combination not feasible under constraint.

Many readers may have observed that the approach to working capital management suggested and illustrated here is similar to the standard procedure for capital budgeting. Indeed, the suggested approach to working capital is consistent with the usual approach to longer-term financial decision-making, provided that benefits and costs are evaluated in terms of changes rather than absolutes. Benefits and costs for working capital changes should also reflect the several linkages that exist between current assets and current liabilities. In long-range capital budgeting, it is usually suggested that the working capital implications of each project being considered should be included in the evaluation. The working capital changes that appear in Exhibit 9-8 should be viewed as *additional projects* beyond those identified in long-range planning.[4]

Many readers may also have observed that liquidity and risk were absent from the illustration, apart from the usual inference that risk should somehow be reflected in the firm's cost of capital. Because liquidity is recognized as an important goal of the firm, alongside of profitability, management must ensure that each combination of working capital changes being considered is also consistent with the liquidity needs of the organization. That can be accomplished through careful cash budgeting, or it can be accomplished by adding a liquidity constraint to the problem of finding the optimal set of changes such as in Exhibit 9-10.

In the preface to this *Guide,* it was asserted that the state of the art of working capital management tends to be a dichotomy between qualitative discussion of institutional procedures and practices, and a series of analytical models. The return-on-investment approach to evaluating changes in the management of working capital would seem to be a useful way of reducing that dichotomy, as well as a way of gaining an overall perspective on the management of working capital. Moreover, we have argued that working capital decisions can and should be be made in a manner similar to long-term investment decisions. In some firms, that may well expand the effort of identifying, analyzing, and evaluating investment projects to other parts of the organization. But only if that is done can Arthur Hanson and other financial managers expect the corrective actions that are proposed for various working capital components to be consistent with the overall financial decisions that are made within the organization.

SUMMARY

Controlling is the way in which management ensures that the firm continues to progress toward its stated goals. Financial ratios for evaluating the status of liquidity and profitability were defined and illustrated. Composite ratios for use in controlling working capital were discussed, and the complexity of trade-offs that result from multiple measures was stressed. Corrective

[4]For further discussion, see H. M. Weingartner, *Mathematical Programming and the Analysis of Capital Budgeting Problems* (Englewood Cliffs, N.J.: Prentice-Hall, Inc., 1963).

actions were identified that can be used to adjust the firm's working capital when results depart from plans. A return-on-investment framework was suggested for deciding what corrective action should be taken. In so doing, working capital management is linked logically to long-term financial decision-making.

Problem 9-1

In Chapter 5, the concept of "operating leverage" was discussed, while here we have considered "financial leverage." Use data from Exhibit 9-1 to show how the two concepts of leverage can be combined.

SOLUTION: The two measures of leverage can be combined by multiplication as follows:

$$\text{Operating leverage} = \frac{\text{gross profit}}{\text{earnings before interest and taxes}}$$
$$= \frac{\$3,894,200}{\$660,900} = 5.892$$

$$\text{Financial leverage} = \frac{\text{earnings before interest and taxes}}{\text{earnings after taxes}}$$
$$= \frac{\$660,900}{\$352,400} = 1.875$$

$$\text{Overall leverage} = \text{operating leverage} \times \text{financial leverage}$$
$$= (5.892)(1.875) = 11.047$$

Operating leverage reflects the cost structure of the business, or the relationship between variable and fixed costs. In contrast, financial leverage reflects the capital structure of the business, or how the firm is financed. Overall leverage combines the two in a consistent fashion.

Problem 9-2

What happens to financial control if management has only one identified goal (e.g., return on equity)?

SOLUTION: For the case of $N = 1$ goal, then there are exactly $2^1 - 2 = 0$ trade-offs required. Evaluation space (see Exhibit 9-7) would be one dimensional as follows:

The value P^* is the current position. Any change either will be an improvement (region 1) or a worsening (region 2). There are *no* possible trade-offs.

Problem 9-3

Near the end of Chapter 9, it was asserted that the ROI for changes that *reduce* the firm's investment must be *less* than the firm's cost of capital in order to be attractive to the firm. Construct an example to verify that assertion.

SOLUTION: Change 2 in Exhibit 9-9 provides a convenient example. The benefit of changing the firm's collection network is to reduce the firm's total investment by $50,000. The cost is $7,000 annually. For the single change, the return on investment would be

$$\text{ROI (change)} = \frac{(\$7,000)}{(\$50,000)} = 14\%$$

This value is *below* the firm's 15% cost of capital. Combining the project with the firm's total activity, we have

$$\text{ROI (before)} = \frac{\$150,000}{\$1,000,000} = 15.0\%$$

$$\text{ROI (after)} = \frac{\$150,000 - 7,000}{\$1,000,000 - 50,000} = 15.05\%$$

Hence, the effect of the single change is to *increase* the firm's overall ROI.

Problem 9-4

Redo the bankruptcy test for Crescent Corporation, but use the projected financial statements for 1978 (Figures 1 through 19 in Chapter 2).

Problem 9-5

Select a firm that is of interest to you. Calculate measures of liquidity and profitability for each of the past several years and ascertain the trends, if any, in those aspects of your firm. If Dun & Bradstreet data can be obtained, evaluate the management of liquidity and profitability of your firm relative to its industry.

Problem 9-6

Recall the example in Exhibits 9-8 through 9-10. Suppose that management decides to include a fifth alternative: change 14 which has to do with changing payroll procedures. Specifically, management is considering a change from a manual to a computerized system for payroll disbursements. The estimated benefit is to increase before-tax annual profits by $9,700. The estimated cost is the $60,000 annual cost of a time-sharing computerized system *plus* a systems analyst to operate the system. How would that additional project change the optimal solutions obtained in Exhibit 9-10?

SUGGESTED READINGS

Altman, E. A.: "Financial Ratios, Discriminant Analysis, and the Prediction of Corporate Bankruptcy," JOURNAL OF FINANCE, September 1968, pp. 589–609.

Drucker, P. F.: MANAGEMENT: TASKS, RESPONSIBILITIES, PRACTICES (New York: Harper & Row, Publishers, 1974), Chapter 39.

Grass, M., (ed.): CONTROL OF WORKING CAPITAL (Epping, Essex: Gower Press Limited, 1972).

Helfert, E. A.: TECHNIQUES OF FINANCIAL ANALYSIS, 4th ed. (Homewood, Ill.: Richard D. Irwin, Inc.,), Chapter 2.

Schleh, E. C.: SUCCESSFUL EXECUTIVE ACTION (Englewood Cliffs, N.J.: Prentice-Hall, Inc., 1955), Chapters 4–5.

Smith, K. V. and D. K. Eiteman: ESSENTIALS OF INVESTING (Homewood, Ill.: Richard D. Irwin, Inc., 1974).

Weingartner, H. M.: MATHEMATICAL PROGRAMMING AND THE ANALYSIS OF CAPITAL BUDGETING PROBLEMS (Englewood Cliffs, N.J.: Prentice-Hall, Inc., 1963).

Weston, J. F.: "Financial Analysis: Planning and Control," FINANCIAL EXECUTIVE, July 1965, pp. 40–48.

——— and E. F. Brigham: MANAGERIAL FINANCE, 5th ed. (Hinsdale, Ill.: The Dryden Press, Inc., 1975), Chapters 2–5.

GLOSSARY

Acquisition Cost. Fixed cost to the firm of replenishing inventory stocking points.

Available Ratio. Cash and equivalents of the firm minus compensating balances, divided by current liabilities minus notes payable.

Average Costing. Accounting method of inventory in which cost of goods sold reflects the prices of all items in inventory.

Bankers' Acceptances. Drafts drawn against deposits in commercial banks with payment at maturity guaranteed by the bank.

Basis Point. Yield of .01 percent.

Business Risk. Uncertainty inherent in the operations of a business firm.

Capacity. Ability of a credit customer to pay for a purchase by a designated due date.

Capital. Financial resources of a credit customer that provide backing for a credit purchase.

Cash Break-even Point. Level of sales per period for which cash revenue from sales just equals the total cash outlays of the product or business.

Cash Budget. Financial statement that compares cash inflows with cash outflows for each period during a planning horizon in order to determine when additional cash is needed or when excess cash is available.

Cash Flow. Dollar value of earnings after taxes plus depreciation.

Cash Ratio. Cash and equivalents of the firm divided by current liabilities.

Certificates of Deposit. Negotiable certificates issued by commercial banks for time deposits placed by corporations.

Character. Honesty, integrity, fairness, and other human traits that cause a customer to want or intend to pay for a purchase.

Collection Period. Accounts receivable of the firm divided by average daily credit sales.

Commercial Credit. Sales on credit by a business firm to other business firms.

Commercial Paper. Promissory notes sold by commercial banks, finance companies, and industrial firms in order to obtain needed financing.

Compensating Balance. Average account balance which a commercial banker requests that a borrowing firm maintain during the life of the loan.

Concentration Account. Bank account that is used to affect the zero-balance accounts of the firm, and also to compensate the commercial bank for services rendered to the firm.

Consignment. Arrangement whereby a supplier forwards merchandise to a retailer without actually selling it to the retailer.

Consumer Credit. Sales on credit by a business firm to individuals and families.

Corrective Actions. Ways in which financial managers can improve the working capital management of the firm.

Cost-Balancing Model. Analytical model that solves the problem of minimizing total costs associated with inventory replenishment, or with other working capital components.

Credit Policy. Authority for making credit decisions, exact terms of credit sales, and guidelines for selecting credit customers.

Credit-Scoring System. Multivariate statistical procedure for categorizing potential credit customers into good credit risks and bad credit risks.

Current Ratio. Current assets of the firm divided by current liabilities.

Denomination. Unit of transaction for buying or selling a marketable security.

Discounted Loan. Business loan for which the interest payment is made in advance, with the principal being repaid at the maturity of the loan.

Dunning. Periodic reminders to a credit customer that the bill has not yet been paid.

Du Pont System. Detailed breakdown of return on assets that is used for financial control.

Earnings per Share. Earnings after taxes divided by the firm's outstanding common shares.

Economic Order Quantity Model. Square-root formula that minimizes total inventory costs, but under rather restrictive assumptions.

Excess Yield. Yield on a marketable security minus the yield on a riskless U.S. Treasury bill.

Factoring. Procedure whereby a business firm sells its accounts receivable to another firm that specializes in collecting accounts.

Factoring with Recourse. Selling of accounts receivable wherein the selling firm is responsible for making good on uncollected accounts.

Factoring without Recourse. Selling of accounts receivable wherein the buying firm (i.e., the factor) accepts the full risk of the accounts being collected.

Field Warehouse. Procedure whereby inventory used as collateral for a loan is kept off the premises of the borrowing firm under the control of a bonded warehouse operator.

Financial Leverage. Extent to which debt is used relative to equity in financing the firm.

Financial Risk. Uncertainty faced by the owners of the business as debt financing is added to the firm's capital structure.

First-in-First-out. Accounting method for inventory in which cost of goods sold reflects the prices of items purchased earlier in time by the business firm.

Fixed Cost. Type of cost which does not vary with the level of output or activity of a business.

Float. Time delay between the moment of disbursement of funds by a buyer and the moment of receipt of funds by a seller.

Flow. Change in the level of a working capital account during a period of time.

Funds. Value within the organization.

Holding Cost. Variable cost to the firm of inventory held, including storage, safety, shrinkage, and the opportunity cost of investment made by the business firm.

Inventory Turnover. Cost of goods sold by the firm divided by inventory.

Last-in-First-out. Accounting method for inventory in which cost of goods sold reflects the prices of items purchased later in time by the business firm.

Line of Credit. Agreement whereby a commercial bank agrees to lend the borrower on request up to a specified amount during a period of time.

Lockbox. Procedure whereby a firm rents a post office box and entrusts its management to a commercial bank in order to process more quickly cash payments from the credit customers of the firm.

Lockbox Collection System. Series of lockboxes strategically placed so as to reduce negative float.

Marketability. Ability of an investor to sell a short-term issue to another investor.

Marketable Securities. Securities that have a short maturity and are issued by the United States government, government agencies, and various organizations within the private sector of the economy.

Maturity. Length of time until the principal amount of a marketable security is paid back to the investor.

Maturity Factoring. Selling of accounts receivable wherein payment to the selling firm is delayed for a period approximately equal to when the receivables should be paid by the buying firm.

Money Market. System of telephones and teletypes that interconnect a network of security firms specializing in high-quality, short-term marketable securities.

Negative Float. Value of the length of time a business firm must wait in order to use the funds which are paid by the buyer of the firm's products or services.

Net Credit. Accounts receivable of the firm minus accounts payable.

Net Working Capital. Dollar sum of the current assets minus the dollar sum of the current liabilities of the business.

Open-Account Financing. Firm purchases materials or parts and pays at a later date, depending upon the billing procedure used by the supplier.

Operating Leverage. Extent to which fixed costs are used relative to variable costs in the firm's operations.

Permanent Levels of Working Capital. Levels of current assets and current liabilities that persist year after year and are not influenced by short-range fluctuations in business activity.

Positive Float. Value of the length of time a business firm can continue to use funds that are owed to its suppliers.

Price-Earnings Ratio. Price per share divided by earnings per share for the firm.

Prime Rate. Interest rate charged by commercial banks on loans to large, financially strong business firms.

Profit Break-even Point. Level of sales per period for which sales revenue just equals total costs plus a designated dollar profit goal.

Profit Margin. Earnings after taxes divided by annual sales of the firm.

Public Warehouse. Procedure whereby inventory used as collateral for loan is kept on the premises of the borrowing firm.

Quick Ratio. Current assets of the firm minus inventory divided by current liabilities.

Receivables Turnover. Annual sales of the firm divided by accounts receivable.

Regular Break-even Point. Level of sales per period for which sales revenue just equals the total costs of the product or business.

Repurchase Agreement. U.S. Treasury bills that a security firm agrees to repurchase from the business firm at a specified price and time.

Return on Assets. Earnings after taxes divided by total assets of the firm.

Return on Equity. Earnings after taxes divided by total equity of the firm.

Return per Share. Appreciation per share plus dividends per share divided by beginning price per share for the firm.

Revolving Credit. Procedure in consumer credit wherein customers are billed monthly for credit transactions during the prior month.

Ride the Yield Curve. Strategy for trying to increase the yield from marketable securities by speculating on changes in interest rates prior to maturity.

Seasonal Dating. Business firm places an order for seasonal goods, but with shipping and billing to occur later in time.

Shortage Cost. Variable cost to the firm of not being able to fill orders from customers.

Simple Interest Loan. Business loan for which both principal and interest are paid at the maturity of the loan.

Stock. Level of a working capital account at a point in time.

System Cost. Cost of deciding what to do with respect to a working capital component.

Temporary Levels of Working Capital. Week-to-week and month-to-month levels of current assets and current liabilities as a result of fluctuations in business activity.

Term Loan. Business loan for which periodic payments to the lender include both interest and repayment of principal.

Trade Credit. Short-term financing provided to the firm by its suppliers and shown on the balance sheet as "accounts payable."

True Interest Cost. Annual percentage cost to the borrowing firm of the funds actually available for use by that firm.

Variable Cost. Type of cost that varies with the level of output or activity of a business.

Working Capital. Dollar sum of the current assets of the business.

Working Capital Loan. Short-term loan, usually with a maturity of a year or less, that is made to a firm for the expressed purpose of investing in accounts receivable and/or inventory.

Yield Determination. Way in which the investors in a marketable security earn a return on their investment.

Zero-Balance Account. Bank account that is deliberately managed to be at a zero balance at the end of each day.

INDEX

Accounts receivable, 115–140
  collection of, 131–132
  management goal, 118
  monitoring, 127–131
  rationale for, 115
  responsibility for, 116
  return on investment, 134
Accounts receivable collection, 131–132
  collection letters, 131
  dunning, 131
Accounts receivable monitoring, 127–131
  aging schedule, 129–131
  collection period calculation, 128–129
Accruals (see Payables and accruals)
Alexander, D. H., 214
Altman, E. I., 226n., 242
Average-cost accounting method, 143–147

Bacon, J., 65
Bankers' acceptances, 98–100
Bankruptcy test, 226–227
Basis point, 103–104
Baumol, W. J., 106–108, 114
Beckman, T. N., 140
Benton, J. B., 90n., 91
Beranek, W., 20, 65, 108, 114
Bierman, H., Jr., 105n., 114
Break-even analysis, 34–39
  cash, 36–37
  profit, 36–37
  regular, 34–37
Brigham, E. F., 114, 226n., 242
Brown, R. G., 30n., 65
Buffa, E. S., 156n., 171
Butterworth, J., 140

Cash, 67–92
  benefits vs. costs of managing, 82–84
  definition of, 69
  management goal, 72
  operating motive for holding, 67–68
  precautionary motive for holding, 68
  rationale for, 67–68
  responsibility for, 68–69
  speculative motive for holding, 68
Cash balances, 84–89
  concentration account, 88
  zero-balance account, 86–89
Cash budgeting, 37–39, 54
Cash collection, 72–78
  lockbox, 73
  regional banking, 73
Cash disbursement, 81–82, 184–187
  remote point disbursing, 81–82
Cash equivalents, definition of, 93
Cash flow:
  definition of, 3–8
  operating cash cycle, 70–72
  policy cash cycle, 70–72
Cash mobilization, 78–81
  depository transfer checks, 80
  Federal Reserve Wire System, 80
  personal couriers, 80–81
  Western Union Bank Wire, 80
Certificates of deposit, 98–100
Cole, R. H., 140
Commercial credit, definition of, 116
Commercial loans, 197
Commercial paper, 98–100, 196–197
Compensating balances, 197
  use of, 210
Composite ratios, 224–227
  bankruptcy test, 226–227
  Du Pont system, 224–226
  operating cycle, 224

Concentration account, 88
Consignments, 179
Consumer credit, definition of, 116
Controlling working capital, 215–242
   composite ratios, 224–227
   corrective actions, 233–234
   liquidity ratios, 217–221
   monitoring financial ratios, 227–230
   multiple trade-offs, 230–233
   profitability ratios, 221–223
   rationale for, 215–216
   responsibility for, 216–217
   return on investment, 235–239
Cost of capital, 71
Cost-balancing models, 105–109, 150–165
Credit, purchasing on, 176–177
Credit analysis, 121–125
   capacity as a factor of, 121
   capital as a factor of, 121
   character as a factor of, 121
   conditions as a factor of, 121–122
   four C's of credit, 121–124
   sequential, 124–125
   traditional, 121–124
Credit policy, 116–127
   changing of, 132–134
   definition of, 116
   establishing, 116–118
   terms, 118–121
Credit-scoring systems, 124–127
Credit terms, 73, 118–121

Davey, P. J., 140, 191
Davis, R. C., 24n., 65
Denomination, definition of, 97
Depository transfer checks, 80
Depreciation, contribution to cash flow, 5–7
Disbursement analysis, 184–187
Drucker, P. F., 21–22, 65, 242
Dunning, 131
Du Pont control system, 224–226

Economic order quantity (EOQ) model, 152
Eiteman, D. K., 223n., 242
Electronic funds transfer system (EFTS), 89–90
England, W. B., 177n., 191
Excess yields, 104

Factor, 199
Factoring, 199
   maturity, 199

Factoring (*Cont.*):
   with recourse, 199
   without recourse, 199
Farrell, P. V., 191
Federal agency issues, 98–99
Federal Reserve Wire System, 80
Ferber, R., 30n., 65
FIFO [see First-in-first-out (FIFO) accounting method]
First-in-first-out (FIFO) accounting method, 143–147
Fisher, D. I., 91, 114
Fixed cost, 34
Float, 71–72
   negative, 71
   positive, 71
   schematic calendar, 82–84
Flow, definition of, 8
Forecasting procedures, 24–32
   expected outcomes, 30–31
   financial simulation, 31
   freehand forecasts, 26–27
   least-squares forecasts, 27–30
   percentage-of-sales, 30
Forrester, D. K., 81n., 91, 185n., 191
Forrester, J. R., Jr., 81n., 91, 185n., 191
Foster, R. S., 140
Freehand forecasts, 26–27
Funds, definition of, 2–3
Funds flow, definition of, 3

Gitman, L. J., 67n., 81n., 91, 97n., 114, 185n., 191
Goals, 12–16
   business firm, 12–15
   financial management, 15
   liquidity, 15–16
   managerial, 15–16
   profitability, 13–16
Goudzwaard, M. B., 15n., 20, 66, 214
Grass, M., 242

Hadley, G., 171
Hamel, H. G., 198n., 214
Heinritz, S. F., 191
Helfert, E. A., 65, 226n., 242
Higgins, R. C., 140
Hutson, T. G., 140

Inventory, 141–171
   accounting methods for valuation, 143–147
   average cost, 144
   first-in-first-out (FIFO), 143–144
   last-in-first-out (LIFO), 144

Inventory (*Cont.*):
  control systems, 166–167
  cost-balancing models, 150–156
    inflation effects, 160–162
    purchase discounts, 158–160
    replenishment, 156–158
    seasonal demand, 156
    uncertainty and shortage, 162–165
  costs, 149–150
    acquisition, 149
    holding, 149
    setup, 149
    shortage, 150
    system, 150
  different types of, 143–147
  finished goods, 143
  management goal, 149
  optimal purchase quantity, 152
  rationale for, 141–142
  raw material, 143
  responsibility for, 142–143
  return on investment, 155
  strategy implementation, 165–167
  work-in-process, 143

Johnson, R. W., 114, 129n., 140, 191

Kirkpatrick, C. A., 171

Last-in-first-out (LIFO) accounting
    method, 143–147
Least-squares forecasts, 27–30
Levin, R. I., 171
Lewellen, W. G., 129n., 141
LIFO [*see* Last-in-first-out (LIFO)
    accounting method]
Line of credit, 197–198
Liquidity, 15–16
Liquidity ratios:
  available ratio, 220
  cash ratio, 220
  collection period, 221
  current ratio, 217–219
  days sales outstanding, 9, 221
  quick ratio (acid-test ratios), 219–220
  receivables turnover, 220–221
Loans:
  discounted, 197
  secured, 205–206
  simple interest, 197
  unsecured, 207–208
  working capital, 197
Lockbox:
  collection system, 74
  definition of, 73

Lockbox analysis, 74–78
Lordan, J. F., 91, 214

McAdams, A. K., 105n., 114
Magee, J. F., 171
Marketability, definition of, 97
Marketable securities, 93–114
  bankers' acceptances, 98–100
  certificates of deposit, 98–100
  characteristics of, 97–100
  commercial paper, 98–100
  cost-balancing models, 105–109
  definition of, 95
  federal agency issues, 98–99
  management goal, 97
  primary securities market, 99–101
  rationale for, 93–95
  repurchase agreements, 98–100
  responsibility for, 95–97
  secondary securities market, 99–101
  strategies for managing, 109–112
  U.S. Treasury bills, 97–100
Maturity, definition of, 97
Maturity factoring, 199
Mehta, D. R., 20, 124n., 140, 171
Miller, M. H., 108–109, 114
Money market:
  asked price, 101
  bid price, 101
  definition of, 100–101
Moses, E. A., 67n., 91, 97n., 114
Multiple discriminant analysis, 124

National Data Corporation, 79–80
Net credit, 174–175
Net working capital, definition of, 2

Open-account financing, 178
Operating cash cycle, 70–72
Operating leverage, 135
Orgler, Y. E., 92
Orr, D., 108–109, 114

Payables and accruals, 173–191
  management goal, 176
  rationale for, 173
  responsibility for, 176
  supplier relationships, 187–188
Phoenix Hecht Cash Management
    Services, Inc., 74n.
Planning working capital, 21–66
  computerized systems, 54–62
  costs of too little, 31–32
  costs of too much, 31–32
  efficiency vs. effectiveness, 22

Planning working capital (*Cont.*):
   forecasting procedures, 24–32
   new projects, 32–39
   ongoing projects, 39–54
   rationale for, 21–23
   responsibility for, 23–24
Policy cash cycle, 70–72
Primary securities market, 99–101
Prime rate, definition of, 103
Profitability, 13–16
Profitability ratios, 221–223
   cash flow per share, 222
   earnings per share, 222
   price-earnings ratio, 223
   profit margin, 221–222
   return on assets, 222
   return on equity, 222
   return per share, 223

Ramamoorthy, V. E., 20, 191
Remote point disbursing, 81–82
Repurchase agreements, 98–100
Return on investment, 134, 155, 235–239
Revolving credit, 178–179

Schleh, E. C., 242
Searby, F. W., 80n., 92
Seasonal dating, 179
Secondary securities market, 99–101
Short-term borrowing, 193–214
   appraising potential of, 205–208
   collateral arrangements, 198–199
    factoring, 199
     with recourse, 199
     without recourse, 199
    field warehouse, 198
    maturity factoring, 199
    public warehouse, 198
   compensating balance, 195
   cost of, 199–205
   lender relationships, 208–211
   line of credit, 195–197
   management goal, 196
   rationale for, 193–195
   responsibility for, 195–196
   sources of, 196–198
    commercial banks, 197
    commercial finance companies, 197
    commercial paper, 196–197

Sinnickson, L., 191
Slater, S. D., 92
Smith, J. E., 65, 92
Smith, K. V., 223n., 242
Sorge, B. W., 20
Stancill, J. McN., Jr., 20, 66, 114
Steiner, G. A., 66
Stock, definition of, 8
Stone, B. K., 131n., 140
Sweetser, A. G., 191, 214

Taubert, W. H., 156n., 171
Trade credit:
   cash discounts, 182–184
   cost of open account, 180–182
   disbursement analysis, 184–187
   types and terms of, 177–179

U.S. Treasury bills, 97–100

Variable cost, 34

Walsh, F. J., Jr., 198n., 214
Weingartner, H. M., 239n., 242
Western Union Bank Wire, 80
Weston, J. F., 15n., 20, 66, 114, 214, 226n., 242
White, I. T., 67n., 91, 97n., 114
Whitin, T. M., 171
Wilson, F. C., 66, 171
Working capital:
   definition of, 2
   organization goals relative to, 12–16
   permanent levels, 7
   temporary levels, 7
Working capital management:
   definition of, 2
   scope of, 8–14

Yield determination, definition of, 97
Yields:
   basis point, 103–104
   calculation of, 101
   excess yields, 104
   yield to maturity, 101–102

Zero-balance accounts, 86–89